Ten Years Inside

Tom Scott

Whitcoulls Publishers
Christchurch London

Acknowledgments

I wish to thank the *New Zealand Listener,* in whose pages most of this material first appeared; also *Straight Furrow, Open Government Report, The New Zealander* and the *Sunday Times.*

First published 1985
©1985 Tom Scott

Whitcoulls Publishers
Christchurch, New Zealand

All rights reserved. No part of this publication may be reproduced, stored in a retrieval system, or transmitted in any form or by any means, electronic, mechanical, photocopying, recording or otherwise, without prior written permission of the publishers.

ISBN 0 7233 0738 5

Typeset by Jacobson Typesetters Ltd, Auckland
Printed by Tien Wah Press (Pte) Ltd, Singapore

To my father, Tom Scott senior, from whom I inherited my sense of humour and bad table manners. Also to the subs on the *Listener* who have wrestled valiantly with my spelling, syntax and lapses in taste this past decade.

Contents

My first meeting with Tom Scott was about 10 years ago, when he turned up in the *Listener* office, bare-footed and in blue jeans, late for an appointment. The slightly bemused expression on his benign face was exaggerated by the lopsided angle of his spectacles, which were held together by sticking plaster (or was it that their frame was almost split and the plaster appeared on a later visit?). I also think he had with him his infant son who scrabbled happily around the office floor while we talked: this must have been the first time I heard the expression 'househusband', which was Tom's description of his occupation.

I had only recently taken over as editor and was looking for fresh talent. The past achievements of former editors Oliver Duff and Monte Holcroft could not be used as security blankets for a successor. The magazine needed a great deal more vitality and a re-statement of its traditions for a new generation of readers. So I encouraged hundreds of would-be writers and journalists to try their hand at whatever they thought they could do best for the magazine. If that sounds all very nice, the actual process, beneath its inviting talk and vague blandishment, was not really like that at all. Most of the hopes and dreams it stirred had to be dashed. That was the price of finding what the magazine needed.

Tom was invited to the office because several sources had mentioned his name as a capping magazine comic. In those days the very literary virtue of the *Listener* made it prey to a good, grey, dull earnestness. Stereotyped and pedestrian attitudes of mind were shadowing its pages; it was growing old. I was looking for humour as one antidote to this condition, also aware that for a tight little country some truths are effectively conveyed only by a jester. That is why New Zealand produces good cartoonists. Nevertheless, it was hard to define in advance what exactly the magazine needed in its new writers: you cannot write a prescription for originality; you must hope to recognise it when it comes your way.

Tom presented no difficulties of recognition for me, although for quite a while he was to bedevil and exasperate the sub-editors; and not just because of his attitude to deadlines. They alleged that he suffered from some form of dyslexia. I had to admit that his construction and form could be wobbly. But this was only the ruffled surface of his early writing. Beneath it glittered fresh insights and perceptions, presented in a way that blithely dismissed the conventions of accepted journalistic practice. He made strengths of whatever limitations he discerned in himself (most of us hide such things), often proclaiming his ignorance and playing the fool — and yet, marvellously, he revealed truths that were straight from home and the heart. He would report matters of great temporary moment by taking his acute awareness of his background, recollections of his school and university mates, of his country town and family, especially his Mum, and relate it all to what he saw going on in Wellington. He moved his readers from a familiar life which they shared with him (there's a little or a lot of Tom Scott in most of us) to a trusting acceptance of his reactions. And he made us laugh.

Sending Tom to be the *Listener*'s first ever Parliamentary columnist was, in the eyes of some friends of the magazine, a reckless gamble. It never seemed that way to me. Parliament's journalistic image, for far too many people, was that of an aloof, rather boring institution, from which emerged predictable reporting and a flood of ministerial hand-outs. Only somebody like Tom could change that. He did, brilliantly, making Parliament a warmly human place in which fallible mortals grappled with their exalted tasks. Of course in shattering the rules of conventional reporting, he seemed to get away with murder. But that was because his writing was imbued with honest wonderment as well as an obvious affection and genuine feeling for his subject. He often used words as a cartoonist uses his drawings, for a sharp, immediate effect. Those home truths of his were made infinitely more acceptable because they were conveyed with an engaging grin.

In the beginning I was never quite sure whether Tom wanted to be a cartoonist or a writer. He resolved that conflict by succeeding as both.

Tom has changed over the years, as is evident in his columns. He most certainly does not give the misleading appearance of being a bare-footed country boy; that guise, which never fooled me for a moment, has given way to that of a brogue-shod, sports-jacketed urban celebrity. He now moves around the corridors and streets of power cheerfully exuding a power of a different sort; he has even been known to give luncheon lectures to bureaucrats. The innocence and wonder of his early days had to go, of course; but in compensation his intuitive insight and comic sense are supported by the observation and knowledge that the past decade has given his pen. He remains true to his roots, thank goodness. It is a joy to me as a reader, no longer his editor, to see him toss aside the mantle of being a famous panjandrum, expert on current affairs, and with a chuckle tell his home town and old mates just what is going on in a silly world.

Have I any criticisms? Well, I believe that like all mavericks and originals, he is never at his best hunting with the pack. And I always regret those rare occasions when it seems to me that he is surrendering his talent to a cause; there are always plenty of other people around to push barrows. Again, my fingers itch for an editorial pencil when I think he may be confusing his readers by not clearly separating his reporting of fact from what he is weaving as fantasy to caricature a situation. I experience the same itch when he is recording with unqualified certitude information he could have received only at second-hand.

But these are the niggles of a former editor who wants one of his favourites to be just about perfect. Tom is as near to that as his magazine and country can ever hope to enjoy.

Ian Cross
Wellington

In 1972, quite by accident it seems now, I found myself tutoring in anatomy and physiology at the School of Occupational Therapy at the Central Institute of Technology in Petone. Looking back I can't understand why I wasn't put off by the name. It sounds like one of those asylums the Soviets maintain high in the Arctic Circle exclusively for dissidents. My sense of isolation could hardly have been worse if it had been. The students were all girls and I was the only male on a staff made up largely of spinsters. Everyone was very nice but, alone in my tiny office preparing lessons on the muscles of the hand, looking up occasionally at the seagulls wheeling over the playing fields, I couldn't escape the feeling that life was passing me by.

Things picked up a bit when I became friendly with another tutor across the way called Grant Moffatt. Grant taught biology but politics was his real passion. He was on the Wainuiomata Borough Council, was active in the Labour Party and *actually knew* the local MP Fraser Colman personally. When I gasped at this revelation Grant casually inquired whether I would like to dine some time with him and Colman at Bellamy's. Dinner at Bellamy's! I couldn't believe it. As nonchalantly as possible I replied that I was a starter.

That invitation kept me going for ages. I didn't even know who Fraser Colman was. Not that it mattered. Getting into Bellamy's — the inner sanctum, the holy of holies — was the thing. Anyone could get a guided tour of the corridors. (I had even been there myself once, on a primary school trip. In the same day we did the museum, the zoo, and Parliament, which of course incorporates the best features of the other two.)

Nothing happened for months and I suspect Grant might have been overplaying his hand for he went decidedly vague whenever I raised the subject again, which was just about every time I met him. In the event the election results changed everything. Labour were swept into office with a record majority, Fraser Colman became a Cabinet Minister, and dinner at Bellamy's got lost in the rush.

There were big changes in my life too. I gave up teaching and became a househusband looking after my infant son Shaun. To keep myself sane I did a lot of cartooning on the side and was starting to get published regularly in the *Sunday Times* and other publications when Ian Cross rang out of the blue. My first assignment was a financial writers' seminar, so dull that in desperation I wrote about it humorously and was lucky enough to amuse the great man. More assignments followed, and I sort of joined up gradually, doing bits and pieces until I was working virtually full-time.

That was over ten years ago. Ten years is a long time. For many people in the world it is literally half a lifetime, yet for me it has passed swiftly, and now that the long nights of terror leaning over the typewriter, glass of whisky in hand, have blurred in the consciousness, it has taken on the quality of a dream. Impression has crowded on to impression, place on to place, face on to face, crisis on to crisis, until I might well have imagined it all.

Did I for instance really meet Rob Muldoon in the corridors in the early days and have him yell out, 'Aaah Scott, I saw your stuff in the *Listener* — I didn't know you could write!'

Did I reply, 'I didn't know you could read!'

Did one of his followers say, 'I think he's got you there, Rob,' instantly regretting it when his boss glowered at him?

I sincerely hope so. I have dined out on it often enough but I couldn't tell you if it was *before* or *after* he became Prime Minister.

It's strange, because the five years I spent at university went so slowly, I remember it all with a painful clarity. The tedium of parasitology lab sessions is with me still and all too real.

But I know the last ten years actually happened because I have been poring over the proof preparing this book, leafing through and re-reading over 500 articles and cartoons. Some articles have been a revelation — I can't honestly remember writing them. Others that I recalled fondly were deeply disappointing second time around.

What I have found amusing are the devices and ploys I have used to write almost the same story many times. Our politics don't change that much and the battle to keep fresh and interesting has been the hardest, but changes there have been and I have changed as well. I began a callow youth and have continued into callow manhood.

Good humour should be seamless and with maturity I have better learnt to smooth the edges. Skill and experience have helped blunt the loss of the energy of innocence. I have learnt many lessons. People holding appalling views can sometimes be very decent, and people whose ideology is on the side of the angels can be right bastards. I am more world-weary but less cynical. I have come to respect the outmoded, outrageous, insufferable institution I have covered all this time.

John Clarke, one of the men I admire most in this business, once told me that the role of the satirist was to find holes in the veneer through which a little fun could be poked. In the same class is my dear friend A. K. Grant who, when I repeated this maxim, replied, 'Quite so, old man, and you are that hole in the veneer . . .'

I hope you enjoy the view.

My permanent assignment to the parliamentary beat came in February 1974. It necessitated buying a tie, getting a haircut, and trotting down to the coin-operated photography booth in the foyer of the railway station in search of a suitable likeness for my first press card.

Ian Cross guided me across to Bellamy's to meet some old chums of his in the Press Gallery who could give me some pointers. Bellamy's back then was a ramshackle old wooden structure that leant against the south wall of the main building. It was always busy. You came down ricketty stairs through an air-lock of cooking smells, tobacco smoke and hops. Early evening it had the casual gaiety of a benign riot. The bar was one of those continuous counter affairs you still find at the odd country racecourse. Thin partitions segregated the various castes. At the far end messengers got a bare wooden floor. Next door the press got stained lino. The Members and Guests and Members Only bars graduated to greasy carpet flecked with cigarette burns.

People entered the cubicle befitting their status, hung up coats, tucked briefcases against the walls, and checked the stainless steel warming drawers to see what tasty morsels were left over from lunch. Sometimes there were crumbed oysters and sweetbreads but mostly it was fish in limp jackets of batter, but once fortified they were ready to battle through the crush to the bar.

That first afternoon I nursed a beer and stared about in wonder. It was fantastic.

'Well, young man,' said Cross above the din, 'what do you think?'

I shrugged. 'I guess it will have to do.'

The Midnight Sun of the Recess

Parliament may be in recess, but the decision making continues. Decisions like, 'Is it too early for lunch yet?' and 'Is it too wet for golf?' Sadly, the answer has nearly always been yes on both counts. Nowhere is this tension more manifest than in the Press Gallery itself, reporters languidly complaining from positions of horizontal repose that they are being rushed off their feet.

Part of the problem on the wet and miserable morning I attended was that only two committees were meeting — the superannuation saga and the Local Bills committee. The superannuation hearings have slowed down and the constant friction has now subsided into a dubious camaraderie of mutual battle fatigue. I must confess to you, as I did to an MP on the committee, that I haven't understood any of the submissions. He abused this vulnerable and tender intimacy, by boasting that he understood at least half of what was said. The committee has shifted rooms and the old venue is now the home of an indoor bowls set, and while the grand affairs of state were being decided next door by pale and weary men, the tea ladies, with much laughter, were enjoying a game.

Back in the House I amused myself wandering the deserted corridors looking at the old photos. I spent some time tracing the changes in appearance of various MPs from the early sixties to the seventies. Some, like Kirk and Connelly, have improved with age; some like Finlay and Holyoake, have aged only slowly, while others evidence tragic degeneration. Other corridors are being repainted and ladders and painters are propped up against the walls and canvas sheeting is draped across the floor. If there is any whitewash left over the Minister of Police, Mick Connelly, has asked for first option.

Many MPs of course are overseas — Speaker Stan Whitehead leads one group, Tom McGuigan has now travelled on the same French 'gas turbine train' as ex-Railways Minister, Peter Gordon, did four years ago, and Bob Tizard is to attend a WHO assembly at St Andrews medical school, which is strategically located beside the Royal and Ancient golf course of the same name. Housing Minister Bill Fraser remains the only Minister not to have gone abroad, not even to Australia, which hardly counts anyway. Presumably with the housing shortage the way it is, he is frightened of squatters, should he leave.

It is also the conference season and most Ministers remaining, are busy up and down the country opening seminars and making speeches to assorted groups. The Prime Minister has gone north for a while, for a well deserved rest. His varicose veins were causing him considerable discomfort throughout the first session I am told, and this factor alone contributed much of the acrimony and discord of that period. The operation, although simple enough, can be very painful and he is reported to have told Hugh Watt that if he'd known how painful it was going to be he'd have left them where they were. My mum had her veins done once and she is very sympathetic to Mr Kirk. Mind you, she only had to run a home, not a country. She hopes however, as I think we all must, that they took out the right ones, something they neglected to do in her case, as a specialist confirmed some years after.

I was rescued from my wanderings by a thirsty fellow reporter and we headed off for Bellamy's. He, being a veteran, took a short-cut through the Government lobby.

'Rufus,' I said, for that was his name, 'are you sure we're allowed here?' He reassured me, pointing out that it was out of bounds only during the session. I was delighted. It had intrigued me for months to see people darting in and out of the lobby doors; like all forbidden fruit, it looked inviting from where I sat. During the session the entrances are guarded by grim messengers and only messages and MPs and their secretaries can pass beyond the glass-panelled doors.

It didn't measure up to expectations, being merely a long corridor, one wall lined with books, the other with old couches and deep chairs. At intervals were small, grubby wooden ashtrays on the floor and a high-stemmed brass lily-shaped structure of inde-terminate function. Further along, telephone cubi-cles hung from the wall and at the doorway into the house was a small blackboard for messages. If phy-sically unprepossessing, it is turgid with atmosphere. There is something about its seedy elegance that lends needed humanity to the home of government. The Beehive will lose all of this and will resemble the foyer of a huge advertising agency, which of course in many ways it should. Off the lobby corridor, Rufus found a new room, 'I didn't know this was here.' It was still being painted and must have been walled off previously. Rufus was delighted with his find and believes it might be part of an old stairwell. Around the corner from here is the Members-only billiards room. It is always out of bounds and no intruder has lived to tell the tale. It and the Govern-ment caucus room (which is always locked) remain the only places denied to me.

In Bellamy's the conversation flowed like wine, which isn't bad considering we were only on beer. I like Bellamy's. The gossip, most of it vicious and uncalled for, is endlessly fascinating. I spent some time there chatting to various people and can now report from impeccable sources why Dr Finlay and Sir Keith Holyoake haven't aged as they should have.

Finlay apparently is boot-polishing his hair, cun-ningly leaving some grey streaks in on the sides to add authenticity. This was hotly denied by respon-sible people and I leave it to the public to decide. Sir Keith favours a light golden brown — never having had black hair it would be patently false if he grew some now. The colour concerned runs back across the top of his head and looks, from above, like wet wool. He is also purportedly wearing built-up shoes, all of which is part of a campaign designed to torment the younger, but nearly hairless Jack Marshall.

I spent the afternoon engaged in more idle speculation, which is how many reporters pass the time during the long midnight sun of the recess. There is talk of dumping Hugh Watt, and I would like to caution the would-be saboteurs, don't throw away the baby with the bath water. Hugh is the only person who can perform what I consider a piece of masterly House Strategy. I have seen him pretend to be asleep during question and answer time, while all about, fury and abuse rages. Hugh 'sleeps' on indifferent to the cacophony which only serves to further incense the Opposition. And on this occasion there eventually came a question specifically for him to answer. As it was being read out in a strident and challenging fashion by a Member opposite, Hugh slept on. Then, when the Member had finished, he arose smoothly and swiftly to deliver without notes a lucid and constructive answer before dropping to his seat and pretending to be asleep again. The Opposi-tion was left in disarray.

A number of people are being touted as likely replacements — at last count there were 50 names on the list, but two of these are Members of the Oppo-sition and their chances are slim.

Listener, May 18, 1974

Labour Party Conference: May 1974. My first political conference. An exciting, mystifying event. Particularly memorable in that illness kept Norm Kirk away until the final morning. When he arrived, even with the aid of a walking stick he had difficulty negotiating the steps of the old Wellington Town Hall. He shuffled past journalists shocked into silence by his appearance and was greeted in the foyer by the most electrifying Maori welcome I have ever heard.

The Rustication Ploy

We live, there is no doubt, in turbulent times, times that given full reign would rip the very fabric of democracy from under our feet. President Nixon, the man who brought miraculous peace to troubled Indochina, is under siege in his own office. Agnew has gone. Golda Meir has gone. Pompidou has gone. Heath and Brandt have gone, and now Jack Marshall has gone ... where in God's name will it end?

And who, pray, is safe?

Many and varied are the 'true' stories that have appeared in print promising to tell the 'real' version of what happened, but it is only now, violent passions and thwarted loyalties having subsided, that the real 'real' story can be told.

National Party watchers have pieced together a tale too bizarre to be false — a tale of cryptic intrigue that characterises this vast and largely unknown party. They suggest it began at the time of Jack

Marshall's alleged trip overseas. One story has it that having failed to get the support of the youth groups Marshall attempted to flee the country, but his Jag was intercepted at Rongotai by a militia escort of Bentleys. He was then taken to a large rural consortium in the Wairarapa Province for a period of intense self-criticism. To cover his disappearance, slides of him eating scallops on the Blackpool pier and at other exotic locations were planted in the media in the usual fashion. This was accompanied by a fierce poster war, and of special significance were the ones of banished party hero Sir Keith Holyoake, captioned 'Where is he, now that we need him?'

In the battle of 'ideology' Marshall's 'bridge-building' and 'liberalism' lost out to hardliner Muldoon's 'nihilism and pragmatism'. The rank and file also favoured Muldoon's three-year-plan to Marshall's nine-year-plan.

Marshall's demise came as no surprise to regular observers of the body politic. His was a lonely figure in the House itself. He cut himself off from the activity of his colleagues, his aloof immobility in mute contrast to their incessant exchange of notes, secret signals and knowing grins. He rarely interjected and rose to speak only when necessary, and then spoke slowly, quietly and almost hesitantly. All his instincts and reflexes were those of a man used to being in charge and the passive, strange and unnatural confinement of Opposition seemed to numb him. He appeared dejected by this cruel and unexpected busting and return to the ranks.

If it appeared to pacify Marshall it had the reverse effect on his nuggety second-in-command. He resented captivity and was perpetually restless. Even when perfectly still his teeth appeared to be grinding together. He would often rise and move across to chat to colleagues, something Marshall never did. Blessed with a splendidly fierce appearance he would occasionally slowly scan the Government benches and it would invariably leave the observed looking vaguely uncomfortable in its wake He was, in short, what is known in gangster movies as 'stir-crazy'.

Had it been a prison canteen I could easily envisage Muldoon leading the rioting and the throwing of food.

There was a feeling that National was sinking and that Jack was prepared to go down with the ship, draped perhaps in a Union Jack and toasting the Queen. This pessimism was not shared by many in both the Labour Party and the National Party. Some in fact, with nostrils fully flared, could smell victory. Could it be that Labour, unused to power, having been denied it so long and having suffered atrophy of their original fighting spirit, would repeat their previous term of office and bow out without an encore?

Marshall was prepared to let this happen; Muldoon it was said, could force it to happen. They would need to fight of course, and fight dirty; after all they were outnumbered.

The bell has gone and already round one is more exciting than the preliminary bouts.

At about this time, by sheer coincidence, Muldoon's book came on sale. This was not, as many have blackly suggested, necessarily to Muldoon's advantage as far as book sales went. The first batch was already assured of sell-out and the extra demand could not be met. The next reprint, however, is out in a couple of months and if the coup had taken place then it would have been much better timing. Perhaps Jack knew this and deliberately stood down when he did to kill the later sales. Probably not, but it would have been a neat trick if he had.

The book-launching itself was a gala affair. On the strength of anticipated sales, drink and food were provided in the foyer of a large bookshop. It was very select, only the press and a few invited guests. There was one attempted gate-crashing at about 6.30. An old lady couldn't believe her luck and decided to buy some books even if all the other shops were closed.

Eventually the guest of honour climbed on to a soap box and gave a short address. He was brief enough and stepped down to considerable applause. Then, while the rest attacked the remains of the food and drink, a few lined up to receive autographed copies. I joined them and suggested he inscribe it 'to the fabulously talented, warm and witty Tom Scott', but he let me down with an ambiguous taunt that will haunt the title page for generations of my grandchildren to come.

Having now acquired best-selling author status Muldoon will probably be treated with further awe by some on the Hill. Like Finlay's doctorate and O'Flynn's former QC status it will separate him slightly from the mob.

Since the change in leadership the House has been witness to some ugly incidents and there are signs that many Labour men are alarmed at the change.

Can victory be snatched from the jaws of the Socialist demon? Not unless, say the experts, pensions are cut by over half, taxes rise by over 200 per cent, inflation runs at 50 per cent per annum, Police Commissioner Sharp is murdered by a gang of crazed typists, Bill Rowling is convicted for pushing heroin to blind boy scouts, and Norman Kirk has a sex change.

Listener, August 3, 1974

The day before Norm Kirk died I'd been at a reception at Parliament quizzing Jonathan Hunt on the state of his leader's health. An obviously relieved Hunt told me that Hugh Watt had not long before informed caucus that the PM was on the mend and only needed rest. Indeed Hunt was more interested in dropping hints about a story he was intending to go public on next week. In the end of course, there was only the one story next week. A story dominating the press, radio and television until Kirk's coffin was laid to rest in the Waimate graveyard.

It was the most extraordinary week I have ever witnessed on the Hill and with the falling rain came a cloudburst of grief of stunning intensity. Like the rain it left as suddenly as it came. Sorrow is like a splinter through the heart and I have often wondered if Labour would have fared better in the '75 elections if even a little piece of the splinter had been left in place. Labour were too anxious to put Kirk behind them. There was no attempt to inflame the old chest pains and he was hardly mentioned on the hustings. Significantly, on the campaign trail in Rotorua Rob Muldoon made a well publicised detour to pay his respects to Kirk's widow, Dame Ruth. If there was any legacy to tap Muldoon certainly wouldn't pass up the opportunity.

The cartoon is from the *Sunday Times*. I wandered in off the street with it and editor Frank Hayden published it. Many readers complained that it was insulting but it is my favourite drawing of Kirk.

That Big Man

If I sat all day wondering what people thought about me or how I'd like them to think about me, I wouldn't get any work done. I leave that to the news media. They don't really know what to make of me either, but they say all sorts of things which entertain even if they don't inform.

The late Prime Minister talking to David Exel

Looking back on it, the chief regret of my brief time as a Parliamentary reporter is that in all those months I never saw Norman Kirk at anywhere near full strength. Even though obviously unwell, he was, right to the end, a commanding figure in the House. His mere presence seemed to charge the air of the chamber with a strange tension and expectation.

He always entered the floor of the House through the side door and they were especially grand arrivals if he did so behind a group of shorter colleagues. He would pause to joke with people like Joe Walding and Bill Fraser and even when in considerable pain he would reach his bench grinning broadly and before taking his seat he would turn and give an exaggerated wink to those in the back rows behind him.

It was the performance of a captain telling his men they had nothing to worry about. If he rose to speak he was granted a respectful and immediate silence. Few dared to interject and members from both sides of the House would pay close attention, some even abandoning, albeit momentarily, their beloved newspapers to do so. Should he begin to shout the Press benches filled, as if by magic, to overflowing. The surplus not able to write notes would stand about grinning excitedly to one another.

As his health deteriorated those occasions gradually became less and less frequent . . .

It began with the varicose vein surgery in April. Eager to return to work, he denied himself an adequate recovery period and complication followed complication. It was to become a familiar pattern. Part of the problem lay in the difficulty involved in forcing an intensely inner-directed man to rest properly. As his great strength and energy eroded so did party morale. Kirk felt this keenly and in private he would rage about his invalid status and fume at the terrible fatigue that dogged him.

Not long after the Labour Party conference, *Inquiry* reporter George Andrews met him in the car-parking basement beneath Parliament. At the time he hadn't resumed full duties and could walk only with the aid of a stick. Laden with a couple of brief cases and some notes, he was only able to move slowly. Finally George plucked up enough courage to offer some assistance.

Kirk shook his head. 'George, I'll carry these bloody things even if it kills me.'

On June 10 he was cleared for full duties, but this failed to quell the growing public anxiety. Bizarre and grisly speculation circulated both boardroom and factory floor. Following minor surgery to treat an ingrown toenail, and well aware of the wild conjecture, Kirk joked grimly with reporters that the same incision, so as to allay suspicion, had been used also to remove assorted tumours.

It was against this background that we were told on August 28 that he was to enter the Island Bay Home of Compassion as part of a well justified, six-week period of complete rest. For some it was proof at last that he was seriously ill; for others it promised a chance for a proper recovery. For all, just two days later, the announcement of his death came as a sudden and cruel shock.

I learnt through a terse Sunday headline.

'Kirk dies aged 51.'

Whenever I relaxed or was diverted, this message came back swiftly to jar and startle me. It greeted me in the morning and kept me awake at night. Friends complained of a similar phenomenon. It must have been some kind of mental teleslide designed to convince a stubborn corner of the unconscious, for it stopped the afternoon he was buried.

And yet for all my piety now, the news at first left me with only an academic, and reflex sorrow. 'Isn't this bad news for the country?' I thought; 'How sad for Mrs Kirk,' I thought, and I hurried down to Parliament on the Monday morning, pen and paper ready.

In the foyer there was an air of hushed, reverent chaos. Workmen in shorts and boots had been there since four in the morning — they jostled for space with messengers, television crews and servicemen. Outside on the concourse a crowd began to quietly assemble. As the hearse drove up the first strains of the Maori lament moved the base of public grief from one of polite containment to one of free expression.

Together with Pacific Island groups the Maoris served over the next three days as a powerful catalyst for pakeha sorrow. Their palpable despair acted as a vast emotional poultice and all those within hearing distance who had any feelings on the matter could feel them being tugged to the surface.

I came as an observer and became, in spite of myself, a participant.

Over 30,000 people came to file past the casket, some from as far away as North Auckland. Many had to queue in the rain for over an hour before being able to pay their respects. Many brought young children.

'I wanted them to pay their respects to a great man.'

'Well it's history for them isn't it? They've said goodbye to a man who'll be talked about for many years.'

Most children were quiet, silenced by their parents' grief, but a few asked questions.

'What were the soldiers doing Mum?'

'They were changing the guard Michael.'

'Was that anything to do with Christopher Robin?'

'No dear, it had nothing to do with Christopher Robin.'

The scale and the depth of the mourning for Norman Kirk has forced many commentators into a new assessment of the man. The public reaction was almost without precedent and certainly beyond expectation.

We all knew he was important, but we didn't realise he meant that much to so many people.

That's one of the problems with experts: often they're the first to know but the last to understand.

Just six weeks ago people around Parliament House would have told you that Norm Kirk was going out of fashion. If it was true, no one bothered to tell the rest of the country. Parliament can be a cloistered, cosy place of petty victories, incestuous intrigue and much sound and fury, much appreciated there, but meaning little just a hundred yards away on Lambton Quay.

Norman Kirk understood the importance of places like Lambton Quay. His affinity for the ordinary New Zealander cut him off from many of his colleagues who through accident of birth, choice, education or elevation to Parliament, were clearly not common folk. A gap developed between him and the rest of the Party, and although respected and even, as Dr Michael Bassett put it, 'loved' by them all, he was essentially a loner. His successor, the extremely capable and amiable Bill Rowling, is very popular with his colleagues, which implies that he is more cut off from the public.

On the Tuesday afternoon the House sat, in its formal and pedestrian way, to pay its own tribute to the fallen Prime Minister.

Three of the most moving speeches came from Opposition spokesmen.

'Fifty-one,' said a pale Brian Talboys, 'is too young to die.'

'I find it very difficult to accept that that big man will not walk through that door and enter this chamber again,' said Sir Keith Holyoake, and at this Colin Moyle and others wept openly.

'He graced the office of Prime Minister,' said Jack Marshall.

Holyoake and Marshall went on to talk of the warm and courteous working relationships they had enjoyed with Mr Kirk, both in Government and Opposition.

Any misunderstandings, said Sir Keith, were due to 'human frailty' and not to any political 'oneupmanship'. Marshall too stressed the need for mutual respect between the leaders of the House. He went on to suggest that often such relationships were mystifying to their 'more rabid supporters'.

At this Peter Gordon looked up at Jack with a grin and then stared across at Muldoon, who in turn stared sourly straight ahead. It confirmed what I suspected, both speakers had been rebuking, ever so indirectly, their own leader. The message was clear — desist from this unseemly and vulgar collision course, for it does no one much good.

This was only a small part of their tribute, however. Both men went on to generously praise the achievements of Mr Kirk's all too brief term of office. Implicit in their tribute was the acknowledgment that Norman Kirk had a greater hold on the country's imagination than they could ever have hoped for.

Listener, September 28, 1974

Idiot Box to Ballot Box

Justin stepped back moodily. The only sound came from his suede trousers as the legs brushed past each other. Not satisfied, he consulted the light meter before dropping it back into the tangle of hair that sprang from the vee of his bodyline silk shirt.

'From the top again team,' he said wearily. 'More vaseline on the lens of camera two please Gavin. Right, let's roll it!'

Once more the giant studio filled with the sound of birdsong, acoustic guitars, lush orchestral strings and a babbling brook. And over the crest of the massive polystyrene hill and down through the field of flowers staggered a squat and instantly recognisable figure. Encumbered by an ankle length white satin kaftan and with his vision partly impaired by a long flowing blonde wig, he had some difficulty keeping up with the heavily sedated palomino mare.

'Smile!' shouted Justin. 'You can do it! That's right. Fantastic!' It was the Leader of the Opposition.

And that, if malicious gossip and ugly rumour is anything to go by, is what Colenso Communications are attempting to do with Rob Muldoon's image. I can't see it myself; white isn't Rob's colour.

Mind you, another impeachable source has it that, should the economic situation really worsen, we can expect a 'no more Mr Nice Guy' approach from Bill Rowling. Apparently he has been filmed standing barefoot in artificial snowdrifts delivering pieces to camera on the need for a strong man at the top while pulling the heads off live chooks and having his teeth removed without anaesthetic.

Perhaps it is prudent at this juncture to examine closely the role of television in the shaping of public opinion and political destinies: the debate, as Peter Jenkins of the *Guardian* puts it, between the 'idiot box' and the 'ballot box'.

Conventional wisdom has it that television, during election campaigns, does not change people's minds, but provides them with information which merely serves to reinforce voting intentions formed over long periods of time.

However, this reinforcement theory only works in a stable political environment and, in Britain, where successive governments have made it patently plain that the place is unmanageable, party allegiances are beginning to dissolve. The swinging vote is now up to 30 per cent and those people are the ones open to persuasion by argument or event.

Television, both in current affairs and party propaganda, becomes the most important factor in determining how these people will eventually vote.

It will be some time yet before New Zealand reaches that happy state, but this does not mean that television campaigns are unimportant here. They began grooming themselves for this new and exciting breakthrough in communications back in 1963.

There were no portable video machines then and the National Party, quite appropriately, trained its front men using photo-finish gear from a local race course.

More important than the equipment though, is the instructor. Both parties like to obtain the services of a big name from television, preferably, of course, a current, current-affairs star. This isn't always possible and over the years light entertainment men — which, when you think about it, isn't so bad — have had to fill in.

The advantages of a known man are that it makes the exercise seem more real. It's flattering to meet the people anyway, and there is consolation in the knowledge that even impartial media stars have their price. The stars involved are not compromised to any great extent as all involved have a vested interest in keeping it secret.

For the stars themselves, the money is good — up to $15 an hour in some places and they can expect about $200 for a weekend's work. The other attraction is that it allows them the flattering opportunity to show off their skills, to talk about themselves and the media, and to tell very powerful men not to mumble and to sit up straight.

The work, I'm told, can be tedious and repetitive. All new candidates have to be interviewed and after the playbacks, group discussions on how they can improve their performances are held.

Senior men, of course, have a more rigorous training programme. A circular heralding such a session, last December, for Opposition frontbenchers stressed that 'A good television presentation is *absolutely critical* to your success . . .'

As preparation for the weekend they were all asked to do a short assignment. They had to pretend that they had been given two minutes of peak television time, on election eve, to persuade the country at large to vote National. 'What,' they were asked, 'would you say?' and 'How would you put it across?'

I guess we'll have to wait for the repeat screening in November before we have a chance to see how they *do* put it over. Reports will have been made of the weekend but these will be tucked away securely in party headquarters.

They usually begin with a general introduction reaffirming the advantages and the limitations of the medium and, when enriched with prose like 'Television is not a toy' and 'Television must be exploited, not cynically, but realistically', they can be very entertaining as well.

After this come the individual assessments and it seems that the biggest problem is the inability of some MPs to be themselves on television. The second biggest problem is the inability of others to be anyone else.

Like school reports the remarks are tempered with

cheap sentiment and you have to read between the lines to get the real picture. When someone is said to need far more work, that their eyes still wander and that their answers are vague, you can safely conclude that they were awful.

Along with advice on how not to look shifty and insincere, there are instructions on what to wear and words to avoid. Blue shirts are advised, spotted ties are disapproved of, baggy suits (except when discussing MPs' salaries, says one report) are a no-no. Hair, when present, should reach the ears, side-burns are encouraged, sun-glasses are out and pipes are optional. All members should avoid words like 'precognition' and Labour men are instructed against use of the word 'socialism'. National members have been told repeatedly not to talk of their trips abroad with the family.

On the purely behavioural side, MPs are instructed against standing on the studio chairs, falling off the studio chairs and lying underneath the studio chairs. Glasses, when worn, should not be looked over the top of, or taken on and off, or sucked thoughtfully. Noses should not be wiped on sleeves, heads should not rock back and forth and torsos should not swivel.

If that weren't enough they're also told how to 'manipulate' the news media. The weekends, they're told boldly, are traditionally slow times in terms of television news, and as a consequence the television news teams are often only too glad to report your press statement, or better still, send a dozen camera crews around to interview you.

We shall return to this subject when the campaign warms up. I've got my ghost-writer doing the research right now.

Listener, March 29, 1975

1975: my first rejected Listener *cover. I think the main objection was to the depiction of Muldoon as King Kong. To get back at the* Listener *I decided to turn it into a poster that would make me rich and teach them a lesson. I must have ended up with about 200 of them stacked in my garage. Still they came in very handy as presents, and this creased remnant is the only one I have left.*

Cartoons were not a regular feature of my early political columns. Although I was primarily a cartoonist when I joined I wasn't always given the space to include a drawing, which I regretted because cartoons were easy and writing was often a nightmare.

One day Ian Cross called me into his office to show me an Auckland University law faculty publication with a drawing of Karl Marx on the cover. It was by a guy called Bob Kerr and Cross wanted to know what I thought of it. I said I thought ,it was good and Cross informed me that he considered me more of a writer than a cartoonist and believed that my dabbling in the latter was slowing down my development in the former. He intended to hire Kerr so I could concentrate solely on my writing.

I wasn't sure if he was kidding. 'Bloody hell you will!!!' I said, 'Not if I've got anything to do with it!' I said this to myself, you understand, and left the office outwardly unconcerned but inwardly seething with hurt, anger and resentment. I was determined that if cartoons were to become a regular feature on my page then I would draw them.

Overnight, almost, my drawings improved enormously. I put in a lot more effort, which may have been what Cross had in mind all the time.

Bob Kerr was hired and we became friends but he never got to illustrate my work.

Termination Consternation

It was left to John Luxton, the Opposition member for Piako, to crystallise the issue. The Hospitals Amendment Bill second reading debate had, you understand, raged for nearly a week and over 50 speeches had been heard and lawyer had clashed with lawyer, doctor with doctor, father with son and old friend with old friend when the said honourable gentleman got the Speaker's call and rose to address the House.

'It would appear,' he said, with his customary caution, 'that some members support the Bill and some are against it . . .'

The majority, however, were in support and eventually the Bill was given a second reading and moved into committee to be amended to allow abortions to be performed in licensed private hospitals. The Highet amendment passed 57-10, supposedly without coaching, got full Opposition support and considerable Government support.

This Government support came in the face of very loud protestations from some senior and presumably influential Government Ministers. Not all the anger however was directed exclusively between Government members. A very flushed Air Commodore Gill took great exception to an amendment proposed by his former leader.

'I'm surprised that the Right Honourable member for Karori would want to procrastinate . . .' Pausing, perhaps to let the shock waves of delight and horror rebound across him, he added sarcastically, '. . . perhaps I shouldn't be surprised.'

The recent two weeks recess, while much appreciated, may not have been long enough to let all the wounds heal.

Some members it is feared will go into battle on the homosexual law reform issue not fully recovered from the last exchange.

Gerard Wall, sponsor of the Bill, after the required preliminary niceties, opened the debate declaring that it was not his purpose to argue the pros and cons of deciding whether a baby's life should be sacrificed in favour of the mother.

A tall, pale, gaunt man, he spoke slowly and softly without reference to notes, staring all the while, unblinkingly, in the direction of the Speaker. It was one of those rare moments of real drama in the House. The Bill had been many months in preparation.

The gallery listened silently and attentively at first but as Dr Wall's speech progressed a discernible rustle of annoyance began to mount in the gallery. Phrases like 'overseas countries are revolting in horror' and 'that disease must not flow into our country', when discussing alleged abuses following liberalisation of the law overseas, drew sharp gasps of anger.

He went on to cite some case histories from the many he had received in the mail, 'to show', as he put it, 'the more blatant occurrences'.

The first concerned a mother of four, who in spite of difficulties each pregnancy had later been able to laugh about her ordeal with her family doctor. A fifth pregnancy had been terminated and the woman was now, for the first time in her life, on tranquillisers.

'I suppose,' said Dr Wall, his voice thick with rage, 'that was for the good of the mother!'

He asked if New Zealanders were a special breed of people in that they could resist the abuses that existed overseas. The time, he suggested, to stop the flood was in the first rush. Failure to do so he predicted would mean a future with people wringing their hands in regret.

The Leader of the Opposition, when he rose to give qualified support for the Bill, inherited a hostile gallery. On the claim that the female sex alone should decide the issue he decided unwisely to jest with the gallery.

'. . . some are what are loosely termed feminists, people whose objective, they tell us, is that there should be no differences . . .' This was greeted with groans and quiet derisive laughter and he continued with less confidence '. . . They should be interchangeable in every way, which is biologically impossible.' Further audible scorn added to his embarrassment and he finished his speech with his usually impeccable timing in shreds.

The Attorney General was the first to oppose the Bill. In a speech which was labelled by many journalists as 'brilliant' and by other members who disagreed as 'cruel and unkind' or 'very clever', he attacked the Bill on the grounds that it was premature and mistimed, devious in intention and sidestepped the real issue, which was the uncertain nature of the law.

The master plan then decreed that he would be followed by the Minister of Health with his more practical objections to the Bill, and completing the triple play the Prime Minister would follow with his 'unacceptable in the circumstances of the moment' speech.

Unfortunately the Speaker was not party to this game, or else, in the heat of the moment he chose to ignore it; and the PM had to speak an hour or so *before* the speech his own speech was meant to follow.

Being, as it was, a free vote, there were no whips in operation and when a member resumed his seat the Speaker chose the next speaker from the forest of applicants that sprang to attention and demanded to be heard. The luckless McGuigan did this consistently but lost out early to Air Commodore Gill and Norman Douglas.

Of all those who supported the Bill, Douglas was the only one to attempt to define a point *in utero* where human life could fairly be considered to begin. Jeered at unfairly from above because of his difficulty in pronouncing 'electroencephalogram' (EEG), he continued angrily to suggest that as the cessation of EEG waves are used to denote death, surely the onset of such brainwaves in the foetus at 43 days must denote the onset of life.

A little later the Opposition's Logan Sloane demonstrated similar courage.

'I'm not one to have 10 bob each way. I'm not worried about the gallery or the votes I might lose!' he declared bravely. (Understandable really — he's retiring at the end of this session.)

Logan went on to insist that he spent five years overseas fighting for the right to life. It was to become a popular claim, those who didn't go overseas to fight for the right to life came into Parliament specifically to do so.

Mary Batchelor came next to oppose the Bill.

'You're sick!' shouted Logan, but he happily modified this to 'unwell' when a Government member raised a point of order.

In an emotional, close-to-tears address, she pointed out that those in the House had a free vote, while those outside didn't have that choice.

'For God's sake, Sir, let us give women themselves a chance to exercise their consciences!'

In spite of earlier warnings the gallery applauded loudly.

Unfortunately the tension which made the first night so exciting never returned and the days of debate that followed were listless by comparison. In spite of the arguments, both for and against, having been well covered, most members felt obliged not only to stand up and be counted but to be listened to as well.

On the wider issue of abortion, the stand many of them took was to one side. The majority clung to the neutrality of the law as it now stands and voiced approval of the Wall Bill provided it would later be amended.

There were highlights however.

Like Mat Rata's declaration: 'I value life whether it's one beginning by conception or otherwise.'

Or Alan McCready's mistake: 'There are good private hospitals like Calvary and Bowen where abortions could be done.'

Gordon Christie's surprising revelation: 'Any change in the law should be carried out by women.'

The anguish of Mike Moore sitting tight in a marginal seat: 'How can we represent the divided consciences of our electorates?'

The candour of Ken Comber: 'I do not profess to be King Canute.'

The prize for the best and most well-sustained highlight must go to Sir Keith Holyoake. His speech was a gem: wordy, irreverent, agile, cutting and full of common sense. Using his age to great advantage he stated on at least five occasions that the debate was likely to be the most abortive of the year. Amidst all the solemnity, coming from anyone else, such a remark could well have been considered outrageous and tasteless.

'Man,' he began, 'is emotional and logical and when I say 'man' I include woman.'

Sir Keith ventured to suggest that most of the speeches heard would, in any other debate, be ruled out on the grounds of tedious repetition; but seeing that every member felt obliged to speak, he would too, although he wasn't sure why.

'The Bill as it stands,' he boomed, 'is not acceptable to any member of the House.'

He went on to explain why he would vote for the second reading.

'I will examine all the amendments clause by clause and, who knows, I may even think of some myself.'

The final result was hailed by the supporters of Dr Wall as a great victory. They came out of the House euphoric and triumphant.

One reporter had great difficulty questioning some members on the wider implications of the victory. He complained later that the only response was one of 'Yeah, but we closed the Auckland Clinic.'

This, however, in the opinion of Alan Highet and others, is, as yet, by no means certain. Indeed, many observers who favour liberalisation of the law felt that they too could claim the result as a minor break-through. They argue that no speaker insisted that abortions should never be performed. The SPUC lobby's support of the Bill acknowledges the need and desirability of abortions being performed in certain circumstances.

The only logical and absolute, if also cruel and stupid, stand, is to insist that abortion is always murder and that it should never be performed whatever the circumstances. Of necessity all other stands are arbitrary except for the equally fatuous, diametrically opposed view that holds that abortions should always be performed irrespective of the circumstances.

Listener, May 24, 1975

Festive Occasion

Well, the National Party conference has come and gone, and this year, to use the words of one delegate who wore dark glasses all morning on the final day, it was easily the most social ever.

National sense a big election win and many in fact came to celebrate the victory they're certain will be theirs in November. The Muldoon bandwagon which needed a push start last conference was this year crowded with delirious supporters and it hurtled through the four days of festivities without pause, forcing many into performing prodigious feats of rationalisation in an effort to get aboard. It's an impressive juggernaut and judging from the speed it was travelling at when I last saw it, it will be difficult to stop in November and irrespective of who wins there is sure to be blood on the tracks.

There were, however, a few churlish bystanders from rural electorates who avoided getting aboard, on the grounds that it was really little more than a streetcar named disaster. They were part of a shrinking minority and elsewhere the mood was of confidence and optimism.

I talked to a lot of candidates and even those in hopeless seats were predicting victory. A typical conversation went a little bit like this:

' *How do you think you'll go in November?'*

'Well Tom I think, and I mean this most sincerely (or 'no hype' if they were from advertising), I've got it sewn up. You must remember that a majority of 18,000 is hardly safe these days, especially in a State House area.'

'Yes but last time you polled 78 votes, coming in last behind the Revolutionary-Suicide-Mechanised-Unit candidate from Uganda.'

'That girl made a lot of extravagant promises last time, Tom, and I know personally, for a fact, that there are 83 pretty disillusioned voters from that quarter who won't make that mistake again.'

'But surely when the Labour man was found guilty of bigamy and white slavery in the last week of the campaign . . . '

'True, but times change and thanks to the dynamic chairmanship of George Chapman and the dynamic leadership of Rob Muldoon the party has never been in better heart. Our funds and membership are up and we've got more members and funds than we know what to do with. We've even stopped raffling off-shore islands. I've talked to all sorts of people from all walks of life and they want Labour out. They're tired of Socialist mismanagement.'

However, in spite of the appalling state of the economy, there were few visible after-effects of this Socialist mismanagement on the first night of the conference. The evening began with cocktails and ended with a sumptuous buffet dinner, with a short interlude in the middle devoted to a witty speech from Brian Talboys. If National do win in November and if they run the country only half as well as they run their conferences then we are all in for three glorious years of gluttony and alcohol poisoning.

They are very friendly people too, the Nats, and many came up to interrupt my disgusting behaviour at the tables to welcome me home. 'Are you still writing for the *Listener*, Tom?' asked one senior party official. 'We haven't seen you for some time.'

'Yes,' I replied, 'I start again soon. I cut my trip short to get back for this.'

'How nice,' he said.

Out in the locker room I was accosted by a nice old lady who accused me of writing about all the fur coats last year.

'Don't forget to mention,' she said, grinning broadly, 'that some of us make all our own clothes.'

One wall was filled with assorted fur coats and stoles and I promised to point out that half of them had been run up on the old homestead treadle and that the other half were out on appro.

The rest of Friday night and a substantial part of Saturday morning were spent fighting to remain upright in the James Cook.

Most of Saturday was devoted to consideration of remits either in committee or open session and as these were candidly admitted to have only a tenuous relevance to final policy I felt no remorse when I stayed away.

Elton John has said that Saturday night is all right for fighting and at the leader's rally the leader came out doing just that. Half an hour before the counter-punching began, the Town Hall was filled to overflowing and the surplus had to move to the adjacent concert chamber and watch it all on closed circuit TV.

The big crowd was noisy and good humoured and they took their lead from the Island Bay delegation in the gallery who came equipped with posters, banners and hundreds of white balloons (presumably because the technical problems of releasing hundreds of doves indoors are manifold). They led the crowd through a ragged chorus of 'Why are we waiting', which as well as heightening the sense of vaudeville, raised a moot philosophical point.

Rob entered to a deafening standing ovation, and for at least five minutes the hollering, whistling and chorus of 'Mighty Muldoon' to the stamping of feet, continued unabated. Muldoon looked genuinely dazed by it all and it was only after a quick sing-along of 'Why was he born so beautiful, why was he born at all' that expression returned to his face. They then sang 'For he's a jolly good fellow', and this tribute was repeated throughout the conference for other officials.

The green astro turf of the Houston Astrodome and the succulent aroma of a thousand cattlebeasts roasting slowly on spits was absent but it was still a very creditable first attempt at a Presidential rally.

What followed has been widely reported. For over an hour National's leader attacked, among other things, the Government's record in housing, immigration, control of inflation, and broadcasting.

He began by thanking the Northern Maori group for giving him a rosette with pois on. For this mention of Maoris he got a tremendous ovation so he went on to add that soon all pois would have three balls instead of two to indicate that all our assets have been pawned. He got a big laugh too, when the attractive daughter of the publicity director carried his coloured charts on stage.

'Northern Maori didn't give me her though,' he said, quick as a flash.

'By my arithmetic,' said Muldoon pointing to one area of the chart, 'We have a $993 million deficit.' Actually, using the other figures on the chart, it should have been 992, but I always say what's a million dollars between friends.

The rest of the speech was devoted to pointing out things like the fact that the PM has no spinal cord, Mat Rata spent five years in standard two and that Dr Michael Bassett can eat bananas sideways. It was essentially the same speech he has given all across the country. Only the foam had been changed.

When he finished, he got another standing ovation but it seemed to lack the enthusiasm of the first and another chorus of 'For he's a jolly good fellow' broke out.

The people beside me left very happy. Others weren't.

'I have been a member of the National Party all my life,' said an elderly lady, 'and that was nothing more than a p—poor circus.'

She didn't sound as if she'd been a National Party supporter all her life.

Listener, August 16, 1975

Call of the Land

Maori land is a complex legal question. It can be held under Maori title or European title and no one seems to know *exactly* how much land the Maoris have left. The arithmetic, though, is easy enough; once they owned over 66 million acres, now they have about three million acres.

The Treaty of Waitangi, which promised the Tribes undisturbed possession of their lands, also granted the Crown exclusive rights of pre-emption, and it worked so well that by 1891 the 66 million acres had been whittled down to 11 million.

The Maoris dug in a little after this and even with new and improved legislation the total could only be reduced to four million, and for 30 years legislators despaired of reducing it any further.

Like pest eradication officials they resigned themselves to the fact that there would always be Maori land they couldn't get. It wasn't until 1967 and the Maori Affairs Amendment Act that a determined effort was made to break the deadlock and it worked very well under difficult circumstances.

Labour came to power in '72 promising the earth. To date they've given 42,000 acres of it back and two sacred mountains have been returned to their rightful owners.

Predictably the timing and implications of the great Maori Land March were not appreciated by the Minister of Maori Affairs and Land, Matuia Rata, or his staff. The organisers at the start hoped for 50,000 marchers and the Minister's special assistant, Dr Pat Hohepa, threatened to resign if more than 12 arrived in Wellington. Seven hundred miles and one month later it was clear they were both wrong. The grounds of Parliament were crowded though and in reply to taunts from some of the young marchers, Dr Hohepa conceded wanly that he had too much work to finish to resign then and there.

In the bitter cold and a light drizzle that led to the collapse of some small children, pakehas and Maoris shivered together as the march leaders presented the Prime Minister with a Memorial of Rights signed by 60,000 people. One well-meaning lady stepped out of the crowd with a home-made sign, lime green on hardboard, 'Love be with you — wonderful people' and the same giant Maori warden who was later to order the press about, sent her crestfallen back to the sidelines.

There were grumbles that Parliament should have remained sitting for them (it never sits on Mondays anyway) but most marchers were pleased with the big turnout of MPs.

A group of young marchers, many of them members of Nga Tamatoa, were not happy with the verbal assurances and they protested angrily. 'Go home to your TV sets, gutlessness and apathy' said one to a horrified group of Maoris who felt that the

MP's should understand how we feel about our land, after all, most of them tend to worship the ground they walk on...

good PR work of the campaign was about to be ruined. A young Child of God with a vacant happy face, hoping to succeed where white-haired march leader Whina Cooper had failed, stepped forward to him with some soothing literature. He tore it in two, handed it back and told her to take her pakeha rubbish home.

'How many are staying?' asked another young leader and about 17 hands went up.

'Not many, are there?' he laughed. But later that night when some tents had been pitched nearly 40 people remained.

Anxious to avoid a damaging confrontation, Acting Speaker Jonathan Hunt said he was prepared to let them stay a reasonable time. He talked to some reporters of a 'secret solution' (waiting perhaps for a freak 400mph wind or a sudden onset of the next ice age to drive them away) while asking others if they had any ideas. He was in the awkward position of having to solve the problem smoothly and he was inundated through the mail with contradictory advice.

All the first week the sit-in continued peacefully, with the leaders declaring themselves prepared to remain two years if necessary to get written assurances from the Government that not one more acre of Maori Land would be taken by legislation.

An embassy tent was set up and ministers of defence and publicity appointed. These two appointments tended to clash, as the minister of defence, armed with a club, went around casually putting the wind up photographers.

While a few went out to work to pay for provisions, the rest held rap sessions on the steps of Parliament, chatted to well-wishers, sang songs and performed chants. It was also planned that others would go to Government departments and libraries to research information for submissions to select committees, but as most involved were shy and unsophisticated young people, the project never really worked at all.

The camp-site and the Ngati Poneke Marae across the road from Parliament were kept clean and tidy — the only people dropping cigarette butts seemed to be television crews and chauffeurs.

The only problems at first were the loud-hailer effects on shorthand typists and the man-hours lost on the Beehive construction site every time a chant or challenge was performed. But at the start of the second week Hunt felt it was time to formally request that their personal effects be removed from the grounds.

When they refused this request and turned down a compromise proposed by two Wellington lawyers, it looked as though a confrontation was inevitable. The District Maori Council was then asked to talk to the group. This took place on a wet Wednesday afternoon; that morning almost everyone had retreated to the Ngati Poneke hall. Bare and spartan like a country hall, a little oasis of timber surrounded by steel and glass, it reverberated with laughter and song and a strong sense of purpose.

At one table 25-year-old David Ruru, a Te Roopu Ote Matakite leader, sat writing a press statement. Fierce and gentle in turns, he looked up every so often to curse when small children interrupted his concentration. Veteran protester and candy-floss king Jim Andrews waddled out of the kitchen. 'I'm here,' he offered, 'because this thing is the nearest thing to ... to ...' 'Heaven,' suggested Ruru helpfully, and Jim sat down to recount his latest exchange with his old adversary, Speaker Stan Whitehead.

Ruru, a Ngati Porou from Tolaga Bay, gave up his job to go on the march and he wants the pride and strength of the march to continue. Much of his radicalism stems from the two years he spent in America as a Mormon missionary working mostly on Indian Reservations in Montana and Idaho. He feels that if the Maoris don't make a stand now, one day soon they will be as lost and broken as the American Indian.

Elsewhere in the hall a group was learning Maori songs, a smaller group was planning the long trek to Tauranga and out the back the cooks were preparing tea. That night they had two sheep — they weren't always that lucky but shopkeepers had been kind. One gave all his unsold pies and someone else had donated a fridge. Any donated fruit was divided up amongst the children.

In the middle of 'Oh happy day', Ruru's cousin Greg Whakataka interrupted the choir to point out that there was a confrontation that afternoon: 'You can sing your pakeha songs later.'

A group of high school students turned up illegally to sing to the gathering and the press were asked to keep their identity secret. The impromptu concert was a little rough but quite moving and across in the Maori Affairs Committee room in Parliament the District Maori Council sipped tea and said firmly that the protesters could come to them. 'We don't go anywhere,' said one of them icily, 'We make the rules here.'

The council seemed to think that the press were responsible for the whole thing and they insisted that if the press boycotted it the protesters would all pack up and leave within hours. Eventually the two parties met on the steps and Ruru told them that it was wrong that the Government should send them to do its work. Reading from the statement he'd prepared that morning, his anger and sincerity were invincible and both groups eventually joined in song.

Hunt made another request the next day and that night on the cold steps the talk and laughter was a little muted. 'I come from a land of eternal sunshine,' said one of the Aborigines softly. Highlight of the evening was the arrival of a bread van, laden with hot bread. Six loaves were tossed off before the driver raced off guiltily into the night.

It was probably the long bitterly cold Labour Day weekend that did the trick, and 16 days after their arrival 50 marchers turned around to march north.

Their demand that not one more acre of Maori Land be taken by legislation forever and ever, while worthy in intent, is patently unrealistic.

A Government can no more guarantee that than it could sign a piece of paper banning cot deaths.

Te Roopu Ote Matakite probably realise that, and they'll be back next year better prepared.

Listener, November 22, 1975

The Blamed and the Blame

The final caucus of the third (and last?) Labour Government lasted almost a full day. And guarded by a solitary messenger the members came out towards the end of the morning session to carry back the crates of alcohol stacked by the door.

Defeat hung heavily on the shoulders of senior men like Warren Freer and Martyn Finlay. They've spent most of their Parliamentary careers in Opposition and the latest rejection was the cruellest and most unexpected of all.

Freshmen Richard Mayson and Ian Quigley, tieless and casually attired, were their normal hearty selves and Aubrey Begg spoke for the others when he said fiercely that he'd be back.

The next morning the Nats, in defiance of convention, moved across to occupy the same room. Down came the sacred photos of the Labour deity and up went a picture of Churchill. Rob Muldoon, an impatient Moses, couldn't wait to deliver his people to the Promised Land. Three years earlier Norm Kirk had his people pause a while in the desert, just to remind them of what they could return to. As aversion therapy it didn't work well at all.

The incoming Government members were understandably jubilant. For some reason I was greeted like an old friend and I had my arm pumped enthusiastically as if I'd been some help (a disturbing thought). It seems now that there's hardly a senior Nat who didn't correctly predict the result and leave it in a sealed envelope with his secretary. I suspect that this is part of a group strategy to further undermine the confidence of the Press Gallery.

Back in their rooms Labour members sorted dispiritedly through their gear. Rubbish went into large sacks, personal effects into separate cartons and official papers to the Turnbull Library archives. Down came calendars, posters, family portraits and pot plants until the rooms were quite bare.

They had to leave their flats as well, as these too are required by the incoming MPs.

Along with a cut in salary deposed Ministers have to leave official residences, relinquish colour television sets and make do without their two self-drive official cars.

There are others in the building who have to make adjustments too. In Bellamy's messengers congratulated one of their fellows on having Sir Roy Jack to tend again and in the next bar press secretaries fortified themselves in readiness for their new masters. Most press secretaries are career men from the Tourist and Publicity Department and they are quite philosophical about the change in Government. Those who had enjoyed a good rapport with former Nat Ministers had no reservations and a few were openly delighted.

Those politically appointed (even though laundered by the Tourist and Publicity Department) know that their number is up and are busy looking elsewhere for work. One plans to go fishing, another may join a shearing gang.

Private secretaries tend to develop stronger loyalties than the press men and some of them plan to move on. Most of the women in the Government typing pool joined Citizens for Rowling and they intend to follow their man across to the Opposition wing. The Opposition typing pool, equally loyal to their man, will move back.

Shattered at first by the result, the Government typists finally rallied to the defence of their favourite back-benchers who had worked so hard. Their departing masters left them the last of their grog and the long vacuum of the change-over was whiled away in secret sipping. Secret because of their boss, senior Government whip, Trevor Young (formerly secretary of the New Zealand Alliance).

The Press Gallery too will have to make adjustments and in some cases amends. I can see now that I was swayed by Labour's offer of the London High Commission post when Hugh Watt retired. With the assistance of comments from Shirley Wells of Christchurch (my only fan — now gone), I can see the error of my ways. She has cancelled her subscription and has taken the little plastic statue of me off her dashboard. My God, what have I done?

Greed and ambition have been my downfall. If I had any inkling that Muldoon was going to win, Shirley, do you think I would have said any of those things? Of course not.

She ended her long denunciation on a conciliatory note. If we'd lost, she said, this would have been a letter bomb.

Actually, apart from the votes cast having something to do with it, no one is yet sure why Labour lost by such a massive margin.

Dame Ruth Kirk blames those in the party with brains, which narrows the field down somewhat. Many of the old guard feel that the 'technocrats' wielded too much power; in fact they weren't 'technocrats', they were school teachers and they were out-technocrated by the Nats at every turn.

What they need are some proper technocrats, not in Parliament but down at the Gestetner rooms which serve as party headquarters.

Others blame the low turnout but even a turnout of '72 proportions would have salvaged only a few seats.

Labour in trying to woo the middle class vote left its working class support behind. National were quick to spot and exploit the gap:

'Good morning Madam, I'm from the Ajax Research Unit and I'd like to know what worries you about New Zealand society today?'

'Fancy wanting to talk to me . . . Well if you really want to know it's these bloody Pommy wreckers in the unions, bloody coconuts and the price of mutton flaps.'

Three days later.

'Good morning Madam, I'm your local National Party candidate . . .'

'Clear off, we're all Labour here.'

'And I'd like to talk to you about the three things which really worry me about New Zealand society today: immigration, English militants in our trade unions and the appalling cost of meat.'

'Gosh . . . you'd better come in then.'

Leadership was an issue and all the attacks on Muldoon merely confirmed him as a working class hero. I know of some bikies in Palmerston North who intended to vote National because blokes like them needed a strong man to tell them what to do. (In many ways it was like the 10 o'clock closing referendum. I knew a number of alcoholics who were violently opposed to a change in the law on the grounds that if it was changed they would never get home to their wives and children.)

Some MPs have rather sourly tried to blame SPUC and the Catholic Church for their defeat. Analysis of the results shows that conservatives and progressives suffered equally at the polls. The public obviously resented the great moral issue debates and Labour took more of the blame than National.

There was no Catholic conspiracy either. One Labour stalwart took his sister, a nun, to vote in the Island Bay electorate, instructing her to vote for O'Brien.

She had to confess later that she hadn't followed his advice. She didn't vote National either. Seeing that it was International Women's Year she said she felt she ought to vote for the feminist candidate, Ron Megget.

Ron is a well-known crusader for abortion law reform. If he has any heart at all, he'll keep that information to himself.

Listener, December 27, 1975

In the early days it never occurred to me that it was possible to travel overseas with Prime Ministers. I had just as much fun staying at home and making it all up. In this piece I borrowed liberally from Rob Muldoon's first book, *Rise and Fall of a Young Turk.* Various phrases he'd used to describe politicians he'd met I just borrowed wholesale and modified a little.

Diary of a Journey

JAPAN: Friday, April 23
Hello New Zealand. Well here we are in Tokyo. We flew in from Seoul yesterday. President Park was at the airport to farewell us and I must say for a man of his age his mind was as clear as a bell and he spoke with the confident dignity of one of the great world leaders of our time. He reminded me of Keith Holyoake and the late Sir Walter Nash. It was an uneventful flight except for the landing. The South Koreans are paranoid about highjackings and they only use North Korean pilots who have defected.

Their training isn't all that it could be, however, and we touched down in a paddy field some distance from Tokyo International Airport and we had to travel the last four miles to the terminal on foot. Bernie Galvin, the head of my department, was something of a disappointment to me. He complained incessantly and actually dropped me a number of times. Good old Frank Corner from Foreign Affairs, however, carried my Press Secretary Gerry Symmans *and* all the luggage without murmur. We lost a lot of our luggage, including four tons worth of press releases about my good self, but we didn't take any of this as badly as the TV1 reporter who lost his comb and pocket mirror. Tam's instamatic survived the impact and she busied herself taking snaps.

JAPAN: Monday, April 26
Phew! Things have been pretty hectic the last few days. I woke up with a boomer of a headache this morning. It's all this fabulous Japanese hospitality; they serve drinks before, during and after all trade negotiations. I had to do some quick thinking this morning to save the Westland beech scheme. It's no secret that the Japanese have cooled on the proposal, so I baited the trap with subsidised road and rail transport, up-graded port facilities at Westport, and cheap, guaranteed water and electricity.

The Japanese, as I said in my book, are very businesslike, but when on the defensive their lack of understanding and knowledge is abysmal. I could see they were folding and I hit them with the clincher, free with every 100 tons of wood pulp we will give the Japanese 10 tons of virtually worthless Mt Davey coal. They knew they were beaten but good sports that they are, they threw their hands in the air in mock delight and clapped each other on the back.

Tam went shopping for aspirin and took more lovely snaps.

JAPAN: Tuesday, April 27
Had an audience with the Emperor this afternoon; a truly impressive old man whose mind is still as clear as a bell. He spoke with the confident dignity of one of the great world leaders of our time and he reminded me somewhat of our own Sir Keith and the late Walter Nash. I think it's fair to say though, admirable as he is, he will never be leader of the British Labour Party.

We talked about the war and he asked me if I spent any time fighting in the Pacific theatre. I humoured the old man and told him that I'd spent a lot of time fighting in the Parnell Roxy before and after the war, but I couldn't help thinking it was no wonder they lost the war if they spent all their time picking fights at the movies.

JAPAN: Wednesday, April 28
Our last night in Japan. We went sightseeing around the nightclubs, leaning out the windows of our official limousine and yelling 'hot-pies' at the late night shoppers. It was just like being on a Parliamentary delegation all over again. Tam insisted on coming and we had to smash her camera.

CHINA: Wednesday, April 28
This morning we touched down in Peking and I remarked to our official interpreter, as we descended the steps, that Red China isn't really red at all. It's sort of a muddy-brown colour. I also told him that I came with an open mind as a leader of a country that believes you can't have a vast country out of the mainstream of world events. He thanked me graciously and said China was grateful for my visit, as it prevented their close call with international obscurity. He also hoped that my open mind wasn't open at the front and open at the rear. Obviously something was lost there in the translation.

It's a vast place, China, and as I said to Bernie, you could take all the South Island and all the North Island south of Auckland, and drop them in China and do everyone a favour. The streets were wide and clean and crowded with cyclists and our guide pointed out the spot where Joe Walding did his trick cycling. I replied with a chuckle that most New Zealanders were impressed at the time, as it was commonly believed that Joe couldn't chew gum and push-bike at the same time. Our guide laughed too, and said that my reputation as a trick cyclist had preceded me. Everyone, he said, still talks of how fast you back-pedalled on China after coming to office. Again I think much of the sense was lost in translation.

CHINA: *Thursday, April 29*

Went to a banquet last night in the Great Hall of the People, held in my honour and hosted by the new Premier. There were hundreds of guests all dressed the same, which is the cause of the protocol mistake I made. I inadvertently spent three hours discussing foreign policy with the head waiter and eventually asked the Premier for a second helping of sweet and sour pork.

The waiter, incidently, had a mind as clear as a bell and reminded me of either Keith Holyoake or the late Sir Walter Nash, I can't remember which.

CHINA: *Friday, April 30*

More top level talks today with top officials. Usual exchange of gifts took place. They gave us a lovely jade chess set and a set of rare Ming vases over 3000 years old and absolutely priceless. I gave them a plastic collapsible Maori Pa, a Peter McIntyre watercolour and an almost new copy of *Colin Meads — All Black*.

Confidentially and off the record, I asked if they could confiscate Tam's new camera. They were very sympathetic but there was nothing they could do.

CHINA: *Saturday, May 1*

This morning, we saw the May Day parade. It was fantastic. Hundreds of thousands of people marching past the official podium waving flags, smiling, and chanting slogans of undying loyalty. I remarked to Bernie that that was New Zealand the way I wanted it. Tam took lots of lovely snaps.

CHINA: *Tuesday, May 4*

We've spent the last few days visiting communes and factories and I must say I was impressed with the self-criticism programmes. If the New Zealand press boys did more of that it would leave me more spare time. We saw a play last night about night-soil. Apparently — you wouldn't read about it — they use buckets at night instead of toilets and they toss the stuff on to the cabbages in the morning. I have sworn not to eat coleslaw for the rest of my stay here. Saw an acupuncture demonstration yesterday, it's nothing new really. I shoved a garden fork through my foot once and it's been numb ever since.

I saw the underground defence system in Peking, too, and now that Russian missiles can reach our shores perhaps our unemployed this winter could dig some tunnels for us.

While attempting to hide Tam's camera last night, I tipped some things out of the wardrobe and when I put on the light the floor looked like a potter's wastepaper basket. All I can say is that they don't make rare Ming vases like they used to.

Listener, May 15, 1976

Socialist Security

With pundits predicting a blood-bath of recrimination, with Labour being notoriously prone to allowing its domestic quarrels to spill into the street and wake the neighbours, it was universally feared that, at its 60th annual conference, the New Zealand Labour Party would somehow ritually disembowel itself.

At no stage, however, were the floors awash with blood. The only bleeding that you'd notice was on the last night when the Onehunga MP, Frank Roger, got into a fight with a Samoan taxi driver. And even that may be seen as a gesture for the working man's vote, so effectively stolen from them last November by Rob Muldoon.

It must have been agreed beforehand that enough blood had been shed during the elections and on the first day the delegates who streamed into the town hall, as well as being the best dressed ever (at their finest they resembled Nats down on their luck), were all sweetness and light.

In the foyer, where the press half expected to find the mutilated bodies of General Secretary, John Wybrow, and whizz-kid Roger Douglas, suspended from the ceiling on piano wire, delegates were greeted by fresh-faced youngsters selling party ties and badges, copies of the constitution, revivalist literature, and 'C'mon Bill' T-shirts.

This folksy goodwill, quite uncanny in a party that had just taken a hideous beating, survived four days of what was at times excruciatingly tedious debate, and the only real danger faced by Conference was that the enthusiastic first-timers might go crazy with boredom.

There were many of them, mostly from new or revitalised branches (since the election 21 new branches have been registered) and, for the first time, tables jammed with delegates ran the entire length of the hall. Also for the first time, branch members had the numerical strength to defeat a union card vote. (Such was the demand for seats at the Conference, a professor of law attended as a delegate for the Nelson Biscuit Packer's Union.)

This enthusiasm and relative discipline was no accident of course, and if at times the Parliamentary Labour Party has appeared to be permanently out to lunch, the party leaders have been extremely busy out on the road. In the weeks leading up to the conference Rowling clocked up hundreds of miles and he claims record attendances at small branch meetings all over the country (300 people crowded into the Richmond hall, 500 at Temuka).

If Rowling recovered well from the November humiliation, many of his senior men and closest aides took a long time to shrug off the feeling of personal rejection, and at times it was obvious to most in the Gallery that her Majesty's loyal Opposition were grief-stricken to the point of inertia. Important decisions weren't made and good ideas were squandered. The protest on the steps of the General Assembly Library, at the Government's failure to call Parliament, was originally planned for the week of the PM's departure abroad, but vacillation delayed it somewhat and then half-hearted advertising drew a crowd of 2000.

Nelson was Rowling's first real test and Conference was to be his second. In recognition of his hard work, Conference gave him an enthusiastic reception and his leadership seems safe until next year at least, or until Arthur Faulkner writes a book, whichever comes sooner.

Rowling's caution, humility and conspicuous decency weren't in high demand last year, but many party strategists feel that the new PM, in his own inimitable way, will eventually make such qualitites politically fashionable again.

Encouraged by giddy increases in membership and a generous response to its appeals for funds, the Labour Party seems to have already decided it can win in 1978, with more of the same. Better organised, better packaged but essentially more of the same.

This was the message Rowling smuggled around the branch meetings and this was incorporated in his keynote address to Conference.

It was a long speech, well constructed on the whole and less verbose than his campaign material. It began with a bitter attack on the new administration and went on to list the achievements of the third Labour Government. Rowling's delivery was better than normal too, and occasionally he had the audience, who were only too keen to stamp and cheer, applauding furiously. He will never be a spell-binder, however, and his speeches lack the delicious anarchy and uncertainty of the PM's.

Once, when he insisted firmly, 'We shall overcome', the audience erupted into applause and raised fists, some even standing, and Rowling could only blush as if to say, 'Did I really say that?'

Labour feel threatened by Values and part of the speech was, in effect, a pitch calling the Labour voter home. Appreciative perhaps, that Labour's bemused indifference to its youth and women's groups has led to defections, Rowling devoted some time to women's rights, urban maraes and the Ohu scheme.

'We have *virtually* stopped the alienation of Maori land,' he said proudly at one point.

'Virtually! What does he mean, virtually?' I whispered to the reporter beside me.

'They must have reached the sea,' he replied.

Most of the speech was a list of the things Labour apparently had no need to apologise for and the most curious remarks came very early on. Rowling reminded Conference that last year he had told people they could choose between a Government

A socialist always leaves the last bun for someone else, never pulls the wings off butterflies.. and more importantly being a socialist means never having to say you're sorry!

which cares, and a jackboot on the back of their necks.

'They took the option, and my word they are paying for it now.'

It was reminiscent of his sentiments at the FOL Conference. There he quoted Burke and Barnum in explanation of Labour's defeat. Barnum, of course, insisted that there was a sucker born every minute. Bob Tizard extended the metaphor and compounded the sin when he followed Rowling at the FOL Conference. He quoted W. C. Fields to explain Muldoon's tactics; namely — never give a sucker an even break.

Which means of course Labour didn't make any mistakes worth worrying about and that the defeat was a ghastly mistake brought about by the apathy and stupidity of us, the general public.

Labour, however, did make mistakes and they weren't all purely management faults either. A change of managers and more money, especially when the new Government is under such fire, is soul-searching enough for most people.

All political parties tend to admire the simple wisdom of the common man when they're in office and resent it when they're not, and National too, took the easy way out in '73 and blamed the people. (A mad Irishman of my acquaintance to this day insists that the PM is mounting a holy crusade against working people as punishment for voting Labour in '72.)

Back in '73 National faced calls for a return to basic principles and Pollink, a ginger-group, was established, but eventually it came to nothing and National stormed back into office through judicious disregard for many of their basic principles.

Labour faces the same pressure and a Labour ginger-group has been set up, and it seems destined to suffer the same fate.

In Labour's case a return to basic principles means a return to socialism, a thought which makes the hairs on many Labour palms stand on end.

Although the word socialist is a perfectly respectable, even honourable word in most European democracies, down here in the world's first welfare state it seems to have acquired the same emotional loading as the word faggot.

Unfortunately, at this year's conference there were many articulate young men and women (which only made it worse) who want the Labour Party to come out of the closet.

They were irritatingly persuasive and direct and they had many of the old guard twitching badly. The old guard weren't all sure what the word meant (and we heard a number of definitions that would have sent Webster, not to mention Marx, into a slow spin), but they all knew what it spelt, and it spelt disaster.

'You can't tell them you know,' confided Mick Connelly sadly, 'they'll be all over TV tonight ... they don't realise the damage they're doing.'

Conference survived this frontal assault and even applauded the tormentors. Rowling's address offered a definition innocuous enough to satisfy most (it means caring for others and social justice) and as National's economic policies start to bite and a Labour victory in '78 seems less remote the great socialism debate will be put quietly to one side.

In the meantime Labour, as someone once said, remains socialist only in the sense that a whitebait is a fish.

Listener, June 5, 1976

Budgeting at Bellamy's

Were it not for the hundreds of trucks, pushchairs, and shopping-carts outside Bellamy's, being frantically loaded with crates of whisky and gin, you wouldn't have realised that July 29 was Budget day. Working a long hunch I popped into the bottle-store to make a few discreet inquiries. Near exhaustion and perspiring freely, the staff waved nonchalantly at the depleted shelves and solemnly assured me that it had just been another humdrum Thursday. I accept their word unreservedly, although I realise that some might uncharitably suggest that there had been a serious Budget leak. It might help if you knew that Budget night parties are traditional affairs, and it would be a foolish Parliamentary host indeed who didn't cater for at least 400 gate-crashers.

The heavy-drinking MP is an unfortunate and unjust stereotype — I know of three Government members who don't drink, except to occasionally rinse their mouths out with gin. Gin is the favoured opiate of senior cabinet men and ambitious back-benchers can send their colleagues into paroxysms of jealousy by merely popping out of Ministers' offices with the stuff on their breath.

I don't pay such rumours much attention and following the undignified scenes in Bellamy's I slipped away quietly and bought the in-laws a couple of outboard motors; the wife a marine engine; and cousin Nigel a radio, stereo, loudspeakers, amplifier and microphone.

Actually, as budgets go, Muldoon's seventh was a rather dull affair. Knocking the stuffing out of the economy earlier in the year seems to have taken its toll, and his latest effort lacks the maniacal fervour of his best work. In fact, he seems tired of economics and it has always been my belief that when a man is tired of economics, he is right. Economics has never been Muldoon's forte and to ensure continuity he will probably hand the portfolio on to George Gair.

Some weeks before the Budget the PM said publicly that he wasn't sure whether the economy needed stimulating or dampening down. Following a coroner's report, he opted for a 'neutral Budget', and the public galleries were surprisingly uncrowded when he rose to read all 42 pages of it. Tired perhaps, from the long flight home from the South Pacific forum at Nauru, he spoke slowly while Peter Wilkinson handed out documents to his colleagues. For a while most of them were attentive and nodded wisely where required, but one by one they succumbed to yawns as the two-hour address wore on.

There were highlights, of course, and I remember well the ripple of excitement when the PM announced that a 10 cents per bushel rebate on fancy grade pipfruit would go towards helping to keep the fruit pest free.

The most interesting part of the Budget for me was the introductory preamble on international affairs. 'It was,' said the PM, 'most pleasing to hear the Minister of State for Foreign Affairs of the Federal Republic of Germany on his recent visit to New Zealand state positively and with some enthusiasm that his country regarded New Zealand as a European country even though it is geographically remote.'

This is a significant advance for National, which for many years regarded us as a part of Britain, even though geographically remote. It's true that Norm Kirk had some half-baked idea about us being a small independent Pacific nation, but this was impractical and we have returned to the old standing of a country cruelly misplaced in time and space.

The PM went on to say that 'close friendly' relations have been 'restored' with the United States, and it was about then that it all became too much for me and I left the House and joined a few of the other reporters in the Press Gallery smoko room.

I was in time to watch the Olympic highlights in colour and it was great to see Rod Dixon and Dick Quax qualify for the 5000 metres final. The PM is a natural publicist and it seemed strange that he should plan Budget night for an evening most New Zealanders could be guaranteed to be gathered around the telly. One can only conclude that he didn't want this Budget to be extensively publicised; besides the Olympics were providing him with enough publicity as it was.

First Dixon, then Quax, spoke out strongly against the All Black tour of South Africa and the PM's public confession that the team went with his blessing.

The Arab/Africa boycott of the Montreal Games obviously upset our own athletes, many of whom were close friends of black Africans involved. One newspaper quoted Rod Dixon to the effect that New Zealanders in the Olympic village were being harassed by other competitors about the All Black tour, and it got to the stage that some of our athletes stopped wearing easily identifiable training gear. A journalist, too, reported that his job was made easier if he pretended to be an Australian.

At about the same time letters started arriving from journalist friends in London who were also avoiding contempt and odium by posing as Australians. It's all rather ironic really, just a few months ago New Zealanders abroad were making it clear that they had nothing to do with Australia. I found on my brief OE that Englishmen everywhere warmed appreciably when I was able to prove I wasn't from Queensland. Apparently our standing in Europe is now so bad that New Zealanders pretend to be Russian or Ugandan. And Doug Carter, our High Commissioner in London, is pretending to be Hugh Watt.

These stories came as something of a shock to me as I've always imagined our image abroad to be that of friendly, rugged, awesomely powerful and saint-like people. People who wear shorts at the South Pole, who build hospitals in the Himalayas, who sing arias at Covent Garden and whom the rest of the world could look up to and admire.

I also had an image of ourselves at home and that has been taking some knocks as well: there are New Zealanders who object to the siting of the Malaysian diplomatic residence on the grounds that the cooking smells and washing will be offensive; some newspaper cartoonists depict African leaders as primitive savages and sub-humans; a Christchurch lawyer and rugby official talks blandly of sending Africans back to the jungle; and in Parliament some MPs toss racial insults across the floor of the House while the Speaker attempts to defuse some tense situations by saying: 'Two Wongs don't make a White.'

The Olympic boycott could easily have been avoided if the PM had followed the advice of the Foreign Affairs Department. The PM, however, is a creature of instinct and gut reaction rather than logic and planning, and he brings to international affairs a rare and dangerous combination of intelligence and abysmal ignorance.

Weeping softly, Foreign Affairs wallahs have been telling journalists, strictly off the record you understand, of the intense efforts made to persuade our PM to meet with Abraham Ordia. With characteristic firmness the PM refused. Undaunted the Ministry prepared several fallback positions but these too were vetoed.

In turn Brian Talboys, Alan Highet and the Under-Secretary for Sport and Recreation were prevented from meeting Ordia. The PM decided that no Government MP would meet Ordia and senior men from the Ministry were also told to keep away from him. Even last minute plans for Ordia to meet a Foreign Affairs Department tea lady during her lunch break in the basement car park under Parliament were eventually vetoed from above.

The boycott went ahead and in reply to an Opposition question on how many countries pulled out of the Olympics, Brian Talboys was gracious enough to admit he didn't know and suggested they ask the IOC.

The full effects of the boycott are still awaited and it seems that if the Springbok tour goes ahead in '78 New Zealand athletes at the Moscow Olympics in 1980 may be the only people to ask for political asylum.

Listener, August 21, 1976

Thinking Ahead

'A great industry deserves good leadership, common sense before oratory, clear expression before emotive reasoning, and putting the common good ahead of personal ambition.'
Who said that? Was it Gandhi? or Lincoln? Churchill? Disraeli? La Rochefoucauld? O'Malley? The Queen Mother?. . .

Ah yes, I remember now. It was the PM himself, speaking at the Skellerup Young Farmer of the Year Grande Finale.

The PM, incidentally, wasn't placed, but that in no way detracts from what he said.

When I spoke to the judges later they explained that his deportment and somewhat elementary appreciation of agricultural economics had cost him points.

That is not to be disgraced however; today's young farmer is part soil scientist, part veterinarian, part biochemist, and two parts statistician and computer programmer. Poise, grace and public speaking ability also count. Gone are the days when the top prizes went automatically to good looking young men with leather patches on their elbows who could pluck dead sheep and push-start tractors.

High though their standards are, Skellerup are continually looking to improve the competition. Indeed with our trade to the Middle East so delicately poised that one false word could destroy it for all time, Skellerup are strongly considering a section on communication and understanding.

In short, tomorrow's farmer will have to be a diplomat as well. Massey University have wasted no time in accepting the challenge and an old friend of mine, Dr William Broughton, anticipating such a move, has prepared a course in Literate Agriculture.

The following are questions from Dr Broughton's first exam paper in this new area:
1. *'The lowing herd winds slowly o'er the lea.'*
Outline, with reasons, your design for an appropriate herringbone shed to accommodate this situation.
2. *'Hail to thee, blithe spirit;*
   Bird thou never wert.'
Assess from the internal evidence of this statement whether the bird referred to was not a Black Orpington or not a White Leghorn.
3. *'. . . we therefore commit his body to the ground, earth to earth, ashes to ashes, dust to dust . . .'*
Does this seem to you the most efficient way of dealing with stock carcases after culling? What benefits would be gained by the installation of a farm incinerator of adequate capacity?

It remains to be seen, however, if Skellerup incorporate Broughton's trail-blazing material. If they did the PM would probably fare even worse, but although disappointed this year, the PM had the consolation of being voted 'Mr Friendship' by all the other boys and the large audience joined in and roared its approval.

It's understandable really, for in many ways his was the best speech of the evening. He spared no one and quite rightly pointed out that the hard work and faith of young farmers should serve as an example to people in other sectors 'whose vision extends no further than next week's pay packet or the next stopwork meeting, whichever comes first.'

John Clarke, alias Fred Dagg, came in for some oblique criticism too.

'Those characters who continue to lampoon the farmer,' said the PM, 'are not only out of date but displaying questionable taste.' (A brave attack to make at a Skellerup function, when you consider what Clarke has done for the gumboot industry.)

The best part though, was at the start when he said: 'Listening to the four finalists tonight my thoughts were also with the 1000 or so young farmers' club members throughout the length and breadth of the land who took part in the contest at area and regional level.'

That may not seem remarkable to you, but those sentiments were included in the embargoed speech notes handed out to the Press Gallery two days before the speech was given.

In other words the PM, or one of his speech writers, was able to predict with uncanny accuracy the PM's reaction to speeches he hadn't heard. It's often said up here on the Hill that the PM is five steps ahead of his own party and seven steps ahead of Labour; now it seems he is also one or two steps ahead of himself.

The guests at the grande finale would not have been aware of this minor deception, in fact the PM's thoughts as he listened to the four finalists were probably on something like the next day's travel arrangements.

To be fair there is hardly a prepared speech or press statement released from Parliament that does not include fibs of this kind.

Press statements are a powerful political tool in that they allow Ministers to make claims and predictions without the terror of immediate cross-examination. They take some time to process, and when the press come back muttering about anomalies, errors and contradictions, you fob them off with another press statement.

The best example of use of the press statement as a manipulative device occurred on Budget night. The PM's department released 12 to coincide with the speech itself and 42 more a few days later. The 54 statements made a stack over an inch high and ran to thousands of words.

(I know the Government is a major shareholder in

Tasman Pulp and Paper, but this is ridiculous.)

The press statements took some time to digest and only rarely did they include more real information than the Budget itself.

That is neither here nor there, but what is important is that it got other Ministers into the act and made it seem like a team effort; it gave the impression that the Government had spared no effort to make itself clear (when in fact much of the fine print was still obscure); and it kept the Press Gallery fully occupied wading through it all.

There is a definite art to making a successful press statement, but most ministerial press officers get by on the basic assumption that the press are both congenitally lazy and stupid.

A good press statement keeps relevant facts to the minimum and is programmed to allow easy processing by the slovenly recipient.

Usually they begin, as in the case of the Budget statements, with an appropriate platitude to the effect that the Government 'recognised', 'appreciated' or 'understood' something monumentally obvious like 'the greater part of New Zealand's export income arose from livestock products.'

Then comes the announcement, often just a reiteration of what was in the Budget.

Next, the important part. A warm little homily or message from the Minister to show that he understood just how the changes would affect those involved.

To show that these should be printed they are surrounded by quotation marks and to make it easy for the journalist they are included in the statement as if excerpts from a speech.

Duncan MacIntyre is especially good at these and his press statements are full of 'We want to get these diseases cleaned up . . .' and 'The sooner we can solve the opossum problem, which is more complex than people realise, the sooner we shall eliminate the disease.'

The press aren't just invited to include the quote, they're also supplied with qualifying remarks as well, and the 54 budget press statements are littered with 'the Minister stressed', 'the Minister emphasised' and 'the Minister commented.'

Printed verbatim, the public would incorrectly assume these phrases to be those of the journalist, when in fact they are invented by the Minister or his press officer.

Most press statements from both parties tend to be cynical and self-serving. What is desperately needed — to quote the PM — is:

a little more common sense before oratory, clear expression before emotive reasoning, and putting the common good ahead of personal ambition.

Listener, August 28, 1976

Bluff and Counter-bluff

Anxious to impress my younger brother, who, coming from Marton, understandably has grave reservations about Parliament and its relevance to anything outside Wellington and/or the 18th century, I recently took him on a grand tour of the environs.

He was, I'm delighted to say, impressed with both the building itself and the obvious high regard in which I was held.

Mind you I had taken the precaution beforehand of hiring a Speaker's wig and gown from the Wellington Repertory Society and this helped considerably, and unaware of this deception brother Micky grinned happily in my wake.

Anxious, too, to show I hadn't let fame and glory go to my head and that I was still a man of the people, I engaged startled tea ladies and cleaners in conversation. Things were going really well until I met an old friend in a back corridor.

'My dear boy,' I said in my best Sir Keith Holyoake voice, 'how are you?'

He finally broke free from my two-handed handshake and replied as follows.

'Well,' he said pensively, 'like any mature, rational, sensitive, well-adjusted human being ... I'm very depressed.'

He was referring of course to the presence of the USS *Truxtun* in Wellington harbour.

I should point out that he's something of a nuclear-free-zone wallah, and before I had a chance to reassure him about how ANZUS had just been salvaged·from near ruin under the Labour administration, he began insisting that the *Truxtun* had run aground in Oslo harbour and that a sister ship, the USS *Belknap*, had been destroyed in a collision.

He had no real proof of course and I started to point out the advantages of nuclear powered vessels to him, the first being that when sailors fall overboard at night they're easy to find as they glow in the dark.

More importantly too, from a public relations point of view, the crewmen exposed to radiation leave fewer illegitimate babies behind in foreign ports and whenever a sailor jumps ship the tiresome old routine involving dozens of men and hundreds of bloodhounds has been replaced by three men with a strong geiger-counter.

Like many of his ilk he had no stomach for cold logic and he held on grimly to his primitive fears and superstitions.

'You overlook,' he argued, 'the random accident factor ...' And he went on to point out a deceptively plausible chain of events.

'Imagine,' he said, 'a seagull that has eaten a polluted fish from the Point Howard sewer outlet. Fighting off nausea, it climbs across the harbour towards the shelter of the city.

'Directly above the *Truxtun* it faints and plummets down to block an important airvent.

'Sitting in his lonely cabin a weeping petty officer has just received a letter telling him that his wife has committed adultery with the entire Los Angeles Rams. Grief-stricken and suicidal, he begins to asphyxiate.

Close to death he staggers from the cabin and runs amok with an axe.

'Attempting to stop him, an over-zealous gunner fires at him from point-blank range with a surface-to-surface nuclear missile. The whole ship goes up and Wellington with it.'

I had to concede that superficially at least, he had a pretty water-tight argument. I contended however that the over-zealous gunner would probably opt for a surface-to-air missile in such a situation, but it was a minor technicality that only a military man like myself would appreciate.

He went on to argue that the presence of the *Truxtun* would make the capital a nuclear target for the Russians if a global confrontation broke out.

If true, that would be quite unacceptable to most New Zealanders but I'm positive Auckland would make an admirable substitute. No one in his right mind would strenuously insist that Auckland be saved and should an American ship be tied up there during a nuclear holocaust, Russian sadism being what it is, it would probably go unmolested.

At about this point brother Micky and I set off to see the contentious ship for ourselves.

I must say I never really appreciated the term 'battleship grey' until after I'd spent a fruitless couple of hours peering across the harbour in search of the *Truxtun*. It blended well with the mist and was smaller than I had expected, but none the less menacing for all that.

It bobbed silently in the swell for almost a week before departing and in that time polite and clean-cut sailors came ashore and New Zealand policemen secreted about the wharves went aboard for the occasional meal. They enjoyed the visits and the good food made a change from the greasy chicken that has become standard fare for the extra policemen called into the capital this year.

At the wharf gates a happy band of protesters braved the poor weather and invited passing motorists who agreed with them to honk their horns. About one in five seemed to agree, while an equal number slowed down to shout 'Freeze you bastards', or 'You wouldn't even know what you're demonstrating about.'

Transport Minister Peter Gordon praised their efforts and suggested to reporters that in future the trade unions should protest in the same way.

It was an unexpected gesture, but understandable as the Minister had spent the weekend attempting to restore the Cook Strait ferry service.

Parliament was unexpectedly busy over the weekend in question and various meetings ran into the night. In spite of threats of tough Government retaliation the unions concerned held firm over the weekend and were privately delighted that they'd got the PM's senior press officer excluded from some of the meetings.

The unions argued on the Sunday that the ferry ban could only be lifted by a meeting of all the members involved and at a press conference after the stalemate Peter Gordon, flanked by Hugh Templeton and David Thomson, assured the nation that he would be bringing a number of proposals to Cabinet the next morning.

That was all very well, but he unnerved a lot of people when he said the final decision would be made as a result of the collective wisdom and experience of Cabinet as a whole.

Predictably enough, the PM's midday Monday press conference was crowded with over 30 journalists and photographers.

'I hope,' said the PM drily, 'what I have to say won't disappoint you too much . . .'

The Government, he said, had tough measures planned to deal with the union ban and the Government intended to make it clear that the country would be run from Parliament and not Trades Hall, and that the Government, not the unions, would determine the country's foreign policy.

The FOL has argued that the Government had plenty of warning about the waterfront ban and that in bringing the *Truxtun* to Wellington in the middle of the school holidays the Government deliberately precipitated an industrial crisis.

The PM made it clear that the Government accepted no blame and argued that the ferry ban came as a shock to both the Government and some of the unionists involved.

Earlier, however, Gordon told journalists that the Government had taken a gamble that the ferries would remain in operation and it had lost out in the game of bluff.

The PM planned a 3.30 press conference for later that afternoon but as the unions delayed reaching a decision on the ferries (the second round in the bluff) it was cancelled and we were told that Gordon would have one at 5.00. This was later amended to 5.20 and at about 5.25 the weary Minister came in to read a prepared statement.

Four days after it had promised tough action the Government conceded that there was little it could do to end the strike without exacerbating an already explosive situation.

Instead, the Government planned new industrial legislation to outlaw political strikes and make them subject to penalties. In addition the public as well as the Government will have the right to seek injunctions from the Industrial Court for an immediate resumption of work.

The draft bill will go to the Industrial Relations Council for comment and after that to a parliamentary select committee.

Facing a barrage of questions, the Minister reacted tartly to suggestions that his strong words early in the dispute had merely been 'bluster'.

'Ask me that in two weeks time,' he said, jutting his jaw.

Questioned about the origins of the proposed legislation he insisted that it had only been considered recently, yet there is some evidence that it has been some months in the wings and that the Government was merely waiting for a suitably dramatic moment to introduce it.

If speculation about some of the provisions of the legislation is correct then the Bill will be considerably more dangerous to the country than the occasional nuclear warship.

Listener, September 18, 1976

'And I'm the Queen of Sheba'

It doesn't happen very often, but apparently one recent Thursday evening, here in the capital, they tried to close the public bar early down at the Royal Tiger. The details are unclear, but it seems that while some mystified reporters, who had received anonymous tip-offs, milled outside, about 60 Black Power gang members, 12 policemen, and a group of nervous regulars jockeyed for space inside. Things were getting dangerously tense until a small, powerfully-built man, obviously not used to being crossed, sauntered casually up to the bar.

'I'm the Prime Minister of this country,' he is reputed to have said, 'and when I want to shout a few friends a beer I expect to get served.'

The barman looked across at the policeman in charge. The policeman shrugged his shoulders. 'I think he's probably right,' he said, anxious not to offend.

It was part of a carefully planned walkabout organised for the PM by his own department. This particular meeting had taken weeks to arrange and earlier that afternoon the PM had visited members of the gang at various sites around the capital where they work as contracted labour.

The discussions, as they say in the classics, were frank and meaningful, and in a rare gesture of respect and goodwill, the PM and his crew were offered certain gang privileges.

These the PM graciously declined and at about 9.30 he returned briefly to the House, which was still sitting. A Radio New Zealand journalist cornered the PM's staff about the pub meeting, but he found them tight-lipped about the whole affair. That was because the evening wasn't yet over — later the PM joined them again and they departed in the PM's car to a gang party.

Here they entered rather well into the spirit of things and I'm told it wasn't long before the PM, and the second most powerful man in the country, Bernie Galvin, head of the PM's department, were togged up in gang regalia and tossing off black power salutes.

At this point a police car pulled up outside to complain about the noise and Bernie ripped off his borrowed jacket and tore out into the night.

'I'm Bernie Galvin from the PM's department,' he told the young constables.

'And I'm the Queen of Sheba,' one of them reputedly replied.

Eventually, however, Galvin was believed and the police retreated a safe distance.

A frequent gang complaint is that they are unfairly victimised by the news media. No doubt the PM feels much the same way. Indeed, after leaving the pub earlier that evening, he had returned to the House to call an un-named *Christchurch Star* journalist a liar.

It stemmed from an unsigned piece that claimed

that 'backbench fury' over the overstayers issue had been 'unleashed' in the Government caucus that morning.

Unfortunately the fury the backbenchers had threatened failed to eventuate, and as the story was filed before caucus had finished, it was only partly correct. With Police Minister McCready absent (the man who categorically denied there had been any random checks, the man who said by way of explanation a week earlier, 'If you have a herd of jerseys and two friesians – the friesians will stand out'), and with senior Ministers promising a full investigation and conceding things had been handled badly the backbenchers had much of their anger pre-empted. When they emerged it was fairly obvious that, as the party had suffered enough over leaked reports, mum would be the word.

Along with his specific criticism of the *Christchurch Star* journalist, the PM had some harsh words for the rest of the Gallery as well. 'I'm sick and tired,' he said, 'of the way certain journalists in the Parliamentary Press Gallery are telling lies and inflaming a difficult situation.'

As my lies had yet to be published I had the satisfaction of knowing I was innocent on this occasion. I got my rebuke last week in the form of a letter to the editor, published in last week's issue.

In his letter the PM insisted that he wrote 75 per cent of his famous anti-apartheid speech, and that no foreign affairs expert had been involved, indeed that no one from Foreign Affairs was involved at all.

Of course, I accept the PM's word unreservedly. Someone ought to tell Gerry Symmans, though. Gerry told me that the speech had been the joint effort of himself, Bernie Galvin, Bryce Harland and the PM. Bryce Harland, for those who don't know, and this seems to include the PM, works for Foreign Affairs and is an expert in African and Middle East affairs.

Never mind, we all make mistakes, and the *Christchurch Star* were gracious enough, following the PM's accusation, to admit theirs. But when McCready admitted that random checks had taken place the PM was not so forthcoming.

A friend of mine, however, whose brother-in-law is a Government backbencher, stoutly insists that there were only two instances of random checks. The first involved 400 Tongans and the second 326 Samoans.

The *Christchurch Star*'s mistake was the only Government victory in a long week of embarrassing revelations.

It certainly wasn't Frank Gill's best week and the normally expansive Health and Immigration Minister was surprisingly taciturn. There is still some mystery about his sudden departure from a Cabinet meeting. During Cabinet discussions on the controversy he allegedly left and spent the rest of the day and that night in a private hospital. Cynics insist he went in for a random check but SPUC sources on the Hill tell me he has been under considerable strain lately.

There is some speculation that Gill is becoming something of Burke's bin and is being blamed for all sorts of things, and many are confidently predicting that he'll appointed an ambassador to somewhere sometime in the new year. If the overstayer blitz is too successful, and we need more Island labour – after all, someone has to pick the cotton – he will probably be sent to Tonga to drive them back here.

Martyr or not, there is no doubt that it was his request to McCready, a former regimental sergeant major, that led to all sorts of people getting their marching orders.

The debacle offered the Opposition a gift-wrapped opportunity to score numerous points, and in the snap debate they began slowly with general criticism which eventually gave the Government the courage to demand specific proof. Right at the end, to a perfectly still chamber, this was then movingly provided by Richard Prebble and Gerard Wall.

The PM, surrounded on all sides, fought back with a series of allegations of his own and at one point he called Richard Prebble the worst racist in New Zealand. He later qualified this following an interjection, and Mat Rata became the worst racist in the House.

The Opposition, rather half-heartedly, called for Gill and McCready to resign, but they probably don't want that to happen any more than the Government would like a by-election in Island Bay.

The week not only began badly for McCready, it ended badly as well. A stout opponent of Communism and creeping Socialism, he had the hapless task of introducing some new gun law legislation.

The new Bill will tighten the registration of guns and make it an offence to use imitation firearms for criminal purposes.

I don't want to alarm anyone, but just two weeks ago Peter Gordon was telling us that any legislation restricting a citizen's right to carry arms, was point eight of the Communist take-over plan.

Does this mean our society has been undermined to the extent that Soviet agents now control our Ministries of Defence and Police?

Was the PM's visit to the Black Power gang purely a social call or is the PM aware of the dangers and therefore recruiting a private army?

These are unpalatable questions, but we ignore the implications at our own peril.

Listener, November 20, 1976

Let Me Be Frank . . .

In the late sixties, here in the Capital, Christopher Robin Wheeler, editor of the infamous and sorely missed *Cock* magazine, ran a popular column called 'Who's up who and hasn't paid.' It survived on supplied gossip and anecdote about the rich and powerful and provided a sort of gutter Ombudsman service in that it allowed bitter civil servants, humiliated Parliamentary Under-Secretaries, and fallen Bellamy's waitresses, a form of anonymous redress.

It wasn't always accurate, and it wasn't always sexual in nature, but it was always good reading and every issue was feverishly devoured on the Hill.

Wheeler, of course, was an honourable man, and certain types of rumours were *verboten*. Lack of proof was no deterrent, but consistency was. Provided an MP, for instance, didn't practise what he preached against, Wheeler tended to leave him alone.

Wellington liberals, of course, secretly approved of Wheeler's activities in this field and it's rather ironic four years on to find the same people roundly condemning our Prime Minister for doing much the same thing.

The argument that an underground journal is one thing and the House of Parliament another is, in my opinion, specious. If I can be critical of the PM for a second or two, I do hope that with time, if these revelations about MPs' private lives are to continue, he develops Wheeler's sensitivity and discernment.

Certainly, his latest allegation wasn't as well handled as an attempt last year to discredit another member of the Labour Party. It was the time of the Carmen breach of privilege and the then leader of the Opposition insisted that no one on his side of the House would be bothered by her claim that several MPs were homosexuals. Referring to a Government MP by the office he held, he went on to suggest that he couldn't say the same for everyone on the Government side. Those of us in the Gallery who heard the charge decided not to perpetrate the smear and nothing was reported.

Caught out then, the PM has made no mistakes this year and openly reminds Gerald O'Brien that he has been very lenient towards him. (That the Opposition has made no reference at all to Marilyn Waring's private life is neither here nor there.)

He made no mistakes with Colin Moyle either, and recently he, in his own words, 'cold-bloodedly' accused the former Minister of Agriculture of being picked up by the police for homosexual activities.

The press had no alternative but to print the charge and the Opposition had no real alternative but to walk out of the House.

While a visibly distressed Colin Moyle was comforted by senior Opposition men in Bill Rowling's office, two Government wags caught the mood of the occasion perfectly and moved across, to guffaws of approval, to the vacated benches.

A somewhat ashamed Richard Walls later confessed he'd done it only to break the tension. His companion Norman Jones was not so contrite; the next day he insisted that Moyle got everything he deserved.

Other Government backbenchers shared the Opposition's disgust and their concern was heightened the next day when the PM asserted that Moyle's explanation to the House was at variance with a police file on the matter.

'How many other police files does he have?' said an anguished Michael Minogue, 'and does he have any on us too?'

The paranoia is understandable. Labour are convinced the National Party automatically get assistance from the SIS, and the Nats know that someone hired a private detective to follow a woman suspected to be a senior Cabinet Minister's mistress.

MPs are under more pressure and are exposed to more temptations than the rest of us, and many as a consequence have enough skeletons in the closet to keep a medical school going indefinitely.

These misdemeanours are kept quiet by what nuclear strategists call 'a balance of terror'. Until recently, anyway, any attack on an MP's private life invited immediate and bloody reprisal.

The PM, having led a saint-like life, was the only man capable of casting the first stone with impunity.

The PM, at a press conference following the whole incident, made it plain that he had not seen the police file concerned. In short, he had the courage to rise in the House and attack someone on the basis of speculation alone. Lesser men would have hidden behind a shield of hard evidence. In fact, said the PM, he doesn't see police files in the normal course of events. Apparently the Commissioner comes up to see him and while he looks the other way the Commissioner reads them out loud.

Rumours about Moyle, correct or not, have been in circulation for some time and Moyle himself this year has looked at times like a man waiting for the balloon to go up. As it happens, his apprehension was justified. Indeed, as early as January this year when discussing future leaders of the Labour Party, the PM assured his colleagues that he had enough on Moyle to end his chances.

I was worried at first when the PM said he regretted the whole affair and was relieved a few days later to find he had no regrets. Given time, it will be yet another personal triumph.

Initially, with typical modesty he found that Russell Marshall and Moyle had started it all. To give credit where credit is due, the PM's charge came after he had already accused Moyle of 'effeminate giggles'.

Others have tried to diminish the PM's very real achievements by suggesting that the Speaker should have been firmer. While it's true the PM has tended to ignore the Speaker lately when he rises to object to what the PM has said, the honour and the glory is rightly the PM's.

Others equally tartly claim the whole episode is proof of the need for Parliamentary reform, and again this a specious and irrelevant argument.

I concede some improvements could be made, and I think sawdust on the floor would raise the tone of the place immediately. Not only that, they could play Bavarian drinking songs instead of the *Moonlight Sonata* every time a division is taken.

While the PM's remarks were all right as a 'oncer', if he wishes to make similar charges in the future (he is after all sympathetic to homosexual law reform) he should dress up in women's clothing and lure the MP concerned into the grounds of Parliament and there as swiftly and humanely as possible kick him to death.

That's what the ordinary bloke who believes in a fair go would have done.

Listener, November 27, 1976

When I first joined the Press Gallery I was politely informed by my senior colleagues that 'dog doesn't eat dog'. This maxim, which Randolph Churchill changed to 'son of a bitch doesn't eat son of a bitch', is based on some obscure law of nature which just isn't true — as I discovered in India when a bus I was travelling on hit a dog. It lay writhing on the dusty tarseal a mere few seconds before every other dog in the village descended on it and it vanished in a frenzy of fur and foam.

What my colleagues were getting at was the Press Gallery doesn't write about itself. In short, while every other aspect of Parliamentary life should be subjected to withering scrutiny, the activities of the journalists themselves were strictly off limits. I never accepted that and ignored the ruling when I felt it necessary. It didn't always endear me to the older reactionary elements in the Gallery. Indeed on occasion my eligibility for Press Gallery status was questioned. One year my continued membership was put to the vote at the annual general meeting of the Gallery. Apparently I survived by the narrowest of margins. With my usual impeccable timing I somehow managed to be absent.

Still throbbing with indignation TVNZ's Spencer Jolly told me about it later. 'I was ropeable, mate,' he assured me. 'I told them what I thought — I made my position plain. I told them I thought the whole thing stank.'

'That's very kind of you, Spence,' I mumbled gratefully.

'Yeah, I told the gutless bastards that if the vote was going ahead I wanted my abstention recorded in the minutes.'

Here's Mud in Your Eye

As soon as I saw the tables pushed back to the wall, the kegs, and the large orange NZR tarpaulin spread across the floor, I knew it was going to be one of those evenings.

But then, I should have realised that anyway. The annual Press Gallery/Secretaries dinner is always that sort of evening.

It was like a bad attack of *deja vu* and for a few panic-stricken moments I thought I was back at a Massey party. With the drinking races and compulsory vulgarity, it was just like the vet student picnics I used to attend — except of course that it was less sophisticated. Needless to say, a good time was had by all.

The evening had begun in Bellamy's with an excellent four-course meal and a bottle of wine a head. People drank as if there were no tomorrow, and no doubt the next morning many were disappointed that it hadn't at least been postponed.

With the toasts and choruses of 'For they are jolly good fellows' over, we departed for the tarpaulin upstairs in the Parliamentary annex.

Here, I think it's fair to say, the tone degenerated somewhat. As expected, various groups put on 'turns' or sang humorous ditties they had composed themselves.

Less obsessed than the others, perhaps, by bodily functions and related obsessions, the broadcasting boys (who must, if I intend to retain the use of my legs for the rest of my life, remain anonymous) put on a little play about the Speaker and the PM.

Played with great dignity by a normally reticent journalist, 'Sir Roy' entered an imaginary House and began with the prayer : 'Almighty God . . .'

'Yeah, whaddya want, you stupid burk?' interrupted the young man privileged to impersonate the PM.

Unfazed, 'Sir Roy' continued, announcing that as he had just told the Labour Party they could not hold political meetings in the grounds of Parliament, as such meetings were not allowed, then Parliament itself, being a political meeting, could not sit either, and henceforth Parliament as such would cease to exist.

'But that's undemocratic,' exclaimed the journalist playing Colin Moyle.

'Of coure it's undemocratic, you stupid burk,' replied the 'PM'.

If that doesn't seem witty and sophisticated to you, you obviously missed what went before and what followed. Strangely enough, the more conservative the newspaper chain the more savage and vulgar was their portrayal of the Government, until finally one of the quietest, most orthodox men in the Gallery sang a boisterous ode (to masturbation) that proved so popular he was asked to sing it again.

These Jekyll and Hyde evenings are supposed to have some cathartic benefit and are designed to compensate for another year of enforced servility. The more conservative journalists were understandably in pursuit of maximum catharsis as many had just written glowing pieces about the PM's first year in office.

While the PM undoubtedly found these pieces, which had him firmly and calmly in control, perceptive, hard hitting and objective, I don't think he would have approved the sentiments these people expressed in their amateur dramatics.

I'm sure he would have repeated the criticism he voiced at the National Press Club recently: namely that the news media concentrate on the negative and neglect the positive. Certainly it was a fault of his own address; he tended to concentrate on our faults instead of extolling our virtues.

Apart from that, it was one of his better performances. He put the boot in, but he did so with more grace and wit than previously. He arrived a little apprehensive, according to one of his aides, and he left exhilarated.

I'm not surprised. He walked all over us and the audience, made up mainly of public relations men and advertising wallahs, applauded every put-down of the media with a brainless jubilation.

Not only that, the PM snookered us rather neatly in the speech itself. The press, he said, was always out to score points off him, and while it was a fascinating game it wasn't journalism. With that Catch 22 staring us in the face it would have been churlish and predictable to draw attention to the obvious contradictions that followed.

He blamed almost all of the overstayer controversy on us and insisted that the press had failed to cover the very real positive changes in New Zealand's relationships with the South Pacific.

Under questioning, however, he was unable to say how the press *should* have covered the story, and he could give no explanation as to why Frank Gill was able, on two occasions, to fly around the Pacific without an accompanying press party.

He did stress, though, that he encouraged his Ministers to make themselves available to the news media at any time, on any issue, and to conduct their administration in the same open way that he did. (Television producers would probably tell a different story and TV1's *Tonight* show was once told it would get more co-operation if Simon Walker were to stay away from the PM's press conferences.)

In fact, said the PM warming up, he understood that Malcolm Fraser had just had his first full press conference in some months, while he had two every Monday.

This is true, but you have to remember that certain elements of the Australian press are vastly different from ours. Over there, the print boys show the most courage, and Fraser now prefers to hold two conferences, when and if he has one: one for television which is reasonably soft, and one for the print people some of whom go for the jugular, which is all right, as the cameras aren't present to record it all.

Indeed, the Australian newspapers have been much harsher to our PM than we would ever dare.

Phillip Adams in the *Sydney Morning Herald* once wrote: 'I won't say that Muldoon's a right wing simian who walks around with his knuckles dragging on the ground ...' and Bill Guy in the *Adelaide Advertiser* at the time of the Montreal Olympics said this of our leader: 'The performance of Robert Muldoon deserves a plastic medal ... he has proved himself a redoubtable champion in the political pentathlon — which comprises hypocrisy, provocation, pig-headedness, confrontation and vindictiveness.'

It's no wonder really that poor Malcolm Fraser only holds the occasional press conference. There is so much concentrating on the negative I think I would, too. Back home, we're nowhere near that bad, and many journalists obviously took the PM's remarks to heart and produced wrap-up pieces for our leader's first year that must rank with the finest accentuate-the-positive writing produced anywhere.

A number of pieces have appeared, too, which have the PM discussing the respective merits of various Cabinet colleagues. Colin McLachlan is a worrier. Frank Gill is probably the best administrator in Cabinet, and Harry Lapwood is doing better than many expected.

What is interesting is the scant mention given in these interviews to George Gair, Les Gandar and Brian Talboys. The PM's favourite backbenchers have changed slightly too, and the formerly wildly promising Jim McLay, who at a recent caucus spoke out on behalf of others against the PM's behaviour in the House, got no mention at all.

Next year, with the Beehive nearly completed, the annual Press Gallery/Secretaries dinner will be held in far grander surroundings and the PM, too, will eventually move to a magnificent new office.

I just hope that we both rise to the occasion.

Listener, January 8, 1977

Walking the Gauntlet

The 41st annual conference of the New Zealand National Party has come and gone. These pagan festivals are always difficult to comprehend, let alone summarise, but I think one delegate came dangerously close on the final morning. 'I want,' he said enthusiastically, 'to congratulate the Government on the steps he — aah, *they* are taking.'

It was a mistake anyone could have made. The Prime Minister, both off and on stage (even when the great head slumped forward on the chest), had dominated proceedings.

Mind you, to be fair, something or someone had to, and he was certainly helped by the July Front and the rest of his team.

Mid-term conferences are like that. The Government has been in office long enough for delegates to expect progress in all sorts of areas and the next election is too far off for the Party officials to seriously threaten people with it. It's even more difficult to liven things up if the economy you promised to correct is showing all the signs of being terminally ill.

The conference began unpromisingly with delegates streaming into the chilly foyer of the Dunedin Town Hall to be handed information sachets and offered cheap tea-towels of the leader. The equivalent conference three years ago had flowers on stage and a new car being raffled in the foyer. Anyone handing out paper in the foyer then had probably come in off the street and was quite properly treated with suspicion.

Included in the information sachet this year was a plug for a local health club offering wholemeal cakes, nuts, dried fruit, herbal teas, honey, pollen, yoghurt, vitamin pills and mineral supplements.

The sinister counter-culture implications of this little advert baffled and disturbed many, until it was realised that Dunedin is the cheap whisky capital of New Zealand, and with three days of reckless consumption coming up it was felt that delegates should know where to get vitamin B in a hurry.

Flight delays ensured that the conference started with the vast hall barely half full, but Mayor Barnes was equal to the occasion. Against a stark background of dark blue and of large photographs of crayfishermen, container cranes and an oil rig, he began as if his recent knighthood were still in need of ratification.

'I haven't seen this hall so bright before,' he gushed. 'We needn't be so despondent after last night. The Government is doing its best and it's a jolly good best, too — this is no time for destructive criticism.'

George Chapman, who'd just seen the Budget swamp his conference, reserved his destructive criticism for the Opposition, and — good sport that he is

— greeted his leader warmly as 'the man of the moment'. In his address he argued that socialism, be it democratic socialism, national socialism or some other variety, always put the state first, whereas National put the individual first.

In an otherwise tightly constructed speech it was a convenient semantic lapse. Democratic socialism is to national socialism what Sir Edmund Hillary is to flower arranging. (Once during a student riot in London a policeman charged at one bystander with truncheon aloft. 'Don't hit me,' the man pleaded, 'I'm an anticommunist!' 'I don't care what sort of communist you are,' replied the constable, hitting him.)

Chapman, dogged every year by media accusations of stage management, had personally selected this year's remits to give a guardedly controversial tone to discussion from the floor.

They wouldn't have turned an eyebrow at any other party conference but in the light of the Budget, some bordered — by National Party standards — on mutiny.

The result was a strange mixture of sycophancy and defiance.

The PM, who resents faint praise as much as mild criticism, finally intervened on the question of tax relief for the single-income family, to say that it was a problem in families with young children and if the conference wanted him to provide more relief then perhaps they could suggest where the money should come from. Chapman tried twice to put softening amendments through, but the critical remit was passed narrowly.

Coming back from dinner that night, delegates had to brace themselves for a long walk down an avenue of protesters shouting 'Tory, Tory, Tory' and 'Fascist, Fascist, Fascist'. Many in the press found it an exhilarating experience, as demonstrations in the Capital have become so civilised and lifeless these days. Some of us knew many of the demonstrators but this counted for little when we found that the gauntlet of abuse included us.

'Gosh, they're an ignorant uncouth mob,' raged one delegate when he'd reached the sanctuary of the foyer. 'I came in behind Ian Fraser from TV1 and they were calling him a fascist.'

It's no coincidence that Sir Keith Holyoake got a similar welcome here in 1971. There is a growing resentment in the deep south at the wealthy indifference of Wellington and points north.

For the most part it was a good-natured crowd, with some placards calling Bert Walker's ignominious DPB cutbacks the 'Wife Retention Scheme' and some delegates waving cheerfully at their tormentors and treating it all like a West End opening. But crowds become mobs very quickly, and one Cabinet Minister achieved this alchemy by bullocking his

way through with unnecessary vigour, much like an All Black prop after the last oyster at a parliamentary reception.

Inside the foyer he looked around for someone under 40 and settled on Stephen Pearson, immediate past president of the Young Nats.

'Your friends,' he bellowed. '... I pay $35,000 a year in tax to support people like them. If I had a machine-gun I'd mow them down.'

The PM, spurning police suggestions that he enter quietly through a side door, had his car driven up to the front entrance. The crowd surged closer shouting 'OUT! OUT! OUT!' while he sat in the car for nearly two minutes. The way was clear all the time and the delay, apparently advised by a party official, served only to anger the crowd.

The PM finally emerged grim-faced but not frightened and strode purposefully into the hall, with a pale and badly shaken Mrs Muldoon in his wake. Surrounded by reporters feigning concern, he calmly laid the blame for what he called the worst thuggery the country had seen for some time on Wallace Rowling and the Labour Party.

Ten feet away one of the 'thugs', crowd marshall and Values Party member Doug Sheppard, was apologising to a weeping delegate who had been accidentally struck. Spotting him when he'd finished,

the PM came across shouting 'Get out, get out', and Sheppard disappeared down the steps and out into the darkness.

If the July Front protest organisers had seriously wanted to embarrass the PM they should have lined up outside the Town Hall and formed a 'dole-bludgers and DPB cheaters Brigade for Rob'. In America the hippies used to enrage George Wallace by turning up to cheer and applaud at his rallies.

Attacking or abusing a leader, however, gives him a wonderful opportunity to rally the troops.

Within 10 minutes the chanting and jeering had eradicated all criticisms of the Budget, and the beauty of it is that the PM didn't have to organise it himself. (Idi Amin, for example, every time food prices jump another 200 per cent, has to arrange an unsuccessful assassination attempt. It's a chilling thought, but imagine what would have hapened had the Roman Centurions merely asked Jesus Christ to move along. Christianity as we know it today wouldn't exist.)

On stage the PM was given a standing ovation when he declared, 'The day we have a prime minister of this country entering by a side door is the day we have anarchy'. Outside, however, the police were busy playing down the incident. The crowd, while noisy and abusive, had been orderly most of the time. Only two arrests were made; two eggs and one flour-bomb were thrown. On that basis, even at $35,000 a year it seems our Cabinet Minister still isn't paying enough income tax.

Inside, Lance Adams-Schneider had the hapless task of deputising for the absent Brian Talboys, and there was universal relief when he finished and everyone was able to file in to supper. Nibbling disconsolately on a mince pie, one young Nat could contain himself no longer. 'I don't know what's wrong with this party,' he lamented. 'The food and the girls get worse every year.'

Afterwards, some journalists gathered in a tiny hotel room. I was shaken to see them reduced to sitting in a circle, silently sharing a hand-rolled cigarette with a funny smell. Inflation has hit the news media as well.

National Party conferences are traditionally gatherings devoted to cramming enough fun and games into three days to tide you over the lambing season. It testifies to the night life and debauchery that Dunedin offers, as much as to the party's new mood of earnestness, that the hall first thing next morning was virtually full.

The remit discussion was more predictable than the polite rebellion of the day before. That is, until one farmer dared to suggest that confidence had not been fully restored to the farming industry. Farmers, he said, found it less risky to invest in student flats than in agriculture.

Aware of the potential damage of this remark, the PM spent some time later that night refuting it. The farmer was unrepentant. 'He wasn't with me at the stock sale last Thursday. Guys up my road have got fences falling down, yet they'd rather buy houses in town with their money.'

Unconcerned by the PM's wrath ('We don't mind critics in our party,' said the PM through gritted teeth) the farmer cheerfully expects to be appointed agricultural attache to the New Zealand Embassy on Campbell Island.

That afternoon one remit discussion group rejected a full conference decision by turning down a call for a freedom of information Bill. Hugh Templeton was instrumental in this, invoking the spectre of arrogant bureaucrats undermining the powers of Ministers. Surprisingly, the great champion of freedoms, Mike Minogue, remained silent, and the remit was lost.

It was just one of Templeton's minor triumphs. In spite of his not knowing what a Budget reference to property speculation tax meant, his mana rose more than that of any other Minister, to the extent that the leader referred to 'my friend Templeton' at the Saturday night rally. His speech to the conference on broadcasting was supersaturated with mock humility. When he wasn't paying homage to Cabinet and his leader, he praised generously the men he had appointed to head broadcasting.

Outside in the light rain dozens of policemen, bussed in from Christchurch and Invercargill at Wellington's insistence, defended the delegates from a handful of demonstrators. Back at the Town Hall the seats had been pushed back to allow dancing and the press gathered in a mean malignant huddle, tossing back the free beer and watching the others whirling round the floor.

Saturday night was the conference highlight — the leader's rally. If you missed it, don't worry. It was the same speech he has been giving for three years now. He began with some punishing ridicule at Labour's expense, but there was a long dry spell in the middle and he really had to pull out the stops to work the delegates into a lather at the end. The applause was deafening but, not surprisingly, few could remember much of what he said.

Sunday afternoon a weary, jet-lagged Brian Talboys was visibly rejuvenated by a warm standing ovation and welcome home. But he soon squandered this goodwill with a rambling dissertation on his recent trip to Europe. His fatigue seemed to affect everyone and he had to actually step back from the podium to indicate that he'd finished.

Sunday night belonged to the Young Nats, which is a sort of middle-class Moonist organisation taking in insecure young people and giving them a sense of identity and purpose. In a panel discussion involving six Cabinet Ministers, Duncan McIntyre started the ball rolling by greeting them in Maori and asking them what they knew about the Maoris.

'Young Nats,' he asked, 'have you talked to any Maori delegates? Try and find one or two Maoris and see what they think and you'll open up a new world for yourself.' Every other panelist decided either to speak in Maori or to pay homage to our Maori people. The orgy of tokenism that followed made Bruce Forsyth's *Generation Game* seem enormously dignified.

Afterwards the same malignant huddle of journalists gathered out the back to watch the young Nats disco-dance the whole night through. A few of us got invited to our first real party. It was full of farmers, some of whom had gone without sleep for two days. They were the only group I met who'd come to conference specifically to enjoy themselves.

One lady, whose husband was a staunch Labour supporter, had attended in spite of his vehement opposition. To do so she had been saving the family benefit for months and at 1.30 in the morning she faced a drive home of 100 miles. 'I've got to go,' she shouted. 'I've got nappies to wash and kids to get off to school in the morning.'

With the abortion and homosexual law reform remit discussion providing little fireworks the conference dribbled to a halt on Monday.

In 1975 the PM, with a phrase worthy of Thomas Jefferson, defined the philosophy of the National Party as being a fair go for the decent bloke. At this conference he described it as preserving all that is

best in the finest multi-cultural society in the world.

George Chapman gave it a slightly different emphasis. New Zealand, he said, must abandon the old goals of rugby, racing and beer; the new catchcry must be productivity, profits and exports.

There had been murmurings all weekend for a return to individual initiative and the PM satisfied nearly everyone with his summing up, namely that National was the middle-of-the-road party.

I do hope, however, that the lady who had to drive 100 miles home in the middle of the night — the same woman who told me seriously that she was prepared to die for her leader — will compromise a little and keep to the left.

Listener, August 20, 1977

Don't Stop till You Reach 60

With Sir Roy Jack still convalescing after major abdominal surgery, and with Deputy Speaker Harrison overseas, the heavy burden of running the House fell recently on the slender shoulders of Bill Birch, the senior Government Whip.

Birch is not the most modest of men, but observers are certain that his unusual reversal of emphasis during the opening daily prayer was purely inadvertent. The MP for Franklin began the week solemnly intoning 'Almighty God, humbly acknowledging our guidance in all things . . . ' As the week developed it seemed less preposterous than it would have normally.

Mind you, the PM was overseas too (at the Commonwealth Finance Ministers' conference in Barbados) and as usual senior members on both sides of the House conspired, in his absence, to get things running as smoothly and briskly as possible. Apparently the PM left his luggage keys behind and while he desperately attacked his suitcase with a pen knife and won the admiration of Third World countries with his grimy cuffs and one shiny-arsed suit, back here in Wellington, with the full but not uncritical co-operation of the Opposition, remarkable progress was made on a number of Government measures.

The week began merrily with a ball for parliamentary staff and days later the new banquet hall was in use again for the State Luncheon in honour of the high-ranking goodwill delegation from the People's Republic of China.

For some reason the protocol-conscious Chinese were greeted in Auckland by Defence Minister Alan McCready. The Chinese themselves are masters of the art of varying the size and grandeur of official welcomes in accordance with the importance they attach to any visit, and doubtless after this the next New Zealand Prime Minister to visit China will be greeted by one Red Guard playing a kazoo and another waving a sock.

McCready, who gave the impression previously of not wanting to rest until the last communist was hung with the entrails of the last democratic socialist, proved a surprisingly adept host. Certainly he was more gracious than one of the PM's staffers, who showed me a coin one of 'the Chows' had given him.

The Press Gallery enjoyed the banquet not only for the assurances that China would never seek hegemony but also because it allowed most of them to take the morning off and race north to Levin's Hokio Beach in pursuit of the elusive toheroa. Indeed, the only attack on the media all week came that morning when a giant mollusc attacked Radio New Zealand's Brent Harman. Harman nearly lost the end of one finger and had to decamp rapidly to a doctor's surgery for a tetanus injection.

Elsewhere and in private, the Public Expenditure Committee sat to consider the cost of TV1's *Governor* series. The PM initiated the inquiry and critics who scream about political interference and malice should remember the PM's close involvement last election with the preparation for television of fictionalised political history.

National's seven campaign commercials each had about 55 seconds worth of Hanna Barbera animation. When questioned, party president George Chapman put the cost of these at about $14,000.

That works out at about $2000 worth of animation per commercial — which is more per minute than the above-the-line costs of *The Governor* but still a remarkable budgetary achievement when you consider that Hanna Barbera's animation costs work out at $250 a second today.

In short, by cutting costs and corners with consummate skill, National managed to get at least $70,000 worth of animation done for only $14,000. From the figures I think it's pretty clear that had Avalon demonstrated the same skill and concern they could have paid for *The Governor* by raffling chooks in the staff bar every Friday night.

The week ended with yet another chastening example of budgetary skill, when Bert Walker implemented his long-promised wife retention scheme and reduced the DPB for the first six months from $61 a week to $49 a week. Now there were ingrates who considered the old figure too low and last year one solo mum wrote Bert an anguished letter detailing how her DPB was spent. 'It is not the high cost of living which bothers me,' replied the Minister of Social Welfare pithily, 'but rather the cost of high living.'

Bert is a bottomless pit of such aphorisms and lately he has addressed himself to the subject of poverty. Too many men, he says, are working overtime to buy a second car and a holiday bach. On talk-back radio in Christchurch he wittily suggested that people were so poor these days they could no longer afford petrol for their Jags.

The cause of this flurry of mirth is the recent report of the Social Development Council. Their discussion paper on family finances argued strongly and persuasively that many New Zealand families could no longer adequately meet their children's needs. They defined poverty as insufficient access to certain goods, services and conditions of life that are available to everyone else and have come to be accepted as basic to a decent minimum standard of living.

Bert hastily put out a press statement challenging this definition. The council's references to poverty, he said, should not be confused with the common meaning of indigence — an absence of the essential

means of living.

Food and water, I suppose, and some sort of shelter would be essential to living and unless you were without all three Bert probably wouldn't agree that you were poor.

The report has not received the publicity it deserves and in the House itself the Opposition seem interested only in one section of it. The figures they like quoting (and they are alarming) are the ones that, using a married couple's age benefit as an accepted minimum, show 550,000 people below such a level, half of them children.

During the recent Imprest Supply debate one of the Government research unit economists happened to mention casually to the PM that these figures had been gleaned from Government statistics by economist Brian Easton during Labour's term in office, and the PM quickly put aside his prepared text.

Although Treasury officials and others were involved in preparing the report he launched an attack on Easton and attempted to discredit the report as the work of Marxists and worse: 'This Government is interested in poverty in New Zealand but it is not interested in the academic workings of the extreme left.'

If the Social Development Council's findings are true, and there has been no serious refutation of them, then the situation today can only be worse. Ironically, with half a million children allegedly under the poverty line, full- page ads are appearing in our newspapers inviting the retired to visit Wairakei in the middle of the week. 'Go on,' say the ads against a backdrop of golfing, fishing, wining and dining, 'you've earned it.'

With economists increasingly worried about the long-term feasibility of National Superannuation, Bert Walker has come up with a novel solution. We will import new workers, he says, to help fund the scheme. Unfortunately, they too will grow old eventually, and will need new workers to support them in turn.

Now that the economic balance of power lies with the elderly, the only solution is to increase the superannuation even further and encourage more overseas travel. Hopefully, gluttony, cholera and debauchery would dispense with some of them, and systematic drops in cabin pressure on the flights home could get rid of the rest.

What about the 250,000 children who are poor right now, I hear you cry? Well, I was coming to that. My advice to them is to grow old as fast as they can and not stop until they reach 60.

Listener, October 15, 1977

Blowing One's Cover

It happened about four times in the one evening: middle-aged ladies kept sidling up to me and saying 'Well, who's on the cover of this week's *Time*, then?' – and, before I could answer, adding triumphantly 'Our Rob, that's who'.

Usually I muttered something feebly about it only being the Pacific edition. Not wishing to seem churlish or hurt I refrained from pointing out that *Time*'s Sydney office couldn't confirm that all or even part of the Pacific edition cover-story would appear in any of their other four editions. Nor did I tell them that the equivalent issue of *Newsweek* had chosen to ignore our Rob entirely.

It wasn't just kindness or circumspection on my part. Seeing as how I was deep in the Wairarapa heartland at the time, just about to address the Gladstone branch of the National Party, it seemed the wisest and safest thing to do.

I was invited, you understand, at the height of the flooding. The farmer who rang had to shout to be heard over the sound of hillsides crashing into valleys, and I accepted immediately on the romantic assumption that I alone stood between the farmers and permanent despair.

I could see myself, head bared in the pouring rain, prancing hypnotically round a tiny stage in front of a vast army of men sitting waist-deep in thick mud. Unaided by amplification or notes, I would be bringing hope and laughter to people who hadn't smiled for months.

As it turned out, on the very day that I was scheduled to speak, the head of the Masterton branch of Federated Farmers warned that hill-country farmers might soon find it no longer worthwhile to raise lambs for the export market. I needn't have worried. My hosts were a relatively prosperous and contented lot.

True, some ingrates insisted that Duncan MacIntyre wasn't half the Minister of Agriculture that Colin Moyle was, and one man brought conversation to an uncomfortable halt when he suggested with some bitterness that Muldoon would go down in history as the biggest bloody socialist of all time. Most, however, have put the terrible erosion and high stock losses well behind them, and to keep their spirits up over summer many have astutely gone out and bought jetboats.

The evening went well and I told them truthfully that I identified with farmers, as I, too, had lived at the end of a metal road. The fact that we lived in a rather run-down part of Feilding is neither here nor there, and in no way invalidates this empathy.

As you'd expect, conversation kept returning to the subject of the PM's *Time* cover, and the wife of the electorate chairman confided that it was his face on their teatowels that was really causing her bother.

She had enthusiastically over-ordered at the party's dominion conference and was now faced with the prospect of having to sell her surplus to unbelievers. If she can bring herself to market them as diapers, she should do well.

Judging from John Hamilton's report in the Melbourne *Herald*, the White House press corps won't be buying any. The US President sees a head of state every three days and the press saw our Rob's talks as an occasion for light relief. At the briefing that followed they clowned around, asked only about six questions in all, and seemed interested only in whether Carter had discussed his brother Billy with our Rob. Brother Billy, described once by Rob as a beer-drinking petrol-station attendant, had just made the cover of *Newsweek* (something Rob hasn't achieved) and they wanted to know if anyone had told Rob the good news.

Back here in the House, Labour's Richard Prebble seized on this and started a small notice-of-motion war.

It began on Tuesday with Prebble asking the House to note press reports of the PM's failure to make any media impact. He went on to quote the UPI reporter who had defined obscurity as being 'a visiting head of government from a nation the size of Colorado and having talks with an American President followed by a briefing in which no one wants to know what happened.'

As the PM's public relations trip hadn't got any publicity, added Prebble, the PM should return home immediately and save some of the $70,000 the trip had cost.

On Wednesday he was on his feet again asking the House to note that despite the PM's assurance to readers of his *Truth* column that his visit would be covered by the American news media, it had been almost totally ignored by them. Prebble called on the PM to put the record straight in another *Truth* column and while doing so to spell out precisely the benefits his $70,000 trip would bring to the taxpayer.

On Thursday the Government retaliated, Ed Latter reading out a motion standing in Robert Fenton's name. It asked the House to note yet another premature, blundering denigration of the PM by the member for Auckland Central. As proof of the PM's impact the motion then invited Prebble to see whose photograph dominated the cover of the American edition of *Time*.

Prebble was ready and waiting; before the applause had died he was up with another notice of his own, pointing out that it was only the Pacific edition. Which at 41,000 copies sold as much as *Friday Flash*, and only a fifth of the circulation of the *New Zealand Woman's Weekly*.

He then asked the House to regret that in spite of a

visit to Disneyland and a trip to a dogfood factory in Topeka, Kansas, the PM had failed to make the cover of the American edition of *Time* which has a circulation of four and a half million.

Actually, with a little more luck the PM might have made the cover two years ago. At the time of the last election *Time* commissioned a cover from *Auckland Star* cartoonist Peter Bromhead, but somehow the Australians, who have never had a cartoonist prepare a *Time* cover, got wind of it, and they told Governor-General Kerr, who promptly sacked Whitlam, and we were lost in the rush.

Similar antipathy caused Malcolm Fraser and Andrew Peacock to write to President Carter and Secretary of State Vance respectively about our Rob's threats to give the Russians exclusive use of our 200-mile fishing zone.

Fraser complained that we were playing with fire and he pimped to Carter that it was irresponsible of an Anzus member to encourage any Soviet vessels into the area. At first Brian Talboys denied Fraser's involvement but he finally conceded that the messages were not the dirty work of junior Ministers in the Australian Cabinet.

Meanwhile our Rob stormed through America telling handfuls of innocent bystanders everywhere that while personally it made him sick just thinking about it, thanks to the restrictive trade practices of friends who really should be helping, New Zealand might have no option but to turn to the nasty Russians.

These 'Save me from a terrible mistake' speeches may eventually succeed where skilful negotiations and reason have failed. Who knows, Japan and America might crack in the face of this hideous prospect and quadruple their imports of our beef and butter.

Even if it all comes to nothing and our massage parlours eventually reverberate to balalaika music and reek of cheap vodka, it will have been worth it for all concerned. Rob has a short concentration span and travel provides him with endless bands, motorcades, banquets and brouhaha. He has been away 150 days this year. For many people, while this is not exactly New Zealand the way they want it, it comes close.

Listener, December 10, 1977

The 239 Steps

One hundred and eighteen days after it had started, the 1977 session of the 38th Parliament came to a sour end nine days before Christmas. But for two reasons the MPs might be there still, arguing feebly and peering at wallet-sized snapshots of their families, eyes red with the strain of attaching names to vaguely familiar faces.

First, the PM had no intention of breaking Labour's 1974 record of 118 days. It may seem a minor matter to you and me, but in Parliament such statistics are all-important. Second, Warren Freer led an Opposition walkout on the final Thursday night and in just under 30 minutes the Government was able to pass nine Bills through their committee stages.

The Opposition made their exodus at 2.53 a.m. in protest at the PM's breach of Brian Talboys's promise that the House would rise shortly after midnight. Unfortunately, while he may hold eccentric views on law and order, the Government backbencher for Invercargill, Norman Jones, is also fiercely democratic. Oblivious to the administrative convenience of the walkout, he rose and rather testily queried the validity of legislation considered in this fashion.

The acting Chairman of Committees, Bill Birch, assured him that the House needed only a quorum to continue. Jones would not be pacified. 'I've just come back from Bulgaria,' he said acidly, 'and they don't have an Opposition there either.' He then advised his colleagues that it would be a farce to continue. They could stick it but he was going home.

His old Army buddy, Ed Latter, was dispatched to correct this Awol, but Jones was not swayed by an assurance that all would be forgiven and he would get a huge cheer if he returned. Latter later complained privately to a few journalists that Minogue and Richard Walls had got to Jones first and had convinced him not to return.

National has always prided itself on its team loyalty, so when National MPs start bitching almost openly about each other and walking angrily out of the House, it's clear that things are going wrong.

This has been a long, hard session. More than 200 public Bills have been considered, 17 local Bills were passed, and a further 21 Bills will be studied by select committees during the recess. Fatigue alone, however, is not the root cause of the disaffection. There is a growing feeling that an absurd amount of legislation is being passed. All sorts of Bills — many of which shouldn't be necessary — choke up the order paper, and Sir Keith has developed writer's cramp passing obscure legislation into law.

It's beginning to worry the staff of Government House. Not so long ago a gardener was chasing a Chocbuster wrapper when it blew through a window and into Sir Keith's study. Before he could retrieve it, Sir Keith had swooped down and signed it.

How many of the 239 Bills passed this year on our behalf could you name? More than seven, and you're probably doing better than the average MP. One MP told me he hadn't seen a single copy of one major piece of local body legislation that was passed this year. To his knowledge there were only two copies to go around the Government backbenchers. When the Bill was almost law he hunted through the chamber one evening and found a copy tied up with string.

This may not matter with the War Pensions Amendment Bill but it does matter with other legislation. The Opposition have repeatedly accused the Government of rushing legislation through the House, and a growing number of Government backbenchers share that view.

The Town and Country Planning Bill is a case in point. A huge, complex document, which among other things gives councils the right to get warrants to enter properties at any time of the day or night, using force if necessary, was passed through its final stages on the last day of Parliament along with 20 other Bills.

Earlier, the Government had terminated hearings of the special select committee considering the Bill after only 40 of the 237 submissions had been heard. By way of explanation the committee chairman said he was under great pressure from the whips to report the Bill back. The PM's own department advised the PM in a 20-page brief that it should be held over but all they got in reply was a terse 'seen' scrawled on the cover of their document. He told one of them that he had no intention of carrying that sort of major legislation over into an election year.

Two days before the Bill became law, Bill Birch was advising a Wellington architect that while his suggestions were sound they would not be incorporated into the current Bill — but they were ideal for the amending legislation that would probably follow next session. Perhaps if Bills were unamendable for five years after becoming law, there would be more care and less nonchalance in the passing of legislation.

Government backbenchers not fully disillusioned by all this found the abortion debate the last straw.

Having promised that abortion would be the last thing debated in the session, the PM, without warning, promoted the Bill in question to the top of the order paper at the start of the week. This caught out Martyn Finlay, a leading liberal who had arranged to be in Auckland that afternoon on the understanding that abortion would come up late in the week. In the event it made no difference. The conservatives were better led and better prepared. The liberals held a strategy meeting, decided they didn't have the

numbers, and withdrew all their amendments.

At the very least they should have persisted with Whetu Tirikatene-Sullivan's amendment making abortion a decision for a woman and her doctor alone. This came closer to what opinion polls have shown both the public and the medical profession would prefer. Liberals, however, venerate silly games of compromise and claim false victories. If a Bill called for the amputation of both legs of all criminals at knee-level the liberals would claim as a triumph a successful amendment that lowered the severance point to just above the ankles.

The conservatives knew what they wanted and when they scented victory they rammed home their advantage.

While conceding that some extra amendments didn't help, Birch facetiously suggested that the law was now more liberal than before. A strange claim, really, as the law no longer guarantees a woman an abortion if her baby is likely to be severely handicapped. Rape is only a factor to be taken into consideration, not a ground in itself, and before a doctor can claim that a pregnancy is dangerous to a woman's physical health and wellbeing, he must see if that danger can be averted by any other means. As if that weren't enough, Barry Brill, who also claims the law is more liberal, moved an amendment that may make IUDs illegal.

As the amended Crimes Act became law immediately, and as the certifying consultants won't start work till April, there is a hiatus during which all abortions may be illegal. Justice Minister Thomson sidestepped this problem by neatly suggesting that Parliament just passes law — it is up to others to make it work.

Health Minister Gill may have the answer to the emigration exodus. To be consistent with the Health Department inquiries he has initiated into the running of the now-closed Aotea clinic, he should move to enforce the extra-territorial aspects of the new law.

New Zealand women who obtain abortions in Australia actually break New Zealand law, and shortly all overseas departure lounges may be equipped with random pregnancy testing gear. Any woman whose test is positive must return home still pregnant, or with a babe in arms, or with a certificate of adoption.

Those MPs still under the illusion that the Bill was to be discussed on a free vote were disturbed by the PM's advice to Government backbencher Richard Walls.

Walls voted with the Opposition to oppose urgency and was visited shortly afterwards by his leader, who put his face very close to his, which was uncomfortable enough, and then in a stage whisper audible in the public gallery hissed, 'I want your seat, not because you're the member, but because it's National. You've made a spectacle of yourself and my advice is to shut up!'

Walls's benchmate, Dr Ian Shearer, offended in a similar fashion later in the debate. In their zeal the House passed clause 32, which the Birch amendment was supposed to replace. It requires the leave of the House to recommit a clause, however, and twice Shearer, determined that a stupid mistake should remain part of a stupid Bill, voiced disapproval.

At the first attempt the PM came across and asked him if he knew what he was doing. He told Shearer it was a highly irregular thing to do. (He did it himself in an earlier abortion debate to deny Marilyn Waring the right to table some important documents.) When Shearer offended again the PM looked around, rose, and told the House that certain members weren't aware of what they were doing. At this, Quigley, McLay and others advised caution, and at the third attempt to recommit the troublesome clause Shearer remained silent.

Said Shearer later: 'It's been an extremely enlightening year. I have learnt a lot of good and a lot of bad.'

Haven't we all?

Listener, January 21, 1978

Nineteen seventy-eight was the year I took six months' leave and travelled to England, Ireland and France with my family. I was tired of politics. Karen Jackman took over the column in my absence, with the late Chris Brookwhite doing the cartoons. Karen is a superb writer and I can remember sneaking into New Zealand House and leafing through back issues to read her amazing stuff. She saw things going on that disgusted her — things that I was already beginning to take for granted. It was a valuable lesson. Fortunately for me she didn't altogether enjoy writing the column and I was offered my old job back by editor Tony Reid when she said she'd had enough.

Before I departed Tony asked me for a parting shot. I said I preferred to leave quietly, but he argued I owed the readers an explanation — which I didn't, but vanity got the better of me and I wrote an anguished piece that today I find a trifle sickly. I don't disagree with anything I said. I'm just embarrassed by the high moral tone I adopted. No matter, Tony was pleased with it at the time, but on my return he took me to one side and grinning broadly said, 'I told you writing that article was a mistake . . .'

Tony was a brilliant journalist and no editor I've worked for worried about his staff to the extent he did. He told me once we were both doomed because we were Irish. He would often sigh and say that after 30 the most you could hope for out of life was a tolerable level of melancholia. If he suffered from it he could also cause it in others. When I walked back into his office after six months away he shook my hand warmly then said slyly, 'Before we discuss money and a new contract I should point out that the circulation went up while you were away . . .'

Devaluation

It is dark when I awake. Head throbs. Someone dancing on my medulla oblongata in hobnail boots. Seem to remember going to the pub last night. Rare visit you understand; made possible because all the children are off at grandparents' for the holidays. Someone dancing on my kidneys in bare feet. Not all the children at grandparents'. Baby in bed. Give him old football sock to chew on. What time is it?

Self-winding watch virtually useless since strap broke. I've carried it around in my trouser pocket, but apparently I don't move about enough as it loses 23 hours in every 24. Switch on radio. 'Hit me with your rhythm stick, hit me slowly, hit me quick!' No, it's too early for that. Change station. Just miss bird call . . . Black-backed gull can be heard again at 8.00 a.m. Must be just after 7.00 a.m. Better see who still wants to come. Seem to recall plenty of enthusiasm in the pub.

Two sleepy refusals. Hell, I don't want to drive to the Wairarapa by myself. Watershed conference, this one. Ought to attend really. Ring Dreadon, a former Feilding man and Karori Values candidate in '72. Stout fellow, only half alive from night before and keen as mustard. Be here shortly.

Food? Can't be expected to drive on an empty stomach. I know it will increase the weight of the vehicle and contents thereof, but you can take this energy conservation thing too far. Toss bacon into the pan. The sizzle doing wonders for my headache. Not the sort of food Values would approve. Still, as my mother says, a little bit of what hurts you can't harm you. She says that after the first helping. After the seventh she says, equally profoundly, well we've all got to die of something.

Dreadon not too impressed by this theory. Clutches his seat belt nervously. Keeps asking if I have my licence. Car buffeted by wind on motorway. Has developed unnerving tendency to swerve without warning. The rear suspension is definitely off-colour since I carted bricks in the back. Dreadon upset by strange noise. Eventually trace this to pram bouncing between the last of the bricks and the bag of overdue library books. What time is it?

Oh dear, it's after eight. We're late. This creates an enormous dilemma for Dreadon. Only peripherally involved in recent times, but a deeply committed Values man nevertheless, he believes in a sustainable, diverse, community-based, co-operative, participatory, internationalist, humane society that appreciates that the world's resources are limited and should be shared equally. His brow knots, unknots, and knots again. Step on it, he says quietly, like a judge announcing a sentence of hanging. Using more than our fair share of precious fossil fuels we surge forward and onward up the slopes of the Rimutaka Ranges.

A strange smell fills the car. The smell of hot rust. The oil light burns bright red. Masterton is miles away. There are no garages open in Featherston. I checked the oil only yesterday. The proprietor of a rural gas station whistles when he checks the dip stick. Dreadon drums his fingers on the fibreglass. What time is it?

At last, Masterton! Dreadon checks the envelope of guff the party sent me. There are neat maps of the library in relation to the tuck shop, and copies of various position papers, but no name, no indication at all as to where this school, if it is a school, might be. Typical, bloody typical. The duty constable at the police station is most informative. Rathkeale College, about a mile north on the main road. We'll make it in time for the leadership debate anyway. Dreadon and I debate the issue. Dreadon at this stage is on Margaret Crozier's side. He feels that Kunowski's demands for a more professional, political, disciplined and centralised party clash somehow with Values' traditional virtues. We argue cheerfully. Dreadon has to put up with my abuse – I designed his campaign poster in '72. I repeat my old claim that Values is a post-60s phenomenon that will biodegrade of its own accord, unless it produces another reason for being other than disgust and despair with the two main parties. Somehow, like the women's movement, it thought in the beginning that petty division and feeble rhetoric were only possible with people indifferent to the plight of the whale. That somehow they would transcend the problems of human nature that bedevilled other organisations. You are what you eat and they would eat properly.

Values' support came from defections from both Labour and National, with Values polling well in National Party strongholds, showing that basically beneath the early caftans, buckskin, and handmade boots there beat hearts of pure pinstripe. The 1960s are wearing off though, and people are reverting to type. Values faces a twin crisis – its membership is declining gradually and turning over rapidly.

In the Rathkeale library they are busy deciding who is best fitted to arrest this slide. It won't be an easy decision as there are threatened walkouts whoever wins.

Margaret Crozier has the floor. Slim, pale, yellow flower in her lapel, blue top, ballooning khaki corduroy trousers. A tracheal infection is given as the reason for her whispered, hesitant, rambling delivery. She looks, at times, as if she might cry, and half of the audience with her. The speech judiciously embraces most Values hobby-horses. Feminism, Christianity, activism, local politics, national politics. Not all things were possible, but done one at a time some were. Being an activist gave one a demented third eye. You never saw things in the same light

FORWARD!

again. The audience exchange knowing glances and acknowledge this fresh insight with polite encouraging applause. She was standing to give the party a choice and she needed their support because if she didn't have it, and what she had done had damaged the party, then it wasn't worth it. She comes close to explaining the central agony of the party. 'We are trying to relate the things we are trying to say to the things we are trying to do.' How true.

Tony Kunowski, previously holding his infant son in a green sleeping bag, is called up. ('You should have been here last night,' I'm told. 'We had real catharsis then. Lots of drama. Lots of people angry with Tony.') He is only slightly repentant under interrogation. He says that he plays social soccer on Sundays with members of the working class ('I suppose some Values people,' he smiles acidly, 'would deny that we have one') who consider Values people amateurs who talk esoteric nonsense. Values must make the connections between the economy and social structure; the fuel crisis and unemployment. There were 100,000 gays in New Zealand yet Values only got 40,000 votes. Values had to improve itself electorally to survive. Yes, there were other areas and levels to work in too. He helped set up a Papanui collective that now boasted 40 families. It worked well but the political impact was virtually zero. The main attitude was that it was a good way to eat cheap food. He conceded that he could be blunt at times, but love and peace rhetoric wasn't enough. He would consider his future in the light of how far the party moved to accommodate his proposals.

Margaret Crozier isn't happy with the love and peace stuff. 'I feel put down by that sort of talk,' she whispers angrily. 'That's what the socialists call trashing.' Having earlier conceded that Values was of the left she made it plain it *wasn't* that far left.

Wringing hands about unhealable rifts and debating whether the ballot papers should be ticked or have the name crossed out, the party finally took a vote on it.

It's a Crozier victory by a slim 11 votes. There is relief but no jubilation. Chairer (a label that sidesteps the chairperson debacle) Dave Woodhams holds her in a long, eyes-closed hug. They look like two mourners comforting each other at a funeral. It's an apt image. Over lunch there is talk of forming a new party or perhaps waiting to see how the Labour Party conference goes. Loser Tony Kunowski is strangely relaxed, yet he nearly won it. Before the conference he was rated as losing 60-40. A few more hoarse cliches from Crozier and a little less aggression from him and he would have won it.

The word quickly spreads that the vote was roughly a south-north split. The north, more into lifestyles, as you'd expect from a group based in Auckland, beat out the south led by the Christchurch lefties.

'The whole native forests issue is too important,' confides one delegate, 'to get bogged down in a debate on the crisis of capitalism.'

In the foyer there is a petition calling for the abolition of compulsory education. I express disbelief – after all, compulsory education is what their soul brothers in the third world desperately desire. 'Relax,' says the secretary, 'it isn't in the manifesto.' I check. It is.

Back from lunch, chairer Woodhams wishes Kunowski well and bids him happy gardening. Someone moves that the ballot papers be destroyed. Kunowski may not have won but his legacy lives on. 'Shouldn't they be recycled?' I whisper to Dreadon. Since this morning he has become a Kunowski man. Dispirited and seeing few familiar faces, he wants to know what time it is. Time to go, I reply.

Listener, June 2, 1977

Fine Words

At times, if you half shut your eyes during the Address-in-Reply debate, it was difficult to tell speakers and speeches apart. It wasn't just the usual, merciful brain-numbing that comes with listening to dozens of speeches in a row. (At the debate's end 90 speeches will have been made.) There was also a curious overlapping of sentiment across party lines. While there was still plenty of party politics, most seemed to feel that a pep talk — part sermon, part All Black locker room chat — was required, and that they were duty-bound to give it.

It began with the mover, the Government member for Marlborough, Doug Kidd. He called for New Zealanders to stop fighting one another. A virulent form of envy, he claimed, was the root of all our troubles, and he asked rhetorically, paraphrasing the immortal bard himself, 'Are not our troubles therefore in ourselves rather than in our Government?'

Dr Michael Bassett (Opposition, Te Atatu), back from the wilderness, claimed it was time for healing and co-operation, for coming together, for a sense of national purpose. Bill Rowling insisted that if our people learned to care and to believe again, then they would accept the need to work together to put the country right.

Related idealism had been expressed a week earlier at the re-election of Dick Harrison as Speaker. Rowling and David Thomson (the PM's appointee as Leader of the House) agreed that Parliament's reputation needed restoring this session and a responsibility for that lay with individual members. But within days, after a spate of partisan notices of motion and a welter of asinine interjections, this session was beginning to sound like any other.

However, there were differences too. Restored in confidence and numbers, the Opposition came out with a new aggression and edge to its attack. Rowling began his Address-in-Reply speech with the claim that Labour had received more votes than National and morally National had no right to the Treasury benches. It was only the vagaries of the electoral boundaries that kept them in office. (If that is the case then Labour has only itself to blame. Barrie Leay, National's appointee to the last Electoral Boundaries Commission, gleefully admits that Labour's appointee was naive and poorly prepared and that National got a lion's share of the electoral advantages that the restructuring provided.) Rowling insisted that the Government had been given a vote of no-confidence in November and was now operating without a mandate.

Turning to the Address from the Throne and the section saying that the Government, having raised the level of economic activity, considered a less expansionary policy now more appropriate, Rowling pointed out that last year was a record one for bankruptcies and company liquidations. He attacked the record unemployment and the record emigration, claiming that during the year ending March 1976 the net loss of people was equivalent to the population of Napier. And in March of this year the annual rate had risen to 40,000. (If this loss could be co-ordinated and confined to a single area no one would really mind getting rid of Hamilton.) He made the point that zero population growth and zero economic growth were Values Party policy and this Government had achieved both. He also attacked the fact that the Government had borrowed more than Labour and that Government expenditure was now 44 per cent of the Gross National Product despite the PM's claims that it was now back in the 30 per cent range. Turning to Gleneagles, he asked the Prime Minister to declare whether he sided with the Minister of Foreign Affairs or the Minister of Maori Affairs on the question of sporting contacts with South Africa.

In reply the PM climbed to his feet and said, 'I will now quietly rebut the Leader of the Opposition's arguments.' It was a curious choice of words, but consistent with the PM's new image as a self-confessed moderate. He has claimed at press conferences lately, his tummy resting happily on his knees, that he has never felt calmer in his life, and that he has a master plan for New Zealand. He ignored Rowling's challenges to outline this plan and indeed, as most of his speech was a jolly denunciation of the previous Labour Government, a speech he's given frequently, it seems that he believes more in his own golden past than in the country's golden future. This benign fixation with the past and this calm, where at the very least epileptic panic would be more appropriate, has been explained in several ways. I favour the theory that George Gair is putting horse tranquilliser in his leader's Bellamy's soup, and such massive doses are required that the Minister of Health is desperately contemplating introducing a charge for all prescription drugs.

The PM defended the Government's borrowing record, claiming that under Labour the external deficit was 10.8 per cent of the GNP and last year it was 2.7 per cent of the GNP, which was why we enjoy a triple A credit rating. National may have borrowed more but they did so at a lower interest rate. Once rearranging a multi-currency floating roll-over credit, whatever that is, at five-eighths of one per cent over the London Interbank official rate. So there!

Without siding with either Talboys or Couch, the PM claimed the Government was honouring the Gleneagles Agreement because Sonny Ramphal had said so. (Apparently Ramphal said otherwise to

VOTE FOR THE
CANDIDATE OF YOUR
CHOICE BY DRAWING
A RHOMBOID ALONGSIDE
HIS NAME

SMITH N
JONES L
DAVIES SC
GREEN V

Rowling in private.) When I was in London last year I spoke to friends who worked at the Commonwealth Secretariat and they pointed out that Ramphal's endorsement of the PM was much in the nature of a parent encouraging a child in potty training. Even near-misses have to be encouraged if the child is to ever learn. For all that, the assistant secretary-general of the Organisation for African Unity, Dr Peter Onu, has written to HART expressing concern that the Government has yet to make a stand on the proposed 1981 Springbok tour.

The PM got cross only once and that was at the suggestion that the Government had no mandate. Labour, he said, adopted the principle of vote early and often, and he wondered how many votes around the country would have been disallowed by the Hunua judgment. Taking those votes into consideration, along with the votes cast for the 11 alternative National Party candidates, it was clear that National had more of a mandate than Labour.

This argument was elaborated by the Government member for Kapiti, Barry Brill. Almost certainly denied a Cabinet position by Margaret Shields's temporary victory, and only recently rewarded with the position of under-secretary to the Minister of Energy, he was understandably peeved in his Address-in-Reply speech. He accused the Labour Government when last in power of manipulating the Electoral Act to suit its own ends. He argued that for Labour to claim it had been disadvantaged alone by the disallowance of votes not cast properly was to claim that the illiterate, the drunk, the simple-minded and those of lowest and meanest intelligence were automatically Labour Party supporters. He argued that in Kapiti 180 additional Labour votes were disallowed, and that if you multiplied that by the 88 general seats then overall there were 15,840 additional invalid Labour votes, so quite clearly National took a clear majority of the *valid* votes cast.

In spite of the lofty sentiments expressed in many speeches, the Government took the unprecedented step of denying the Opposition member for Hunua, Malcolm Douglas, the customary extra time in his maiden Address-in-Reply speech, leaving him only 20 minutes in which to defend himself. No one knows just how much hanky panky there was in Hunua, and how much of it was deliberate, but certainly it can't have been on the massive scale the Government claims. Again in spite of the sentiments expressed, the Government blocked an Opposition motion to get Bruce Beetham on to the select committee considering changes to the standing orders and procedures of the House. The leader of the Social Credit Party was further insulted when the reshuffle caused by Malcolm Douglas's replacement with National's Winston Peters resulted in Beetham's being shunted back from a front bench.

It was a sad day for Mr Douglas and it can't have been the most pleasant of circumstances for Mr Peters either. One was cheered by his colleagues as he left, the other by his colleagues when he took his seat.

Peters made the curious claim that if he had revealed to the court all the evidence of malpractice he had at his disposal, a by-election would almost certainly have been called for. He claimed that such a by-election would have wasted time. In the great tradition of by-elections and considering also the unpleasant measures the Government has introduced by regulation this year, it would have been a by-election almost impossible for the Government to win. Under those circumstances, Mr Peters's failure to tell all is also 'hanky panky' of sorts.

For all that, the Government's Bionic Mandate Mk 2, a tattered replica of the early model, has risen to 51 seats, which in our electoral system is more than enough.

Listener, June 16, 1979

Going Through the Motions

Every afternoon at the start of Parliament, after the Prayer, Private Business, Presentation of Public Petitions and Presentation of Papers – none of which take much time – Speaker Dick Harrison enquires if there are any Notices of Motion. It's strictly a rhetorical question and Harrison's voice is a mix of good humour and weary resignation, for barely has the sentence died on his lips than half a dozen or so Honourable Members are on their feet shouting 'Mr Speaker!' There is never a shortage of Notices of Motion.

Surveying the eager faces the Speaker usually gives the first call to the most senior member of the Opposition. It goes next to the most senior Government member and seesaws back and forth until all who want a turn have had their say.

But those of you who have never listened to Parliament are probably wondering just what a Notice of Motion is. Well, don't worry – many who work in the building have the same problem.

Basically, and I'm simplifying here in case any MPs are reading, a Notice of Motion is a piece of information dug up by the Opposition to embarrass the Government and vice versa. There are certain rules, of course. You couldn't announce to the House for instance that another Honourable has to sleep with a rubber sheet on his bed. That would be in bad taste and would lower the standing of Parliament and invite retaliation. Hence the old parliamentary saying, 'Let him who sleeps without a rubber sheet cast the first motion.'

It also goes without saying that you don't just get up and say something nasty and sit down feeling pleased with yourself. There are conventions that have to be observed. Ideally you begin as follows: 'Mr Speaker, I give notice of my intention to move next sitting day, that this House deplores (or whatever) the fact that . . .' *Then* you throw in your nasty bit and sit down feeling pleased with yourself.

All that mumbo-jumbo about 'next sitting day' and 'intending to move' is meaningless, as Members don't rise next sitting day and repeat themselves. Instead their Notice of Motion is printed on the Order Paper and remains there a couple of weeks before being removed. Wednesday afternoons are usually set aside for debate of Private Members' Notices of Motion, but Questions for Oral Answer and the introduction of Bills – if there are any to introduce – are dealt with first. In the time remaining before the tea adjournment only a handful of Notices of Motion, selected beforehand by the Whips, get to be debated. In other words, nearly 90 per cent of the Notices of Motion slide off the Order Paper without being mentioned again. This is often a fitting end for them. If they were all debated later, there is little doubt that MPs would use the device more sparingly.

Government Notices of Motion are a little different again. They can be debated any time the Government decrees, but in all my time on the Hill I can recall only one such Motion – and it was never debated.

It endorsed the Gleneagles agreement and it sat on the Order Paper for all of the '77 parliamentary session. It was never debated, not because the Government couldn't find the time, but rather because it couldn't afford the spectacle of a significant number of its own backbenchers, and maybe a Cabinet Minister or two, voting against it.

The Government thought it had neatly side-stepped the issue, but Gleneagles refuses to go away. While New Zealand rated the sporting contacts issue one of low priority for this year's Commonwealth Prime Ministers Conference, other countries haven't, and some in Foreign Affairs were a little dismayed to find Gleneagles at No 4 on the conference agenda. That dismay stems partly from the feeling that up until a few months ago the PM thought Lusaka (the capital of Zambia) was an Indonesian rice dish cooked with noodles and smoked pork.

Since then the PM has been fully briefed on black Africa and Indonesian cooking (though he now thinks Nasi Goreng was head of the Luftwaffe) and he has begun to express fears for the Queen's safety in Lusaka. Others suggest that Her Majesty will be fine in Lusaka as long as she doesn't loiter near the PM. This is not to say the PM is a marked man. True, other Commonwealth Prime Ministers of about Rob's height and weight have gone on cottage cheese diets and taken to parting their hair differently, but that is neither here nor there.

The biggest fear is that Rob will open his mouth and say the first thing that comes into his head. Diplomacy has never been his strong suit and just because he behaves all terse and abrupt, large numbers of overly sensitive black leaders are going to assume he's terse and abrupt, when nothing could be further from the truth.

The PM's diplomacy or lack of it features on the current Order Paper. Labour's Stan Rodger wanted the House to note with dismay the PM's reported comment to the new US Ambassador to New Zealand that he didn't like lady politicians. Further down the Order Paper his colleague Frank O'Flynn wanted the House to note that while the PM has no recollection of the incident he hadn't denied that it had taken place. O'Flynn wanted the House to further note that Mrs Martindell was especially suited for her new job, as previously she'd been director of the State Department's Foreign Disaster Co-ordination Centre.

Obviously the report of the exchange between the PM and Mrs Martindell was ideal Notice of Motion material. Such gems don't always fall into the Opposition's lap, though Jonathan Hunt did well asking the House to note a *New Zealand Herald* item on Auckland lawyers, in which the claim was made that in a recent poll of lawyers' attitudes to court protocol some 25 per cent filled in the form incorrectly. As the poll was a ticks-and-crosses one, Hunt called on the Minister of Justice, in the light of the Hunua experience, to find out whether or not the votes of those lawyers who had made their intentions clear were counted.

Such Motions fall into the smart alec category.

The Government backbenchers don't have quite the same ammunition to work with. Instead they have to retaliate with limp Motions about the wool clip being up, unemployment dropping momentarily, the success of *Telethon* and a winner from Eric Holland asking the House to note with pleasure the end of five major industrial disputes.

Some people specialise. Paul East and David Thomson take it in turn to move Motions condemning Labour's Richard Prebble (an exhausting and thankless task, but someone has to do it). Their colleague from Kaimai, Bruce Townshend, files a steady stream of Motions, in tandem with Peter Wilkinson, about Social Credit and where it stands on the great free enterprise issue.

For his part the Social Credit leader retaliates with Motions asking the House to survey other legislatures to see how their third parties are treated in Parliament, and Motions on rising interest rates and falling productivity.

These are essentially harmless. Occasionally, though, Motions are used to wage personal wars. Labour's Michael Bassett has filed several that are highly critical of Energy Minister Bill Birch. In retaliation, Chief Government Whip Tony Friedlander filed a reply citing the Gospel according to Matthew and imploring Bassett to cast the beam out of his own eye.

My favourites are irrelevant harmless ones. Dr Ian Shearer moved one recently congratulating the International Whaling Commission on its recent ban on whaling, and Labour's massive David Lange grinned and said, 'Goody, I can go swimming this summer.'

Listener, August 4, 1979

An article I wrote on the PSIS started the worst month I experienced on the Hill. The piece is of no particular interest now except for the fact I was sued for libel as a consequence of it by the Prime Minister, Rob Muldoon. The details are important only in that some of the key details were incorrect. Journalists shouldn't make mistakes – especially when writing about heads of government.

The first I knew of my transgression was when a lawyer friend came round late at night looking sick with worry. I thought he was about to tell me his marriage was on the rocks so I poured him a huge whisky. He took a large slug then told me that the PM had retained the services of the much feared Des Dalgety of the Wellington law firm Bell Gully, with the express intention of hitting me with a writ for defamation.

I was terrified at first but soon subsided into self-pity. I didn't mind defaming the PM so much. Politicians must expect that sort of thing. I figured he would soon get over it, if indeed he was ever hurt to begin with. After all, he was only demanding $10,000 in damages, which meant either (a) he felt sorry for me, or (b) his reputation wasn't too severely impugned as (c) my own reputation was so low any charge of libel from whatever source would be hard to sustain.

I did feel bad about my editor. I had let Tony Reid down. He was very decent about it at first, which only made me feel worse, but as the plot thickened he took to shaking his head sadly, rolling his eyes at the ceiling, muttering darkly about things being pretty grim on the third floor (executive row).

'What do you mean?' I would inquire nervously.

'Don't ask me, pal. Don't ask me . . .' he would sigh, moving away.

Despite my feeble suggestion that we defend the case in court the BCNZ eventually dropped my column one week and published a full apology in its place. Being only the second defendant, being in disgrace, and with the corporation paying all the costs, I was not consulted on the wording – which was largely the work of the PM's people anyway.

The BCNZ's response to litigation is often capitulation and in this instance they didn't have much choice. Still, I winced when I saw the printed apology. It was an excruciatingly humiliating moment but I took some comfort from the fact that while they were at it they at least refrained from blaming me for the Great Fire of London.

The more immediate problem was that the National Party annual conference was about to begin in Christchurch and Tony told me he would understand if I preferred to give it a miss. It was a tempting offer but I knew there was no escaping the ignominy. It would be better to get it over and done with. The joshing began shortly after I landed at Christchurch airport. While waiting for my baggage dozens of National Party delegates wandered across to chat.

'I guess Rob got you there, Scotty?'

'Yeah, I'm afraid so.'

'Gudday Tom, got ya cheque book on ya, mate?'

'No, the bank confiscated it – I'm ten thousand dollars overdrawn.'

'Hey, say something nasty about me next week. I need the money!'

'What a good idea – we could go halves on the damages.'

And so it continued for most of the weekend, reaching a crescendo the night of the social in the Town Hall. I'd been grinning sheepishly and trading *bons mots* for two days by then and was getting a little weary. I joined a group of my colleagues at one of the several bars serving free liquor. We stood in a sullen huddle watching the Nats whirl by in their finery.

I had an almost constant stream of people coming up to clap me on the back and wink at me, and I started asking for double whiskies, but somehow, rather than dulling my senses, they seemed to intensify my anger.

I remember one group of macho young men sauntering up and saying, 'I suppose you're too famous to talk to us.' An awkward conversation ensued but eventually I asked to be excused as I was with friends.

'Oh yeah,' sneered the ringleader. 'Done your bit for the masses! The famous person doesn't find us interesting enough to talk to! He wants to get back to his famous friends!'

The awkward conversation staggered on a bit longer until I could stand it no more and ordered another double whisky while they shouted 'See!' and 'Thought so!' over my shoulder. The pretty girl behind the counter smiled at me and shrugged in sympathy.

Near the end of the evening a colleague came up and shouted in my ear, did I want to go to a party afterwards?

'Why not?' I replied.

'Good,' he beamed. 'It's in your room!'

Although it was news to me, word it seemed had gone out that I was holding a stir of some sort.

By this stage I had decided that the pretty girl who'd been pouring me whisky all night was the only real friend I had left in the world. I inquired casually if she would like to come to a party. She smiled sweetly, then to my secret relief she said she couldn't. Her husband was at home babysitting the kids.

When I got back to Noahs Hotel there were already people in my room. Someone had got a key from the desk. As I forced my way into the crush there were boisterous hoots and yells. No one of course had brought much grog, and I was obliged to be a good sport and ring room service for some whisky, gin and beer.

'Don't worry,' brayed a red-faced young Nat in a checked sports coat and cravat. 'We're going to take a collection.'

OK, SO I GOT SOME FACTS WRONG — SOME DATES WRONG...

OK SO I IMPLIED SOME THINGS I SHOULDN'T HAVE..

GOT YOUR CHEQUE BOOK MATE?

LET'S LOOK ON THE BRIGHT SIDE....

I SPELT 'PM' CORRECTLY...

This they did, triumphantly raising about $50 for a bill which eventually came to $75. I didn't mind at the time. The crowd swelled and people were enjoying themselves.

Some more particularly obnoxious young Nats had arrived, and to escape the din and pandemonium I went out into the corridor where Ian Fraser and some journalists were talking quietly and swopping yarns.

It was very pleasant out there, laughing and passing around the wine. Certainly much nicer than in my room, where the din didn't begin to abate until some time after three. What I didn't know then was that Hugh Templeton and his wife had the room on one side of me and Air Commodore Gill and his wife were on the other side. I was told later that Nastasha Templeton several times begged her husband to get up and complain about the noise, but it seems Hugh's tolerance levels were far too high and he remained in bed, indirectly contributing to the catastrophe his intervention might have prevented.

When the crowd thinned I returned to my dishevelled room. There were only a handful of people left, including Jim McLay and his wife Jenny. She was sprawled sleepily across the bed and appeared most reluctant to leave. I busied myself stacking bottles and glasses and emptying ashtrays while people thanked me profusely. Finally there was only TVNZ's Neil Roberts left.

Neil was a bit the worse for wear — just minutes before he'd had to be stopped unwinding a fire hose in the corridor. It seems he wanted to hose the last of the stragglers out of my room. He was a decent bloke like that.

I was moaning about the state of the room when he said suddenly, 'Jesus, don't those young Nats just give you the shits.' Slumped on a low table I concurred moodily, and looked up to see Neil pluck a heavy black armchair off the carpet and hurl it through the plate glass window. There was a terrible explosion, followed by another crash as it disintegrated on something far below. We were twelve floors up and a strong icy wind surged through the splintered wound. Sheer horror left me momentarily paralysed. I was thinking, first a libel suit now this. But I came out of my trance of self-pity when Neil threw the telephone directory out the window and began looking about the room for other missiles.

Roberts is a big strong boy, but I managed to get a table lamp off him. Wrestling him to the floor I dragged him by his heels out into the corridor. Just opening the door was an experience. The breeze became a howling gale, flattening the curtains against the ceiling. The whirlwind subsided once I'd locked Roberts outside but he immediately began pounding on the door. I had no choice. I had to open the door again. My advice to him that he had to behave himself was lost in the maelstrom, as bending double into the head wind he surged past me and started dragging the double bed towards the window. I restored a modicum of calm by shutting the door, and raced after him. I had to knock him over and drag him by the legs back to the door again, and I was wondering just how often this cycle would need to be repeated when the hotel security men burst in.

I said as calmly as I could that there was no cause for alarm and everything would be paid for. They didn't say much. They could have got very heavy but obviously they assumed I was a Government MP or senior National Party official and things were best hushed up. No point in complicating future dealings with the party.

Neil, who had become unaccountably meek all of a sudden, was led away gently. The man in charge surveyed the carnage and asked me menacingly if I wanted him to find me another room. I shook my head and said I'd caused them enough trouble — it would be fine as it was. He grunted agreement and reached for the door handle, the curtains flapped like sails and he was gone.

It was so cold I had to get into bed fully dressed. Sleep when it came was fitful and tormented. I was awakened early by a phone call. It was Jim McLay, talking in hushed, urgent tones. His wife's handbag was missing — had I seen it? I had a quick look and told him I would ring him back. I searched through the debris but could find nothing. Finally I pulled the bed out from the wall and something thudded to the floor. I retrieved the purse and rang McLay; he said he'd be down in a moment. He wasn't kidding. Barely had I put down the receiver, it seemed, when there was a soft tap on the door.

It was Jim. Peering anxiously up and down the deserted corridor one hand tucked into the small of his back, palm open. I lowered the purse on to the trembling fingers, he grinned nervously and fled to the lifts.

There were more phone calls. The incident was the talk of the hotel. Some thought it had been a terrorist attack. There was a rumour going round that the pressure of the libel suit had been too much for me and I had jumped to my death. I decided to skip the morning and afternoon sessions of the conference and left hastily to spend the day with my old friend A.K. Grant and his lovely wife Liz.

I returned to the Town Hall for the evening session and a burly farmer who'd been at the party came up grinning broadly. 'By Christ, this Senior Whip bloke Friedlander has got his knickers in a twist over this,' he laughed. 'He was giving me the old third degree, I can tell you. He wanted to know if any MPs were there.'

'If he asks you again,' I joked, 'tell him you didn't recognise anyone because no one had their clothes on.'

'Jesus,' he beamed, 'I just might do that — he'd go apeshit!'

Feeling that the worst was over I wandered into the house bar at Noahs late that night. Police Minister Frank Gill sighted me and he got up from his seat and came across shouting angrily that I owed him and his wife an apology. According to Gill the noise of the chair going through the glass had nearly given his wife a heart attack. I explained that while I deeply regretted the incident I wasn't responsible for the chair going through the glass. This wasn't good enough, he spluttered, I had to apologise to his wife personally. I replied that I had already apologised to the hotel management for the incident. He could pass my apology on to his good lady for I was through with apologising personally for something I hadn't done. He got even angrier and said as Minister of Police he could order an inquiry into the whole business and I could find myself in deep trouble.

I got angry too, and told him I didn't take kindly to threats like that. I would remember the conversation and write about it in the *Listener*. As for the police inquiry, he could do what he liked — I was quite prepared for the law to take its course. At this point television producer Derek Fox wisely intervened and led me away. (I heard no more about it, of course, and Gill and I got on surprisingly well after this.)

The next morning I rang Air New Zealand to see if I could get an early flight north. There was one about midday and I booked myself on it. I was wondering whether I should head down to the Town Hall for a bit or just lie about in my room (now fixed) when the phone rang.

'Hallo,' purred a woman's voice.

'Who is it?' I inquired cautiously.

'It's the barmaid you spoke to the other night, remember?'

'Oh yes . . . hallo.'

'I couldn't come to the party the other night, but my husband has gone to work this morning and the kids to school. I'm free for the day. I could come across and see you.'

'No, you can't!' I panicked. 'I was on my way to the airport when you rang . . . I'm running late . . .'

I hung up, rang a cab, checked out, and headed out to the airport two hours early. I didn't feel safe until the plane was in the air — which is unusual for me.

That was a Monday. The following morning I handed in my article on the conference. Of necessity, it avoided all reference to the central disaster. Things are not always as they are written. Mistakes can be costly, and the truth even more expensive.

Around the 80s in Four Days

At the National Party conference I watched the live telecast of the All Blacks being thrashed by the Wallabies in the company of a group of grizzled cow-cockies from Marilyn Waring's Waipa electorate. It was a sorry spectacle and a desolate camaraderie filled the room. Much had been said that afternoon about the 'challenge of the 1980s', but right then there seemed a more pressing need for a decent forward pack. At one point a burly Australian attempted to shred an All Black's ear with his boot. The ladies in the room were outraged. 'That's not a game! That's thuggery!' 'It's all right,' counselled one of the men. 'You don't feel the sprigs when you're fit!'

Somehow, in that simple statement he seem to capture the central philosophy of the party. Rising prices, education cuts, carless days and all the rest of it don't really hurt if you're *fit.*

Well, that's what the 'modern conservative' thinks, and there was also plenty of talk, mostly offstage, about him. What is a modern conservative? No one is quite sure. One suggestion is that 'modern conservative' is essentially a figure of speech like 'virile impotence' and 'tall dwarf'. What he believes is marginally easier to define. For starters he does not believe in the economic theory of John Maynard Keynes but in the philosophy of that other great economist Charles Darwin — namely, the survival of the fittest (and the spoils to the victor).

In his closing address to the conference George Chapman, albeit unwittingly, returned to the sprigs analogy. He blamed much of the country's problems and National's problems on the timid consensus politics of the Holyoake years. In short, the Nats didn't put the boot in hard enough then.

Chapman's remarks were curious in that they implied criticism of senior Cabinet Ministers like Lance Adams-Schneider, Brian Talboys and Duncan MacIntyre, who, along with their boss, were part of the Holyoake machine. They were curious too in that a frequent criticism of the PM is that he runs a one-man band and ought to *return* to the consensus politics of the Holyoake years.

Political scientist Keith Jackson believes political parties debate philosophy when they haven't the courage to debate leadership. Certainly the muttering before this year's National conference indicated a leadership battle, and the rumours gained momentum when the Housing Minister, champion free-enterpriser and heir apparent Derek Quigley, was dispatched to an obscure conference in New Guinea. (Personally, after perhaps a brief Hugh Templeton stewardship, I've got my money on Jim Bolger, who is steadily earning the respect of many in the labour relations field.)

Certainly Chapman's opening address was short of plugs for the boss. The best he could manage was

something to the effect that Rob Muldoon had the full support of the conference for the objectives and philosophy outlined in the Budget. It got no applause and no doves or helium-filled balloons were released. The speech was delivered nervously and hesitantly as though George had something wrong with his throat, but whatever the problem it seemed to correct itself at about 9.30 that night, when his boss left the Christchurch Town Hall and headed for Wellington and Lusaka.

For his part the PM good-naturedly endured several veiled references to his leadership and saved his comeback for the leader's rally. In fact, not much of a comeback was necessary. The withdrawal of the original fiscal regulator proposal had seen to that (though many Government backbenchers were anxious to play down their victory in order to repeat it more easily on other issues). The state-of-the-nation speech also helped immensely. Whenever it came up there were enthusiastic chants of 'Do it again, Rob'.

Still, he tried very hard in his speech to convince the doubters that he was one of them. He stressed his long involvement with the party and told them that the parliamentary team was really one big happy family. He concentrated less on the Opposition than usual, and touched many bases in his long, disordered speech. The old Rob Muldoon surfaced only during the handling of one interjection ('Who let you in? You must be a dropout from that lot outside' — a reference to the small group of protesters in the street).

I got an honourable mention. You may have noticed, more probably you didn't, that my column was absent last issue. Rob referred to the apology which replaced it and he told the hall that I was hiding among them somewhere. Blushing furiously, I had no option but to make a small bow. Later I was swamped by delegates anxious to make apologies because the PM had raised the issue again in his speech.

Truthfully I replied that journalists should not make mistakes. I had made some and therefore I deserved my public caning. Eyes brimmed with tears. One lady said that Muldoon had bailed out the PSIS when he should have let them go to the wall as they deserved to.

(My PSIS story was based on information I received from a man, impeccably placed to know the full story, whom I call 'Deep Throat'. Later, when to my horror, I discovered he was wrong, I vowed he would become 'Sore Throat' next time I saw him.)

The anti-PSIS feeling was merely part of a much larger antipathy to bureaucracies in general and civil servants in particular. Regulations and controls, it was said, were strangling everyone. (Some delegates were honest enough to admit that when it came to scrapping regulations and subsidies, most people wanted it to happen to the people next to them, rather than themselves.)

The party deliberately moved to the right. Many saw it as the only way to win in '81. Boldness was the key. The welfare state would have to be drastically altered — but not so drastically that National would never win another election.

'Where,' asked one bemused delegate during a panel discussion, 'does this leave the wage and salary earner?' Norm Jones was quick to the microphone. 'The National Party looks after those who look after it.'

A few years ago the buzz word at National Party conferences was 'biomass'. This year everyone's eyes lit up at the term 'microprocessors' — they were part of the challenge of the 1980s. Barry Leay, in a compellingly seductive speech, mentioned them frequently. Them and Margaret Thatcher, who was just as *wonderful* and *fantastic* and *incredible*. His was the best leadership speech of the weekend. Totally ignoring all evidence that ran counter to his thesis, he saw New Zealand's potential as *amazing, incredible* and *fantastic*. He told the hall that in a decade God-zone could be in the world's top three for wealth and prosperity. The hall trembled at the prospect of a jetboat in every freezer. And as for forestry, in the 1980s there would be a world shortage of timber and we would have the Arabs over a log.

Mind you, as Bill Birch pointed out in an earlier speech, while there was cause for optimism there was also a need for discipline and restraint. Mindful especially of the latter, the Young Nationals gave youth everywhere a lead by holding their caviare evening by candlelight. It was a tremendous gesture of sacrifice. If more wage and salary earners can be persuaded to hold their caviare evenings by candlelight, then New Zealand will indeed stride boldly and with dignity into the challenging 1980s.

Listener, August 18, 1979

Quick, Before it Depreciates

In politics and advertising, how things are said is often more important than what is said. And what is said isn't always what is meant. Thus Harold Wilson stopped talking about 'wage restraint' and opted for the much nicer-sounding 'planned growth of incomes'. And Aussie Malcolm, former advertising executive, now the Parliamentary Under-Secretary to the Minister of Labour and Immigration, prefers not to talk of crowded refugee camps in Hong Kong, Thailand and Malaysia. Instead he favours the lovely phrase 'primary refuge', and undercrowded New Zealand, which has clearly indicated its desire to take more of the Vietnamese boat people, is known as 'ultimate refuge'. Asked why we are not accepting more refugees, Aussie beams patiently and says the questioner doesn't understand the concept of ultimate refuge.

Of course, the demand for good rhetoric far outstrips the supply. Our politicians have tended to ransack Churchill, the Kennedys and, lately, parts of Jonathan Livingston Seagull. At this year's National Party conference Energy Under-Secretary Barry Brill (notice how when you're No 2 you try harder!) borrowed from the language of the People's Republic of China (probably because his own boss is known in some circles as the notorious Gang of One).

He told an enraptured audience that almost 100 years ago New Zealand extended the frontiers of technology to develop refrigerated shipping, a breakthrough that made us one of the richest countries in the world for 80 years. That was the agricultural revolution. Now we were at the brink of our second Great Leap Forward — the energy revolution. Eventually this would make us all extremely rich and once again New Zealand would have 'God's own economy'. This of course would entail massive capital investment, a move away from consumption to productivity, and an end to 'internecine strife over cake-sharing'.

Brill went on to ask if, during this investment phase, we could justify cutbacks in health, social welfare and education spending. (The Housing Minister and Associate Minister of Finance Derek Quigley, seemed to answer in the affirmative recently when he said that we couldn't have new hospitals and a liquid fuels programme. Presumably if you're ill you squirt petroleum jelly on to the offending organ and hope for the best. Part of becoming hideously rich will be an interim period of relative poverty.)

Unfortunately, standing between us and this new utopia is a mountain of red tape, and Brill, arguing that time is money, proposed the streamlining of planning procedures for projects of vital national importance.

Thus, publicly at least, the National Development Bill was born, and a Government caucus committee chaired by Tourism Minister Warren Cooper was set up to develop the proposal. Cooper was the obvious choice for chairman. Long before others joined the bandwagon he was grizzling about environmentalists. He once complained that these days you needed an environmental impact report before you could kick over a cowpat. (It is said that, given half a chance, the former motel owner and Mayor of Queenstown would install coin-operated machines designed to make the Remarkables revolve in time to hidden speakers blaring out German drinking songs.)

Such songs would be necessary, as it is the West Germans who have expressed interest in South Island coal and hydro resources. Dead keen they are apparently with reservations only about our unstable and unservile workforce and our cumbersome bureaucracy. As luck would have it, some of those concerns may be alleviated by the National Development Bill.

The measure is being sold as necessary to take New Zealand into the 80s and beyond. More specifically, it is designed to get the National administration over the '81 election hump. National feel, probably correctly, that if they can give the impression of boldness and authority in the confusing energy area, then a dazed, anxious electorate will gratefully return them to office.

In the meantime, the package has to be sold like some peacetime Manhattan project. Instead of the atomic bomb to teach the accursed Hun a lesson, we're after synthetic petrol to teach the accursed Arabs a lesson, and the accursed Hun will probably put up most of the money to help us do it. This has left the Commission for the Future, supposedly pointing out options, belatedly complaining that the Government seems to have made up its mind before all the future options have been publicly discussed.

Not everyone in the Government's ranks was happy with the Bill; the version introduced by Energy Minister Bill Birch had been through seven drafts. Birch gave the Bill to the Opposition 12 hours beforehand and the introductory speeches were of a far higher standard than usual. For starters it allowed the Opposition time to decide on a stand, something they tend to find difficult, and that stand was essentially one of constitutional law.

Bill Rowling mocked Birch's claim that the Bill merely saved time. He called it a blatant grab for power in that it allowed the Minister to act God and ride over 28 Acts of Parliament. Fraser Colman, in a surprisingly direct speech, made positively mesmerising by the sluggish Warren Cooper effort that followed, said the Bill was the result of 10 years of Government delay. But Labour's best attack came from its young lawyers David Caygill and Geoff Palmer.

Palmer, arms folded across his chest, speaking with such anger and logic that Government members went pale and pretended to busy themselves behind newspapers, declared that the Bill was oppressive, unjust and unnecessary. 'Aw, come on,' cried a lone interjector. 'It is,' continued Palmer, 'government by fiat without Parliamentary control.'

Bruce Beetham, lately accused of fence-sitting, made his position plain – the Bill was potentially the most dangerous piece of legislation ever introduced into the House.

Down the back in the visitors' gallery the Government member for Marlborough, Doug Kidd, who later found the Bill 'exciting', chatted amiably with Brian Bremner of Fletcher Holdings.

Birch, who looked a little shaken by the avalanche of criticism, replied unconvincingly that he was delighted with the Labour attack, as it showed they were anti-progress, anti-development and opposed to using our natural resources. He also accused them of being ambivalent, and went on to claim that at last the Government knew where the Opposition stood.

Barry Brill was more forthright in his defence. Spitting out the words he accused Labour of being in favour of bureaucratic entanglements. The Government wanted to get the country on the road and it wouldn't shelter behind skirts. As for Palmer's suggestion that the Government bring in special empowering legislation for specific works, it wouldn't

have such legislation 'slapped through the House'.

On a division the Bill was sent to the Lands and Agriculture committee. As time is limited not all submissions on the Bill are guaranteed a hearing, and it will return later in the session and get 'slapped through the House' at the appropriate time. Those concerned about the limited time can't be comforted by the fact that Leo Schultz chairs the select committee. In '75 he was voted by some in the Press Gallery as one of the three least effective National members.

Objections to the Bill include the argument that delays in the past have saved governments from terrible mistakes. Such a Bill in '75 would have allowed the then Labour Government to commit itself to nuclear energy. Such a Bill would have resulted in Auckland Thermal No 1 being built. Brill himself conceded that up until recently the authoritative view on natural gas usage was that it should be burned to generate electricity.

Other objections are to clauses 15 and 16, which effectively give the Government the power to ignore the advice of its own planning council and pass Orders-in-Council that can't be challenged in the Courts. Decision-making is streamlined but there is no guarantee that the standard of decision-making will rise.

Listener, October 27, 1979

The Tizard of Was

On Thursday, November 1, Bob Tizard got a pinch and a punch for the first of the month that he neither enjoyed nor expected. By the narrow margin of 20 to 18 votes the Opposition caucus opted instead for David Lange as its deputy leader.

The leadership question wasn't due for formal consideration by the party until next February, but such was the disquiet at the poor showing in the polls that a group of backbenchers, aided by others like party president Jim Anderton, brought the issue forward for resolution this session.

Hastings MP and freshman David Butcher moved the motion putting the leadership ballot on the agenda some two weeks before the fateful morning, and all agreed at the time that the whole thing was to be kept secret.

Normally the Labour Party have the retentive qualities of a colander but on this occasion they even surprised themselves as well as the news media. (Though one Tizard supporter, still a little sour at the result, remarked that as absolute secrecy had strengthened the hand of the Lange lobby, then it must be they who did most of the leaking normally.) The first the media knew of it was when Eleanor Roy, Bill Rowling's extremely capable press officer, strongly advised the Press Gallery to bring cameras to her boss's post-caucus press conference. Alan Hall, TV2's economic roundsman, quickly guessed what was up and rushed a crew to Bob Tizard's office. They caught the fallen deputy hurt and confused with tears streaming down his face.

The Nats, though, have the best intelligence service of all. At their caucus the same Thursday morning they were discussing strategy for the supplementary estimates debate scheduled for that evening, and Marilyn Waring, chairer of the influential public expenditure committee, assured the PM he would have no problem from the Opposition because 'the knives are out'.

She meant of course that Tizard, who would normally play a big role in the debate and even — especially if on form — do considerable damage and embarrass the Government, would be preoccupied. He certainly was. He spent most of the evening with his closest supporters, easing his sorrows and reliving the infamy.

Marilyn Waring's use of the knives metaphor, though later used by Tizard supporters as well (it gained currency when Muldoon ousted Marshall in '74), was considered inappropriate for *News at Six* and two minutes before air time a graphic of a sharp knife inscribed with a Labour insignia was dropped from the bulletin. Reporter Hall still managed to point out that Bill Rowling now had a deputy he hadn't voted for. (Rowling's luck in these matters is not good — years back he voted for Nordmeyer when

Norm Kirk successfully challenged for the leadership.) Rowling can't have wanted that snippet made public, for later that evening he met Hall in the corridors and told him that the story would 'cost him'.

These days we're all fed on a diet of great coup stories from overseas. President Park of South Korea goes to a dinner party and gets shot between the hors d'oeuvres by an old friend, which I am told can be pretty painful. From the Central African Republic come tales of French paratroopers and fridges full of human flesh. The Tizard ousting is comparatively small beer and I like to think of the coup as the night of the pocketknives, as the main challengers for his job were David Lange and Russell Marshall, both good scouts and not at all prone to cannibalism or the reckless discharge of firearms.

The only people hurt were Warren Freer, who seemed to take Tizard's reversal personally; Mat Rata, who had to move back a row to make room for Lange on the front benches, and who has since resigned from the party; and, of course, Tizard himself. Tizard in defeat was much the same as Tizard normally: blunt, honest and almost incapable of putting himself in the best possible light. He was hurt and angry and he made it plain. When Nats walk the plank they hide their rancour behind platitudes about democracy having its say, pledge unwavering loyalty to their new masters, and leave the room either to blow their brains out or plan a coup of their own.

Tizard's pain came from the vain belief that such a reversal could never happen to him, although he had a warning last year when Lange unsuccessfully tested the waters. By general assent he was considered the smartest in the Opposition, edging out Gerard Wall, and in the House itself being edged out only by Rob Muldoon. Faith in his considerable intellect gave him an arrogance that I enjoyed, though some in the Opposition found it made the hairs on their teeth stand on end. He could be quite brilliant in the House and he could be awful: like the night he offered to punch Hugh Templeton on the nose (which would probably have improved Templeton immeasurably, but it's the principle of the thing), and the time he called Bruce Beetham the member for 'Sexual Credit'.

In the end these excesses told against him, though the vote was far too close to give the Lange camp comfort. Broadly it was a battle between the old guard and the newcomers. Trevor Young, who might have been expected to support the status quo, was mercilessly ridiculed by Tizard in the recent debate on the Sale of Liquor (Amendment) Bill, and he voted for Lange.

The announcement that Lange had won the necessary 20 votes for victory was heard by caucus in what one member later described as stunned silence. Some who supported Tizard later indicated they would have supported Russell Marshall had it been a Lange-Marshall battle. The Wanganui reverend only pulled out of the race the day before when he realised he didn't have enough support to survive the first ballot. His supporters, who then included Ann Hercus, crossed into the Lange camp. Five minutes before caucus started, Kerry Burke asked who would nominate Lange and Roger Douglas agreed to.

In view of his reluctance to lobby on his own behalf Lange's victory is a measure of his influence in the House. His is a commanding presence. He has a rich, warm, booming voice and an unfailing sense of humour, and is fast enough on his feet to score the minor verbal victories that are so important to a party's morale. One failing in the House is that he is sometimes too jolly. Some situations require a little gravity and on occasions Lange is too obviously enjoying himself to take things seriously. He is susceptible to the same charge that dogged Tizard: namely, of being lazy if a subject doesn't interest him. (Though Tizard, who resented Lange's standing in the polls, said he deliberately kept a low profile so as not to overshadow his boss. At times his undershadowing was brilliant.)

At 37 Lange will have to acquire a lot of new political skills very quickly. Few doubt his ability to learn but many worry whether at something like 20 stone he has the stamina to cope with the extra pace and stress the position will inevitably bring. The job will involve much travel, a lot of it in Friendship aircraft, and wedging himself into their tiny seats Lange will need every ounce of his good humour.

Some say the vote for him would have been greater had he challenged Rowling, with, say, Marshall as his deputy. With his new power to pick a small shadow cabinet Rowling must acknowledge the new realities and wield a sharp knife. Men like Michael Bassett and Burke from the class of '72 — the 'retreads', Rowling calls them — must be brought forward and the present doughy centre must be relegated to the periphery. That's what Lange will expect. He must have a considerable influence on Rowling: after all, to get his own way all he has to do is lean on him a little.

Listener, November 24, 1979

The Whiz Kids are All Right

Labour Party backbencher, Taupo MP Mr Jack Ridley, has criticised the 'trendy whiz kid image' of his party in a New Year message to his electorate.
Dominion, *3/1/80*

The trouble with all this rain, thought Vera as she wrestled with the knitting needles, was that it made your joints swell and ache something awful, and didn't half make knitting difficult. Still, she knew most of the pattern by heart and could do it now while watching telly. It was mostly repeats at this time of year, but she didn't mind; she tended to miss lots of things in the programmes the first time round anyway.

She blew on her hands and rubbed her knuckles. Outside it was raining. Terrible weather for January. It was supposed to be summer. Still, it was the campers she felt most sorry for. Imagine being cooped up in a tent or a caravan in the rain — it was such a shame for the kiddies, wasn't it?

It was all right for some. They had baches at Taupo where (according to the weather on telly) it was fine and warm most of the time. Yep, real National Party territory up there all right. And the baches! She'd never been inside one, only seen them through the trees from the road, but you could tell just by looking. Carpeted throughout, with eye-level ovens. Some people in this country had better second homes than most people had first homes. It made her cross and she nearly dropped a stitch. She'd asked her Noel about an eye-level oven once and he'd said that if she was dead keen on it, then all she had to do was lie on the floor in front of her old one.

Still, there was always someone worse off than yourself. Vera busied herself with the knitting. She would soon have 10 garments to send to Kampuchea. She knew Asia was hot but she'd read somewhere that it got cold at night and pure wool shorty pyjamas seemed an ideal compromise.

Micky Savage seemed to approve. He beamed down beatifically at her from his honoured position on the wall. Such a nice man. Who knows what he would have achieved if he'd lived? That was the trouble with the Labour Party. It was full of people who either died too soon or lived too long.

'Vera! Vera!' The voice came from behind a giant mound of '78 election manifestos. It was Andrew, the regional organiser. A lazy sod who seemed to spend most of the morning reading the *Dominion,* a newspaper even the severely dyslexic could finish in minutes. He'd been thrown out of medical school but was still terribly ambitious and dreamt continually of becoming a trade union secretary.

'Vera,' he said, 'I've been thinking about those shorty pyjamas of yours. I reckon you could double your output if you stopped putting *Labour and You*

— *together we'll make it* across the chest in different-coloured wool.'

'Well, smarty-pants,' replied Vera triumphantly, 'if it wasn't done in different-coloured wool it wouldn't show, would it?'

She could sense his agitation and frustration through the layers of pamphlets and manifestos, but before he could regroup the phone went.

'If it's for that massage parlour again I'll scream,' said Vera. 'It's bad enough having them come in looking for it without them phoning as well. Say what you like about George Chapman, I bet there won't be a strip club or massage parlour within a mile of *their* new building.'

'Doesn't need to be, does there!' chimed in Andrew. 'They make house calls for them.'

'This is what I've heard!' said Gran from the next desk, woken by the phone and suddenly taking an interest.

'I've got my hands full here, Gran — could you answer it for us?' smiled Vera.

Nervously adjusting her dentures Gran reached for the phone.

'New Zealand Labour here. Can I help you?' A long silence followed, with Gran nodding furiously and rolling her eyes in terror. Finally she cupped one hand over the mouthpiece and turned to the others.

'It's a Dutchman. Not been here long and wants to join a political party. Wants to know if we have any books or pamphlets that explain what the Labour Party stands for . . .'

'Oh dear!' said Vera.

'Says he's rung before. Says he's got stuff from all the parties except us. Says that Social Credit alone delivered a truckload of stuff within minutes of his first call. . .'

'Tell him that such is the demand from new members that as soon as we print the stuff it's snapped up,' offered Andrew helpfully.

'We could send him some *I'm backing Bill* badges and Roger Douglas's paper on tax reform,' added Vera, thinking aloud.

'Too late,' said Gran. 'He's hung up.'

'We really must get something together.'

'I quite agree, Andrew, but the committee in charge can't agree on a date for their first meeting,' said Vera defensively. 'These things take time.'

Before a row could develop Nigel called them in for morning tea. Nigel was gay, which made things difficult at times, but awfully sweet all the same and a genius at raffling chooks in pubs.

At the stained Formica table Andrew sucked thoughtfully on his Cameo Cream and studied the *Dom.* 'I see,' he said finally, 'that Muldoon has refused to condemn Pol Pot outright.'

'Typical! Bloody typical!' sniffed Gran. 'Just what

you'd expect from that man. With that sort of moral cowardice it's no wonder the young smoke the stuff.'

'What shall we do with the last Cameo Cream?' asked Andrew, neatly changing the subject.

'Send it to Kampuchea,' said Vera firmly.

'Raffle it,' suggested Nigel.

'OK,' said Andrew wearily, 'we'll put it to the vote . . .'

Listener, January 26, 1980

Mat Rata, having resigned from the Labour Party, resigns his Northern Maori seat as well, forcing a by-election he contests as leader of the newly formed Mana Motuhake Party. (April 1980)

Paper Tigers

Ask almost any visitor to this country, or someone returning home after a long absence, what impresses them most and they will probably tell you how it's virtually impossible to pick up a newspaper, watch television news or listen to the radio without coming across something said either by or about Robert David Muldoon.

An English friend of mine, brought up on the tradition that prime ministers, like children, should be seen and not heard (and rarely seen), is continually flabbergasted at the sheer range of topics on which the PM seems compelled to comment. He finds it hard to believe that the PM has Cabinet colleagues, for his daily utterances appear to blithely encompass dozens of portfolios. Of course the PM would argue that because he is Minister of Finance other people's business is also his. His latest forays include definitions of what is and what isn't *culture*. He's convinced that most rock music isn't and says he has no intention of relaxing the crippling sales tax on records in spite of what his associate Hugh Templeton might have said. (Having declared opera *culture*, I wonder how the PM would react if Kiri Te Kanawa, with a safety pin in her cheek and her hair dyed an appropriate shade of green, put out an LP entitled *Never Mind the Bollocks! — Kiri Sings the Johnny Rotten Songbook.*)

Not for nothing is the PM known as the 'Gang of One', and with a public profile today easily eclipsing that of Chairman Mao at the height of the Cultural Revolution, it is not surprising that he and the news media should occasionally squabble.

In his last book, *The Anatomy of Power*, the late James Margach, long-time chief political correspondent for the British *Sunday Times*, described the relationship between the government and the press as being one of irreconcilable interests. He contended that the healthiest relationship is one of tension, mutual suspicion and constant hostility. Our own Keith Ovenden has described politics as a conspiracy against the people but most Gallery journalists would consider that an unpalatable definition. As far as our major metropolitan dailies are concerned the conflicts of interest that Margach refers to don't really exist, as the press and the present administration have long shared the same goal: the re-election of National governments.

Rob Muldoon, however, with his non-stop broadsides at the news media, friend and foe alike, has unhinged this automatic loyalty. Even the *New Zealand Herald*, hardly a radical publication, took the daring step a few weeks back of publishing on its front page a large photograph of the PM, glass in hand, staring at a fashion model's legs.

This picture was published days after the PM's release of figures to show that the circulations of several major newspapers have dropped over the past decade. Quoting from the Audit Bureau of Circulation he made the case that newspapers who concentrated on the sensational have fared worse than their competitors.

The *Christchurch Star* and the *Dominion*, papers he's had occasion to castigate in the past, had experienced falls of six per cent and 19 per cent respectively. The PM pointed out that the *Dom's* performance stuck out like a sore thumb.

Television New Zealand's Dennis Grant pointed out, however, that the PM failed to mention that *Truth*, a publication that he himself writes for, suffered a 29 per cent drop over the same period. And Brian Priestley on *News Stand* completed the rout by adding that the *Sunday News*, which is almost entirely based on sensation, experienced a big jump in circulation, and the *Listener* (whom of course it is my great pleasure to have written for these past seven years) experienced a record 140 per cent jump.

In short the PM omitted evidence that was damaging to his case. But when the *Dominion* excised two paragraphs from a long press statement of his that was critical of their reporting of the great methanol debate, the PM declared editor Ted Frost's actions 'contrary to the principles of decent journalism in a modern democracy'. He then banned the *Dom's* Gallery team of Richard Long and Glynis Green from his press conferences.

The PM's disputes with the *Dom* go back many years. I'm sure it's his favourite paper in many ways — certainly it's one he can safely whip. His relationship with Richard Long, the *Dom's* chief Gallery reporter, is more complex. Long is one of the best journalists on the Hill and is not afraid to ask dangerous questions at press conferences. I suspect that the PM quite likes him for that reason alone, though at the same time I'm sure Long has the ability to infuriate him. This he did quite effectively last year when he wrote something of a shock-horror-probe story on the unlocked Cabinet room at the time of the move into the Beehive. The PM reacted swiftly, calling Long's action 'irresponsible' and a breach of the traditional trust placed in the Press Gallery. In retaliation no one was allowed on the ninth floor without checking with his press staff first.

That stipulation was universally ignored.

But the recent ban, while quickly lifted, raises questions that won't lapse with time. I have a particular interest in the subject, as I was banned myself for a time last year. It was when the PM was in his old office. He told the chairman of the Press Gallery that his press conferences were for hard news journalists only, not weekly journalists, especially not that Scott fellow who wrote fiction. (If I wrote fiction how come I got sued for libel? I should have got a grant from the

Literary Fund.) Space then was at a premium and when the press conference venue shifted to the Beehive theatrette I sneaked in the back and to date have been allowed to stay.

Almost as disturbing as the ban on the *Dom* reporters was the response of some in the Gallery. In trade union matters the Gallery has the tensile strength of warm butter, though one is not allowed to say that, as all Gallery matters are strictly confidential. This is a rule which I find perplexing and disturbing. On the one hand journalists are forever calling for a more open society, an end to secrecy and fuller access to information, and on the other we run an organisation more secret that a papal election.

The afternoon the ban was announced the Gallery held a meeting in camera, which, as I didn't attend (deliberately), I can write about. I am told views on the ban varied. A few thought the *Dom* had brought all this on itself and deserved everything it got. Others were all for a total walk-out on the principle

that no one knew when it would be their turn to be asked to leave.

In the centre, however, were those who felt they could only act according to instructions from their editors, and in the end, in the interests of a tenuous unity, a compromise was agreed to: essentially, if the *Dom* people were asked to leave, the Gallery chairman would rise and express the combined concern, but the press conference would continue as if nothing had happened.

In any event private discussions resolved the dispute, with the *Dom* agreeing to print the excised paragraphs if the PM lifted the ban.

Chairman Mao once said that there were times when one should stand firm like an oak and other times when one should bend like grass in the wind. Some in the Gallery demonstrated a complete mastery of the latter.

Listener, May 10, 1980

Unhappy Landings

US CAN COUNT ON NZ, SAYS PM, IF
FIGHTING BREAKS OUT IN GULF
— headline in *Evening Post*

The PM gave this assurance to a team of journalists led by William Randolph Hearst Jr, editor-in-chief of Hearst Newspapers. While such a bold pledge undoubtedly brought joy and hope to untold millions of US citizens in their hour of need, it scared the hell out of me. I belong to a generation of lads who were ritually pruned at birth specifically so that they could fight in some future desert conflict without the inconvenience of trapping sand in their private parts. Immediately I saw myself wading up a giant dune pursued by Arabs either hell-bent on marrying me or holding me personally responsible for the continued existence of the state of Israel.

Dry of mouth and damp of palm I swallowed hard and read on. 'The strongly pro-American leader said that if the US had to resort to military action to protect the Middle East oilfields from Soviet aggression and needed naval and air-staging facilities in New Zealand, they would be granted . . .'

Phew! Thank God for that. You've got to hand it to Rob — he's no mug. A less likely launching pad for an air strike on Tehran than Whenuapai I can't imagine. Still, apart from logistical drawbacks, like being nearly half the world away, such a strike would certainly have the advantage of surprise on its side. With President Carter's luck that probably wouldn't be enough. Some say he couldn't organise a two-car funeral and they may be right. The recent debacle in the Iranian desert seems to confirm that.

I know that planned obsolescence is as American as apple pie, but to lose three out of eight helicopters and a C130 halfway to the final target is carrying faith in capitalism too far. Assuming that a loss rate of three out of every eight helicopters every 300km is normal for the US Navy, to actually get six functional helicopters from Whenuapai to Tehran you'd have to start at this end with a vast armada of 30 million aircraft. Even if they had that many helicopters, which of course is impossible, and even if Whenuapai could hold them all, which of course it couldn't, not even Carter would be likely to consider such a scheme. You can imagine the chaos if he did. Something like 10 million helicopters would go down in the Tasman within 300km of Auckland.

No, Rob's no mug. He knew what he was doing when he made his generous offer. Still, to be on the safe side I'm going to put my feet in the vice this weekend and render myself even more ineligible for active military service.

On the home front things have been quiet on the Hill, with only the visit of Wilhelm Haferkamp, vice-president of the European Commission, raising much interest — and then mainly because Haferkamp's name was at the centre of a controversy over a recent expense accounts scandal. He regularly managed to run up $3000 a day in expenses and one legendary dinner in Washington is supposed to have cost the EEC $30,000. The man has style, though. Another legend has him visiting the People's Republic with a particularly attractive interpreter, who, it transpired, couldn't speak a word of Chinese.

Unlike the much underrated Brian Talboys, who travels to the annual Brussels negotiations with perhaps three others in tow, Haferkamp led a nine-man team here. The crucial talks were scheduled for Queenstown, partly because of the magnificent scenery and partly, some suspect, because Talboys is at his best long distances from Rob.

It's always difficult to measure the success of such meetings and many argue that leaving the visitors with warm impressions of New Zealand is just as important. Sightseeing and visits to farms are therefore part of the itinerary. In the past the farms chosen have tended to be showcases, which probably counted against our negotiating claim that New Zealand would be in dire economic straits if the EEC further restricted the entry of our primary products. To counteract that, Duncan MacIntyre has flown other EEC officials low over barren and rugged hill country to emphasise that God's Own is not one vast verdant flat paddock.

I don't think that is enough. Just as Russia builds model cities for naive tourists to ogle at, we should build model farms that clearly demonstrate our vulnerability. I suggest a farm somewhere inland from Gisborne. You can only reach it by jeep and the EEC officials should be car-sick at least twice. The odd school bus should lie burnt and gutted at the bottom of steep ravines. In places the metal road should fall away to sheer cliffs on both sides. After what seems like years the first of many Taranaki gates should come into view. Eventually, on a barren windswept ridge, the battered weatherboard homestead is spotted. Corrugated iron still patches the windows that were broken when the house was delivered on the back of a truck.

Nappies that will never be white again run the full length of a clothes-line that stretches across two paddocks to a lone cabbage tree. At the back door a dog trained to rip the trousers of well-dressed foreigners does its stuff. In the kitchen an immense woman with tired faraway eyes is clutching a child to her breast with one hand and chopping up a horse's head with the other. She says her husband won't be long — he's just burying dead sheep and their nine-year-old, but it's difficult to hear her over the sound of the wind whistling through the gaps in the sarking.

Eventually, of course, a lot of New Zealand will

actually belong to overseas interests and such visits will be made by landlords rather than EEC officials. Recently a consortium of BP and Fletchers obtained 50,000 hectares near Gisborne and Prince Nawaf Bin Azziz purchased a million bucks' worth of prime Coromandel real estate. The Overseas Investment Commission controls such land sales, but the PM is on record as being keen to have Saudi Arabians in particular invest in New Zealand.

Part of Prince Nawaf's deal was to loan $20 million to the Development Finance Corporation for investment in energy projects. One of the reasons we are so frantic to develop our energy sources is that we want to lessen our dependence on Arab oil. In the process we are increasing our dependence on Arab money. I can foresee a future Opec summit agreeing to put up the interest rates on loan money. They may eventually force us to move around with smaller cheque accounts and endure creditless days. Inflation will continue to soar and finance ministers the world over will say it's not their fault that the bloody Arabs keep putting up the price of money.

The same weekend that Haferkamp et al were chatting against the backdrop of the Remarkables, and the Americans were running around Iranian deserts in the dark, the very sad news was announced that Labour's Frank Rogers had died without gaining consciousness after a massive stroke. Typically he died helping to rescue two people trapped in a car.

There was always something hypertensive and deliciously unpredictable about Frank's behaviour in the House. Bill Rowling described him, somewhat euphemistically, as 'colourful and forthright'. He was that. He had perhaps the loudest voice in the House, a deliberately hazy appreciation of Standing Orders, and everyone liked him. He could be rude and rash, and far smarter than you gave him credit for.

My favourite moment came after National's Neil Austin had given a long and tedious speech on some obscure topic. At the bell he sat down with obvious relief, adding for good measure, 'I could speak for hours on this subject Mr Speaker but my time is up.'

Frank was on his feet in seconds. 'Mr Speaker, I move an extension of time!' Austin went pale at this betrayal, but the Speaker judiciously ignored the request. Frank will be missed.

Listener, May 17, 1980

The Prime Minister has to increasingly come to the aid of his much-criticised friend, Colin McLachlan, the Minister of Transport. (April 1980)

Post-Skinner Behaviourism

I have always thought that trying to summarise a week-long event like a conference is rather like trying to describe the shape of a shoal of plankton. While it's expected of you and it can be fun to try, often it's an empty and artificial exercise. Still, after the recent 43rd FOL conference there was no shortage of delegates willing to volunteer conclusions of their own.

Many saw it as a long overdue move to the left. Tony Neary's people saw it as a *dangerous* move to the left. Some saw it as a moderate and quietly progressive conference. A few came to the extraordinary conclusion that the conference had in fact moved to the right — a complex thesis based on the view that SUP delegates, whose standing was much enhanced at this conference, are essentially conservative trade unionists.

One delegate, his eyes misting slightly behind his glasses, described it in Maori terms. It had been a whanau conference — a family affair. 'People,' he exclaimed rapturously, 'were actually waltzing at the social.' By all accounts the social was the best ever, the highlight being the contribution of the Wellington Trades Council Women's Subcommittee choir.

After their moving version of 'Solidarity Forever' there wasn't a dry seat in the house.

Jim Knox, barely able to contain his pride, described the conference as the best for many years.

Amid this fevered 'born again trade unionism' a friend of mine attributed the new optimism to the departure of Sir Tom Skinner. He likened the FOL to a husband who has just escaped a long unhappy marriage. Formally separated from the cold and loveless Skinner the movement was relishing its new freedom and brazenly sleeping with every passing ideology that took its fancy. Eventually this hollow intellectual promiscuity would pall and the FOL would look around for a nice girl, probably the Labour Party, to settle down with.

Sir Tom, whose memoirs come out in September (purportedly the saga of his many bold stands, entitled *Uncle Tom's Cave-Ins*), was seldom mentioned this conference, and then usually in disparaging terms. ('For years we were led by a knight,' gloated one delegate, 'and we were kept in the dark.') In truth, while outwardly benign and casual, Skinner ran the conference with a ruthless efficiency, stifling dissent and steering discussion away from areas he

thought were best left untouched. Jim Knox, who seems to have only the vaguest appreciation of standing orders, was anxious to erase that legacy. Aided by the calming influence of secretary Ken Douglas, he ran the most democratic conference in years. Certainly many people who had been afraid to say anything in the past made their maiden speeches this year.

Jim Knox's speeches are not noted for their linear precision and clarity. At times his impromptu oratory wanders like a stereo needle across a dirty LP (halfway through one train of thought the needle skids and you end up somewhere else) and at the start many doubted whether he would be able to handle a full conference. At times he rambled interminably (during his opening address one delegate blasphemously moved a lunchbreak) and during procedural wrangles he was liable to pound the table in impotent rage.

Still, at the week's end some feminists who had had to endure a series of inept and sexist remarks were insisting warmly that Knoxie was a 'pussycat'. Following his closing remarks that the movement had to stand firm and have discipline he was granted a spontaneous standing ovation. (In the past he has loyally had to wave delegates to their feet to salute his predecessor.)

Still on cloud nine he was driven to Avalon to be interviewed by Ian Fraser on *Newsmakers*. It was there that he made his famous statement that while socialism was close to communism it was equally true to say that communism was close to socialism. He went on to advocate nationalising the petrol companies and conceded that there were few major differences between himself, Ken Douglas and Bill Andersen.

I know a lot of decent people have not slept properly since then, but it must be remembered that unity was one of the themes of this conference. 'Unity through diversity,' said Bill Andersen at one point. (The SUP have a never-ending supply of such slogans. Sometimes industrial action is rejected on the grounds that the workers are not sufficiently educated. When it suits, the opposite slogan — 'Education comes through action' — is wheeled out.)

It was argued repeatedly that the Kinleith victory was achieved through unity ('Such a small word,' said Knox, 'but it has a ring to it') and at times the conference was determined to push for unity even if it made enemies in the process. In the end there was little real division.

Tony Neary and Knox clashed over the appropriate response to the Government's refusal to grant an immediate cost-of-living order. Two days after the conference had already overwhelmingly agreed on some form of direct action Neary advocated accepting the Government's offer of a special tribunal, provided it met within a month. If the Government refused that, he argued, then direct action should follow. This would allow the Government a dignified retreat and make the FOL the goodies of the piece. Many delegates privately agreed with the moderate Neary but voted against him. It had already been decreed that a vote for him was effectively a vote for disunity.

Neary later led the opposition to clause 15 of the Working Women's Charter, which virtually guaranteed the charter's complete adoption — safe legal abortions and all. While Neary's objections were sincere and moral there remains the suspicion that some rubber workers opposed the clause out of self-interest.

The only other marked division was between the SUP and the Workers Communist League. In their glossy publication on Kinleith, where they share the credit between the workers, Knox and themselves, the SUP accused the Workers Communist League of being an extreme left-wing (Maoist) organisation which labelled the great Kinleith victory a 'sellout'. In retaliation the league put out a broadsheet titled 'Bill Andersen is a liar!' and charged the SUP with being agents of Soviet imperialism in the trade union movement.

More constructively the conference agreed to the setting up of a Maori Resources Committee to examine and make recommendations on the employment problems, discrimination and exploitation faced by Maori youth.

There were moderate and sensible gains in other areas as well, though the movement has yet again delayed addressing itself to the urgent and pressing problem of union amalgamation.

In many ways the movement has its self-respect back and is understandably beginning to swagger a little. The revolution, though, is a long way off. Some prominent unionists are rumoured to own a racehorse and they have no intention of seriously rocking the boat until after they have won the Melbourne Cup.

As for all the talk of nationalisation, this is merely predictable reaction to Government rhetoric about selling parts of the public sector to private enterprise. In short, the status quo remains in a state of dynamic equilibrium. One way of course that the Government can postpone Armageddon indefinitely is to nationalise the horseracing industry. That way the baddies will never win the Melbourne Cup.

Listener, May 31, 1980

Young and Foolish

If the recently married Minister of Lands, Venn Young, has any wedding cake or flowers left over he should send them to Labour's Bill Rowling and Roger Douglas. Just when the Opposition, for perhaps the first time this year, had the Government looking groggy on the ropes and virtually unable to defend itself, fighting broke out in the Labour corner.

Rowling overreacted to Douglas's probably intentionally provocative 'alternative Budget', and at the height of the Fitzgerald loans affair media attention was diverted by the shock sacking of Douglas as shadow Minister of Transport. Ruefully conceding that the timing could have been better, Labour president Jim Anderton dutifully supported his leader, while Richard Prebble gleefully welcomed Douglas to the backbenches.

Resignations are not common in New Zealand public life and the hapless Labour Party seems to have a monopoly on the few that do occur. Colin Moyle had to resign from Parliament a few years back. Mat Rata resigned from the party and Parliament this year. Following a row with Rowling late last year Richard Prebble voluntarily resigned from the Shadow Cabinet.

Nats are not prone to the same fits of pique or principle, which is why Venn Young, even though he was warned it would happen, seemed genuinely hurt and bewildered by the resignation of Roly White, a longstanding member of the National Party, from the Marginal Lands Board.

White, a retired Whakatane farmer and a member of the board since his appointment by Duncan MacIntyre 10 years ago, resigned in protest at the granting of a $200,000 loan to Jim and Audrey Fitzgerald to develop their 930ha property south of Wellington.

The Marginal Lands Board had twice declined to lend the Fitzgeralds any money, but as Mrs Fitzgerald is Duncan MacIntyre's daughter, and as Venn Young — a friend of the Fitzgeralds as well as chairman of the board — once pleaded their case before the board, White resigned, alleging political pressure.

The Fitzgeralds first approached the board last November and were turned down, essentially on the grounds that Mr Fitzgerald was not a farmer and the application therefore did not meet with the board's lending policy. Applicants can appeal against a board decision by approaching any board member and asking for a review of their case, and in January this year the Fitzgeralds did just that by approaching Noel Coad, the Director-General of Lands. Just to make absolutely sure, they quite independently approached Young too. Young wrote to Coad, conceding that the Fitzgeralds were friends of his and outlining the reasons why the board should favourably review their case.

The minutes of the board's January meeting show that Young took the chair to plead the Fitzgeralds' case and extol their virtues, suggested the setting up of a subcommittee to deal with the matter, and then excused himself from further discussion or decision-making because he was personally involved.

The subcommittee reported favourably but the local marginal lands board stood by their earlier objection and the national body upheld their decision and declined the loan. That was in April. Weeks later, citing new information, the Fitzgeralds approached Coad for yet another review. Another subcommittee visited their farm, was impressed with Jim Fitzgerald's mustering skills and fencing, and again reported favourably. Again the local board objected but in June the national body overruled them and granted the loan.

When the story broke, Venn Young told *New Zealand Herald* reporters in the Gallery that the final vote was 8 to 1 in the Fitzgeralds' favour, thus giving the impression that Roly White was a sore loser. As the board only has eight members, someone would have had to vote twice to get that result.

In fact the final decision was only 3 to 1. One farmer representative on the board, Mr Phillips, was absent overseas. The Treasury representative, Mr Lough, has not attended for five years, in spite of a statutory requirement that he or his appointee do so. (In theory they are there to supervise the spending of taxpayers' money. Marginal Lands Board loan money is given at various interest rates, though it is not uncommon for such loans to be written off entirely. In effect the Fitzgeralds just might have got a $200,000 cash grant.)

The Director-General of Agriculture, Don Cameron, voted yes, as did the farmer representatives, Mr Fergusson and Mr Rider. The Minister of Lands did not attend. Roly White voted no. And, perhaps very wisely, Noel Coad abstained.

The close decision alone does not worry some. The Opposition seemed more peeved by the fact that the Fitzgeralds, in spite of owning more than $200,000 worth of property in Wellington, lived rent-free in a ministerial home with Duncan MacIntyre. Others were aghast that they had approached the Marginal Lands Board, usually a lender of last resort, in spite of being offered $75,000 by the Rural Bank.

This Government insists that people show initiative and stand on their own two feet. Mrs Fitzgerald, I think it must be conceded, showed enormous initiative in being Duncan MacIntyre's daughter.

While Venn Young has resolutely denied any wrongdoing Labour's Richard Prebble has talked of impeachment, David Lange has threatened to take legal action against the Minister, and Geoffrey

Palmer has thundered in the House about a stench pervading the land. Refusing to extend the Ombudsman's powers of inquiry to cover the Minister's actions, the PM announced a one-man commission of inquiry to 'clear the air'.

Even a cursory reading of the Marginal Lands Act shows that Young behaved unwisely at the very least. Clause 8 specifically says that members should not be present at any meeting or take part in any discussion if they have directly or indirectly any pecuniary or personal interest in the case. On Ian Fraser's *Newsmakers* programme, in contrast to his almost jaunty appearance earlier in the week on *Eye Witness,* the Minister, unfortunately sweating profusely, tried to argue that personal interest meant pecuniary interest.

He also maintained that he had not been an advocate for the Fitzgeralds, in spite of stressing their good qualities and insisting that they could farm their property successfully if given the opportunity.

Lange says that Young has been more of a fool than a knave, a point of view Young's senior colleagues might share, as several of them declined to respond when asked if they would have behaved as he did. Should Young resign, though? If stupidity were automatic grounds for resignation, both sides of the House would be severely depleted in numbers.

Some have described the whole issue as a mountain being made out of a molehill. If young farmers could do just that, then there wouldn't be any need for the Marginal Lands Board at all.

Listener, July 19, 1980

Commission of Inquiry into Marginal Lands Board affair finds Venn Young acted 'unwisely', and Duncan MacIntyre acted 'extremely unwisely'. (December 1980)

My office at Parliament is really just a desk in the smoko room between the RNZ and TVNZ rooms. I share it with a teleprinter, coffee machine, fridge and a battered, ominously stained couch. Late afternoon the sun beats through the ineffectual curtains and I was sitting drowsily at my desk one day when TVNZ's chief political reporter Dennis Grant strode in for some coffee and mentioned casually that he'd just finished the costings on his forthcoming trip to India and China with the PM.

I responded wistfully that the *Listener* never sent me on trips like that. Dennis almost dropped his coffee.

'No one sends you on these things out of the goodness of their hearts,' he snapped. 'You have to submit a proposal.'

'You do?'

'Yes, of course you do. You make out a case for why they should send you.'

He told me I could use his costings and insisted I got on to it right away. I did as I was told and about half an hour later handed the document to Dennis.

'No, no, no . . .' he sighed, 'I wouldn't give you a taxi chit for this. For Christ's sake you've got to sell them the idea. Build it up a bit. Make it sound absolutely imperative that you go. Don't pussyfoot around.'

With him yelling advice at me about stressing the unprecedented opportunity for the *Listener* and its readers; the unique grouping of world leaders in India; the first Western leader to visit China since the change of leadership; the vital debates on the great issues of the day, I typed away furiously, producing two pages of hyperbole that I found embarrassing, but which Dennis insisted would do the trick nicely.

I must say he knew what he was talking about. *Listener* editor Peter Stewart nearly wrote me out a cheque on the spot. The only conceivable hitch would be getting the PM's approval to be part of his official party. The next morning, quite fortuitously, I ran into his deputy Brian Talboys in a corridor and I told him I wanted to follow his boss around Asia, not as a satirist but as a serious journalist, and did he have any good advice?

'Drop him a note telling him just what you have told me,' he grinned, 'Good luck . . .'

I dispatched a suitably sober and craven letter off to the PM and a day or so later his press officer Gerry Symmans told me that as the PM had scrawled 'seen' on the bottom of the note it could well mean I would be allowed to come. At the very least he hadn't rejected the idea outright.

Over the next few days, however, the news filtering down from the ninth floor was not good. Time was running out and Dennis suggested I sound the PM out personally by dropping a note into the House asking to talk to him in the lobby. I wasn't all that keen.

'Go on,' urged Grant. 'He can only say no.'

I handed the note to a messenger and waited nervously for the man himself. He came out a short while later, glowering. The voice was low and deliberate when he spoke.

He told me I wouldn't be going to China *or* India if he could help it.

My usual response to authority is an inadvertent insolence (it must be genetic – my own children do it to me) and I inquired if he was serious or merely bluffing. He assured me he was deadly serious. I knew that if he refused to have me in his official party I couldn't go to China but I doubted aloud whether he could stop me going to India. He jutted his jaw and fixed me with a piercing stare and told me he could and he would. He'd be contacting the Indian Government and the Commonwealth Secretariat and having me banned.

I scoffed politely and we parted. Going back upstairs I felt quite weak at the knees and in a daze told the others what had happened. Within minutes they were thumping away on their typewriters and, as they say in Values Party circles, by early evening the yoghurt really hit the fan. Poor Peter Stewart, not long on the job, suddenly found himself embroiled in a controversy he could have done without. He was very good about it and insisted the *Listener* would be sending me to India irrespective of the PM's thoughts on the matter. Elsewhere the PM and I were engaged in a bizarre war of words. He claimed I wrote garbage and I riposted that it was garbage of the highest quality.

Next it became a battle of Chinese sayings, with the PM claiming that his reluctance to have me along could be explained by the old Chinese proverb that one rat dropping spoiled the soup. I replied with a quote from Chairman Mao that you couldn't smell the flowers from a galloping horse – meaning that a whirlwind trip through China had only limited value – adding that it was possible though to smell the horse, and often that was enough.

It was a pathetic exchange really, but heady stuff at the time. Things got more serious when the PM took some journalists aside to tell them I threw chairs out of hotel windows – the implication being that you couldn't take me anywhere. While the latter is probably true enough the former was quite incorrect.

Editorially most newspapers took the line that the PM was perfectly entitled to refuse to have me in his official party on the China leg of the trip; it was, however, up to the *Listener* to decide whether I was a proper journalist or not.

The Commonwealth Secretariat and Indian Government, as expected, did not ban me from the regional summit in Delhi. Secretary-General Sonny Ramphal said that the Commonwealth had a long tradition of a free press and he expressed his alarm that this seemed to be declining in New Zealand. As for the Indian Government of Mrs Gandhi they were only too pleased to show how liberal they were on press matters and so, much to the PM's irritation, I cockily boarded the same flight as the official party, bound first for Singapore, then Bangkok and Delhi.

That night in Singapore the feelings of triumph began to subside. Alone in my room while the others were across in the luxury wing getting an exclusive briefing from the PM, I suddenly felt terribly tired and alone. I began to question whether the entire exercise was worth it — for me or the *Listener*. I got into bed wearily and for the first time in years wished my mother was there to tuck me in.

I found out later that my dear, grey-haired Irish mother was just a few miles away. By a coincidence so extraordinary if you read it in a novel you'd barely credit it, my mother was that very night in another, less sumptuous Singapore hotel, returning home from her first trip back to Ireland since immigrating to New Zealand in 1949. She knew nothing of the controversy surrounding my trip but is a free-lance worrier when it comes to her offspring and doubtless she was in her hotel room wondering about her children and putting out vibes which I was picking up. I'm sure that it was because of her unseen, unknown proximity that I slept with my passport and wallet tucked under my pillow and with the door securely latched.

India was a giddy madhouse and I wasn't really alone again until I called into Australia to do an election preview on my way home. It had been arranged beforehand that I would hole up in a Sydney hotel for a few days to finish the India articles before heading to Canberra to do an election preview. Booking into the Decrest in Kings Cross I ran into National Party Dominion Councillor (now party president) Sue Wood on holiday with her husband Terry. We greeted each other like long lost friends and arranged to have a meal together later that evening. We had a nice time. I told them all about India and they told me a bit about the turmoil in the National Party following their shock loss in the East Coast Bays by-election. (I was at a press reception in India when the news of the defeat came through. I related the tale to some Indian officials who immediately burst into big grins. 'It couldn't have happened to a nicer chap,' laughed one of them.) Sue told me that the by-election loss had many causes. One factor had been the PM's treatment of me. Whatever satisfaction this gave me at the time it had all vanished by the time I returned to my hotel room. Alone with my notebooks, sketch pads and typewriter I had to write a story in which I was a participant without dwelling on myself.

Ever since Hillary climbed Everest and modestly confined himself to 'We knocked the bugger off', New Zealanders have expected their countrymen to be suitably coy and reticent about events involving themselves.

Writing about India, I didn't want to seem obsessed about what had happened to me, nor did I want to ignore it entirely — as if it was something I couldn't face. The tone had to be just right and being on my own I had no one to check things with. It proved very difficult and in the space of a few short days I deteriorated into a recluse. I couldn't bear going out and hated eating alone in the dining room so took to ordering all meals from room service but eventually even that was an ordeal and I began darting across the road once a day and buying yoghurt and fruit.

When I had nearly finished I finally ventured out one evening and strolled down the Cross. I felt better than I had for days but I must have looked furtive and desperate for I was propositioned every few yards by various ladies of the night and other gaudy creatures of indeterminate gender. Naturally not wishing to bring home an anti-social disease or guilty conscience, I hurried by. After passing about the tenth dirty bookshop I decided a guilty conscience was something I could live with, and I paused outside one such establishment working up the courage to dash in and buy a whole armful. Taking a deep breath I went in and picked up a Danish publication called something elliptical like 'Thrust' or 'Juicy Lucy', affecting what I hoped would seem the bored nonchalance of a connoisseur who has overdosed on the real thing.

I was just relaxing and had worked out at what speed I should turn the pages to stop my glasses misting over when the discreet, almost studious quiet of the bookshop was rent by a terrible shriek from the doorway: 'TOM SCOTT! YOU OUGHT TO BE ASHAMED OF YOURSELF! GET OUT OF THERE AT ONCE!'

I staggered out, burbling that I only went in to buy *Newsweek* but they didn't have any.

My accuser was a very attractive New Zealand girl in a white jumpsuit, which only made things worse.

'How was India?' she asked.

'Fine, just fine ...' I muttered, wretched with embarrassment.

'Jolly good,' she said, chatting on a bit before bidding me a laughing farewell and melting into the night with her amused friends.

It was the first indication I had that after India my status had changed. The Prime Minister had promoted me in the batting order of public consciousness. Suddenly people who had never read my column or for that matter were only dimly aware that there was a publication called the *NZ Listener* discovered I was a journalist in some sort of bother with Rob Muldoon.

The bother came to a head of sorts shortly after I returned home. The dark mutterings that had gone on within the National Party while the PM had been away suddenly became the colonels' coup and Rob Muldoon found himself fighting for his political survival. He used television in particular quite brilliantly to head off his opponents and with Brian

Talboys in Europe wringing his hands and saying that he didn't seek the position of leader but would take on the job if that was what his colleagues really wanted, the challenge wilted. For a few days though the PM looked genuinely shocked by it all and there was lots of talk privately about him being a changed man, even while publicly he was insisting a leopard couldn't change its spots.

I decided to put the reformation to the test and went along to one of his press conferences, that he had previously barred me from on the grounds that they were for daily accredited journalists only. He looked up at my approach into the Beehive theatrette and said, 'Oh no, Mr Scott,' and asked one of his staff to escort me out.

Somewhat plaintively, not to mention ineptly, I inquired, 'Is this an example of the turned over new leaf?' before leaving.

The PM later complained that this was one of the rudest exchanges he had ever had endured in his long political career. If he wasn't happy with my behaviour, neither were some of my colleagues. Some thought I'd been unnecessarily provocative. I thought it was necessary provocation. I guess what upset them most was they knew even as I was leaving the room that they themselves would later be criticised for not walking out with me.

That particular clip has been shown on television a number of times since then and I think the PM and I deserve some sort of royalty. I still cringe when I see myself, and note sadly that I had a lot more hair then.

Being well known in this country brings no particular benefits unless you enjoy being stopped in the street by dear old ladies who are not sure who you are but think you might have something to do with Dougal Stevenson or Brian Edwards. I can recall though one occasion when the India debacle came in handy. It was a few weeks after I had returned home and we were on our way out to a wedding in Waikanae when I pulled into a service station at the bottom of the Ngaio gorge to fill up the van.

'Sorry mate, no cheques or credit cards,' he said when I went to pay him.

I assured him the cheque wouldn't bounce.

'Oh yeah. I've heard that one before.'

I produced a wad of ID cards and press passes that left him unmoved. He seemed quite prepared to siphon back the petrol should the need arise.

I started to get desperate. 'I was the guy Muldoon tried to have banned from India . . .'

He grinned and patted me on the shoulder. 'No worries mate,' and then, turning to the kids, added, 'Help yourselves to some drinks from the fridge.'

Snakes and Leaders

The scenes in the back corridor of the third floor of Parliament the morning Rob Muldoon attended his first party caucus after his long overseas trip were quite amazing. I have seen nothing like it since the Labour caucus met six years ago to pick a successor to Norm Kirk. There was the same sense of dramatic possibility in the air. Every journalist, television cameraman and newspaper photographer in the building milled about, feeding off and contributing to the tension and excitement.

For some it was too much — thrusting tape-recorders into others' hands, they shot off to empty their bladders, insisting that they were to be called immediately if anything happened. It was obvious that many in caucus felt the same way: assorted members, barely pausing to look at the crowd, emerged only to dart briefly into the toilets. Noting this, some journalists hatched an ingenious scheme to eavesdrop on unsuspecting Nats from a spare cubicle, but the plot lapsed on ethical grounds and through lack of a volunteer.

Would the PM survive or not? He had earlier admitted that his leadership was on the line, a revelation which came as a shock to the few journalists still scoffing at the rumours of a palace coup. Fresh speculation and those strange jokes journalists make at these times rippled through the throng. Hugh Templeton had just had a play-lunch delivered and the sandwiches were all pre-masticated — a bad omen for the Talboys lobby . . . Muldoon was planning a television address to the nation and his staff had been dispatched to find a dog called Checkers.

The caucus ran way beyond its normal length and it was a very subdued Muldoon who came out to admit to a crowded press conference that he was still Prime Minister but that the challenge to his leadership was far from over. He conceded he no longer enjoyed the full confidence of caucus but thought he could still lead National to victory in '81.

'I really do think I can . . .' he added plaintively, sounding for perhaps the first time in his long career diffident and insecure.

The man who set off for India, China and North America some six weeks earlier didn't sound diffident and insecure. But, as they say, a week in Taihape and politics is a long time, and six weeks in Taihape and politics is an eternity . . . especially if you have the misfortune to lose a safe seat in a by-election in the interim.

It would be a gross over-simplification to say that Muldoon's reversals began with the East Coast Bays defeat. There have always been elements within the National Party who find his style of leadership unsavoury, but provided he won elections for them they were prepared to hold their noses and look the other way. Not any more. When the PM opened the by-election campaign with the announcement that harbour bridge tolls were to rise, the reaction was one of dismay. This must have baffled him, as back in '76 when he was slashing subsidies and doubling the price of everything he was applauded for telling it like it was.

Worse than any of that, though, was his refusal to accept any of the blame for the defeat.

Meanwhile, given a long uninterrupted spell as acting PM, Brian Talboys, as his confidence grew, proved to be rather good at it and began to enjoy himself. Never rude or bullying he encouraged everyone to participate in discussions and many members found Cabinet meetings and caucus meetings strangely pleasurable to attend. This, coupled with his mastery in the House, led some people to wonder what it would be like if he were permanently in charge.

The more they thought about it, the more it occurred to them that for the first time in five years a credible alternative to Muldoon as PM had emerged, and they began to lobby in earnest.

Across the other side of the world the PM heard the rumours and refused to take them seriously. When Radio New Zealand's Dick Griffin rejoined the PM's party in Mexico he mentioned that the PM could be in trouble and Muldoon's staff found the idea amusing. The homecoming must have been a rude shock.

Still jet-lagged the PM attended a meeting of the National Party's Dominion Executive, where a succession of divisional chairmen reported on the poor state of party morale and general disaffection with the direction and leadership of the parliamentary wing. In response the PM delivered a 40-minute speech on his overseas trip, with only oblique references to the criticism.

Back on the Hill it didn't take him long to judge the strength of the challenge, and with five of his own people absent he probably knew he was going into the vital first caucus outnumbered, and to make matters worse he had just threatened to sack his Chief Whip, Tony Friedlander, who had committed the unforgivable sin of being seen late at night in the company of Derek Quigley, one of the key plotters.

Muldoon's first ploy was to delay the leadership question until 12.30 p.m., when time was running out. Calling for frank discussion he had to endure some punishing criticism from the most unlikely people. When the catharsis had abated he sent David Thomson to phone Brian Talboys and sound out his opinions on the subject. As both sides had been in contact with Talboys the night before, the PM probably knew what his response would be. The Deputy PM's expressions of loyalty to Rob (provided he made certain changes), and his offer to serve only

if called, blunted the bloodlust somewhat and Muldoon emerged with a week's grace.

His first move was to go public and appeal for public assistance. (If Jack Marshall had taken that undignified step in '74 the public response would have been overwhelmingly in his favour.) Still shocked and stunned by the vehemence of some of the caucus criticism, Muldoon, the legendary counter-puncher, was at this point fighting on pure instinct alone. His own supporters doubted that they would win.

Fortunately for the PM the Social Credit Political League as well as the Labour Party have a vested interest in keeping him where he is, and they responded to his call with a selflessness and alacrity that was truly magnificent. In the PM's language a telegram is a telegram, and buoyed by the reaction he devised the strategy of frightening his opponents into submission by claiming the people were with him.

As a generalisation you could say that the Muldoon supporters in caucus were the weak, the aged, the pedestrian and the frightened. And, as the week wore on and the PM's tactics seemed to prove effective, you could have described the Talboys fac-

tion as the best, the brightest, the young and the very frightened.

Having been dangerously frank in caucus some of them felt they had no choice but to press on regardless. One MP felt that the PM's humble conciliatory performance in caucus was worthy of an Academy Award. But they know he never absorbs criticism willingly, and one MP later described him as a 'rogue elephant', meaning that sooner or later he wouldn't be able to help himself and would lash back at all those who had tormented him. (In changing leaders, as in hunting elephants, the first shot should be between the eyes.)

It all came down to Brian Talboys. In the end he opted for the status quo. To remain the leader Muldoon only had to win narrowly. To become champion, as Muhammed Ali once said, you gotta whup the champion. Finally the 'colonels' didn't have the numbers, but even if they haven't forced a change in leaders there will undoubtedly be a change in the leadership style. Muldoon will never again rule with the same arrogant effortless dominance.

Listener, November 8, 1980

Explanations Deleted

George Chapman paced up and down the huge boardroom of the new National Party headquarters in downtown Wellington. The eyes of the Dominion Council were on him – and what a sad assortment of eyes they were. Some were red from lack of sleep, some from weeping. Others blinked uncertainly as though the dull light that permeated the room was too bright for them. The remainder, which were even worse, were coated in a milky film as if in a trance. It was the look he had last seen in the dark days after the shock defeat in '72. It was up to him as party president to say something bold and reassuring – to pull them out of it.

'Gentlemen . . .' he said, a shade shrilly. He needed a drink of water, that was the trouble, but he couldn't guarantee that he wouldn't spill half the glass down his lapels before he got it to his lips. He always had that problem when Rob was present. He had problems calling his leader 'Rob' for a start. Still, for the sake of the party he always did. Rob was down the back, no doubt enjoying his discomfort. Nothing apparently wrong with his eyes though. Beneath their folds of skin they blazed away calmly, and it was only the knowledge that his boss was short-sighted that gave Chapman the courage to carry on.

'Gentlemen,' he continued, adding one of his famous dry giggles, 'anyone would think you were at a funeral.' They smiled wanly back at him, and as the full implications of his little aside sank home he felt his body sag. He gripped the pointer tightly and advanced uncertainly on the huge wall chart of the North Island.

All over the top half of the island green and yellow flags sprouted gaily like so much moss. 'Here, here, here and here, gentlemen,' said Chapman matter of factly so as not to alarm them, 'we have Social Credit.'

'And here' – the pointer indicated a lonely cluster of blue flags, as Chapman's voice began to break, 'are we.'

He took a deep breath and turned back to the massive rimu table that they hadn't yet paid for. Like the rest of the furniture that they hadn't yet paid for. And for that matter like the whole bloody building, which was his idea in the first place and which they hadn't yet been able to fully let. Still there was no time for that now. Chapman had bigger things to worry about – like whether to lean on the table with his fingers extended or stand back with his arms folded. He opted for the latter. 'Gentlemen – and lady,' he added, suddenly remembering the women's vice-president. 'I'm sure I don't need to remind you of how serious this is.'

'What's happened to the bloody Labour vote then?' enquired someone from down the back.

'That's the problem in a nutshell,' said Chapman softly. 'I'm afraid they're almost done for. Social Credit are taking two votes from them to every one from us. We can no longer rely on them to shut Social Credit out. They have proved as effective against Social Credit as the Polish Cavalry were against Hitler's Panzer Corps. Gentlemen, we are on our own in this one.'

Warming to the military analogy, a dominion councillor wondered aloud if there were any chance of Social Credit advancing too far beyond their own supply lines.

'Afraid not,' said Chapman sadly. 'Their organisation in this area is terribly effective. Their Beetham Dwyer Foundation has raised an awesome amount of money. In some electorates, gentlemen, electorates which in theory are National Party strongholds, Social Credit supporters have raised hundreds of dollars each, while we can't get life-long members of our party to renew their subs – and God knows we don't charge much.'

'Couldn't we get Rob out on the roads with his charts,' enthused one of the PM's toadies. 'Hit them where it hurts with jokes about knocking inflation for six and taunts about funny money?'

Chapman responded slowly, choosing his words carefully. Rob may be deficient in the visual acuity area but there was nothing wrong with his hearing and he could detect treason in a hall full of jubilant applause. 'We have to remember that this November there will be new voters who have never heard of the '51 waterfront dispute, or the Black Budget, or Vern Cracknell . . . Social Credit support is strongest of all among the 18- to 24-year-olds – especially in Auckland. But you can't do battle with an enemy who won't show himself. Gentlemen, we are dealing with a foe as evil, as insidious, as cunning as the Viet Cong . . . it's . . . it's unfair . . .'

In his office on the ground floor of Parliament Buildings, Bruce Beetham was smiling. It was a wide smile, with the lips pulled back to expose his excellent teeth. Some said it was the smile of a Cheshire cat. He personally had never seen a Cheshire cat so he took no offence. That smile was one of his assets. It acted as a counterpoint to the dark bags under his eyes. They worked well together. Even if one part of his face was bright and relaxed, another part was suitably grave and restrained.

Beetham was busy reassuring his closest aides that the latest public opinion polls, putting Social Credit in front of Labour again, did not mean that Social Credit now had an obligation to explain itself fully on all the major issues.

'Are you sure BCB?'

'Positive,' he beamed. 'Positive' was one of his favourite words. 'Our position is that we let the other

Policy? Policy?.. we'll burn that bridge when we come to it!

two parties take up positions, dig themselves in so to speak. We in turn will travel light, suitably disguised, and pop up and down behind enemy lines whenever and wherever it suit us.'

'The other parties won't like that BCB.'

'No, they won't.' His grin if anything widened. The schoolteacher in him came to the surface. 'Look, politics is a game, rugby if you like. Traditionally played between two teams of about 15 players each. One side having perhaps 17 players, being the Government, and the other team of 13 players being the Opposition. Now we have come along with two extra players and they don't like it at all. Better still, we can score at either end and yet, not having our own goal line we can't have points scored against us.'

'Brilliant, BCB, brilliant.'

'How does this affect our policy on youth unemployment BCB?'

'What do the 18- to 24-year-olds themselves think?'

'They're worried sick BCB.'

'Fine. The official policy of the Social Credit Political League is that we are worried sick about unemployment.'

'Aren't we already worried sick about the Springbok tour and the second smelter BCB?'

'OK then, we're concerned and disturbed about youth unemployment. Damn it, do I have to do everything myself around here?'

Underneath the Labour headquarters the operations room was cramped and stale. Jim Anderton briefly contemplated asking Lange to leave and thought better of it. Lange was touchy about his size. It was all Lange's fault anyway, not that he would ever admit it. The news was all bad. Reports from the last of the Labour regions still fighting indicated that hundreds of their best workers were defecting to Social Credit. The end was only a matter of time.

Rowling would have none of that. 'When it comes to the crunch,' he said with a mad laugh, 'the people, the ordinary decent people who make up this ordinary decent country of ours will be with us.' No one could look him directly in the eye.

Listener, March 14, 1981.

The Erebus Error

At 12.50 p.m. (McMurdo time) on November 28, 1979, DC-10 ZK-NZP flew at full power into an ice slope at the base of Mt Erebus on Ross Island, instantly killing all 257 people on board. It was New Zealand's worst aviation disaster and the fourth worst air crash in history.

British newspapers headlined the tragedy with banners about a jet flying into a volcano, making it sound at times as though ZK-NZP had plunged into a crater. They said, without hesitation, that the accident was pilot error. American newspapers were no less judgmental. After all, even the most devoted proponent of the theory of continental drift and plate tectonics would concede that it is the pilot's job to avoid mountains rather than the other way round.

And you can be sure that the beleaguered McDonnell Douglas Corporation, manufacturers of the controversial and much-maligned DC-10, spared no effort to clear their aircraft.

In New Zealand, with everyone still numbed by the horror, such conclusions at first seemed unworthy and premature. Someone had to be at fault, however, and five months after the crash the report of the Chief Inspector of Air Accidents, Ron Chippindale, came as something of a relief. While very critical of many of the procedures of both the Civil Aviation Department and Air New Zealand management, he cited as the probable cause of the accident Captain Thomas Collins's decision to continue the flight at a low level towards an area of poor surface and horizon

definition when the crew were not certain of their position and were unable to detect the rising terrain ahead of them.

Such was the authority and crispness of the Chippindale report that his conclusion that human error on the part of the crew was largely to blame seemed beyond question. At least I said so at the time and received in due course a very sad letter from Captain Collins's widow, Maria Collins, insisting bravely that one day her husband's name would be cleared.

In a stunning reversal the report of the Royal Commission of Inquiry into the crash has done just that, with even greater authority and crispness than the earlier condemnation. While praising the lucidity and scope of the Chippindale report, Justice Mahon in effect attributes human error to the Chief Inspector of Air Accidents himself. The frailty of human judgment is a persistent, if unwitting, theme to the Royal Commission finding. And Mahon's central conclusion — so different from Chippindale's, so mercilessly obvious and logical — just might be subject to the same frailty.

Chippindale, citing the chilling cockpit voice recording which had unidentified people uncertainly enquiring where they were, argued convincingly that the crew were in effect lost, and ploughed on at a dangerously low altitude into a featureless horizon. Although it is nowhere stated in so many words many people — thanks perhaps to the news media — assumed from the Chippindale report that the plane was flying in something like the Antarctic equivalent of pea soup and that Collins's strange response was to descend lower and lower.

A 'white-out' to most of us sounds like flying in thick cloud or falling snow. To correct that misconception, Mahon devotes a lot of space to the phenomenon, pointing out that it occurs so frequently in Antarctica that it is hardly a phenomenon at all. Quoting movingly from his own experiences on the slopes of Mt Erebus on the first anniversary of the crash, he describes how clouds and sun can quickly combine to render the landscape an amorphous white expanse.

All a white-out needs is low cloud and the sun at your shoulder. It can occur in clear air, as the recovered photographs taken by crash victims show only too well. The insidious illusion lay only in front of the aircraft, and Mahon says that even a momentary change in conditions could have alerted the crew and averted the one-chance-in-a-million disaster.

A white-out in one sense could be likened to driving along a road with a giant mirror placed on it somewhere ahead of you. The road would appear to stretch out infinitely in front, and you would recognise the approaching car as your own only when it was too late to swerve.

As Air New Zealand failed to supply their crews with topographical maps of the flight path, Collins spent the evening before the fateful journey plotting his course on the family atlas and describing his route down McMurdo Sound to his inquisitive daughters. Later, without his knowledge, some of the flight coordinates fed into the navigational computer were changed. Instead of the relatively safe passage over the pack ice, the approach to McMurdo favoured by the three air forces who land Hercules aircraft in the area, ZK- NZP was many kilometres to the east, on a collision course with Mt Erebus.

Air traffic controllers at McMurdo, who also thought he was cruising down the sound, invited Collins to descend to 450 metres, where visibility was at least 65 km. Mahon says that the cockpit recording, if confined to dialogue between Collins and First Officer Gregory Cassin, makes it clear they believed they knew exactly where they were — that is, they thought they were flying down the sound, as originally plotted. The only confusion was over reconciling the landmarks of Lewis Bay with those of McMurdo Sound. To them, the featureless slope of Mt Erebus was merely a featureless stretch of pack ice. Technical evidence from the manufacturers of the aircraft's radar confirms that radio waves are just as easily distorted when bounced off dry ice as light is, and the warning to pull up, when it came, was too late.

Mahon says that Collins, believing himself to be on course down the sound, had a 'mental set': he had great faith in the navigation system, and most of the visual evidence confirmed what he believed. Chippindale, believing that the altered coordinates played only a minor role in the disaster, also seems to have had a mental set: he says all the evidence confirms that the crew were to blame.

Naturally Air New Zealand, who have some mental sets of their own, favour the Chippindale report. According to the Royal Commission, there is evidence that they attempted their own white-out. On instruction, surplus copies of key documents were destroyed and the flight bags of Collins and Cassin, recovered from the ice and presumably containing relevant information, later disappeared without trace.

With potentially crippling compensation claims yet to be heard, and the police contemplating criminal charges, Air New Zealand didn't exactly embrace the commission's findings.

At the time of writing, with High Court action looming, it's not clear what sort of managerial shake-up will take place.

A friend on a recent flight from Hong Kong to Auckland reports that individual employees are leading the fight back. Upset that two businessmen were not paying attention to his mime on safety procedures, a steward leant over them at the finish and said pointedly, 'I just hope for your sakes, gentlemen, that this plane doesn't crash!'

Listener, May 16, 1981

Practising Separate Development

Late one recent evening, from high above in the Press Gallery, I spied Ben Couch rehearsing a speech. He sat in a bench with a huge yellow fleece draped over the back of it, and inscribed on the sheepskin was the legend 'Ben'. Someone was making a dull contribution to the Address-in-Reply debate, but the Minister of Police and Maori Affairs was far too busy to pay it any attention. Leaning forward, his brow furrowed in concentration, eyes labouring over the type while his left hand jabbed the air to give emphasis and his mouth opened and closed wordlessly, he looked helpless and vulnerable like a child struggling with difficult homework . . .

Two days earlier in New Plymouth he had told a National Party gathering that the sort of people who condemned New Zealand over the Springbok tour, like the Nigerians, were the sort of people who shot their leaders in the gut. New Zealanders had given thousands of dollars in appeals to African states and he had never seen a thank you letter.

A few days later on Ian Fraser's *Newsmakers* programme he admitted that he supported separate development in South Africa, and also said that he supported both the Gleneagles agreement *and* the Springbok tour. As these last two are mutually incompatible, to reconcile them must require either incredible intellectual dexterity or a vastly reduced rate of blood supply to the brain. But in this extraordinary stand Couch is not alone. Two other members of Cabinet, Deputy Prime Minister Duncan MacIntrye and Minister of Education Merv Wellington, have also managed this incredible feat.

So far, however, they haven't gone that 'extra further step', as Ben Couch would say, and stated on television that separate development is the solution to South Africa's problems. To be fair to Couch, he appeared to be saying that while he was opposed to apartheid in principle, he approved of it in practice in South Africa — because South Africa had millions of problems (22 million of them black and two and a half million of them coloured and Indian). Believing we are all God's children, Couch doesn't believe for a moment that blacks are inferior to whites. No. It's just that some of God's children will have to live apart from some of God's other children.

Watching Couch make a fool of himself and his Government on television was not a pleasant experience, although Ian Fraser was professional throughout and at times quite lenient. I had to remind myself that the bewildered human being on the screen, who looked like a possum caught in the headlight glare of a Kenworth truck, was in fact a Minister of the Crown. The programme raised two questions. How do some people get into Cabinet? And once there what mechanisms exist to remove them?

Couch is an unlikely Cabinet Minister. The Mormon elder, shearing contractor and former All Black was elected MP for Wairarapa in the 1975 landslide. For three years he was a genial and totally undistinguished backbencher, so his elevation to Cabinet status after the 1978 victory surprised nearly everyone. Couch himself joked, 'What have I done to deserve this?'

The PM provides an explanation in his latest book when he says that he always wanted National to have another Maori Minister of Maori Affairs to follow in the footsteps of Apirana Ngata. The PM is full of praise for Couch in his book, calling him unpretentious with a tough-minded integrity. But then it's obvious that the PM thinks highly of all three of his Maori members. He calls them all 'first class Maoris' and claims that the more intelligent Maori achiever is more likely to support National. (This pride is sometimes dangerously close to being paternalistic — the opening sentence of the book attributes much of the good work of the Mormon Church among the Maori people to the fact that they have a rule of total abstinence. He seems to be supporting the notion that Maoris can't hold their firewater.)

The PM admits in his book that he is forever telling world leaders about his Maori lads who hold European seats and how this shows how splendid our multicultural society is. Even for a man who can call Abraham Ordia a clown, the PM is going to find it difficult to boast about a Maori Minister of Maori Affairs who supports separate development in South Africa.

Strictly speaking, in advocating just that, Couch challenges an agreement which his Cabinet professes to collectively support. The PM has always argued, and in fact states clearly in his latest book on page 23, 'A cabinet decision is literally binding on all members; any minister who wishes publicly to oppose that decision must first resign his portfolio.' Instead of calling for Couch's resignation, however, he merely chided his colleague for being 'foolish' enough to go on *Newsmakers,* and once there for being 'too straightforward'. And presumably for falling into the trap of telling the truth.

Although purportedly cool, the rest of Cabinet also rallied around their beleaguered and suitably abject colleague. For some reason, though, MacIntyre was not embarrassed by Couch's remarks. When you consider that a transcript of Couch's admission would have been doing the rounds of Commonwealth capitals within hours of transmission, I would have thought a second statement hard on its heels professing Cabinet horror and embarrassment would have helped alleviate the damage. Along with the concept of collective responsibility there is surely the concept of collective shame, and in declining to publicly admonish the Minister of Police and Maori Affairs, Cabinet must share some of the shame.

In spite of the many calls demanding his resignation, I don't expect Couch to resign. There appears to be no conceivable situation in our political framework now which would demand automatic resignation. No matter what the outrage, you just set your jaw and tough it out. I seriously doubt that some Ministers will stand down even if they lose in November. On current trends a Labour or Social Credit Cabinet could consist of up to 40 men, 20 of their own and 20 Nats who refused to go.

Apart from loyalty, other reasons for not chastising Couch were acknowledged to some extent in the snap debate forced by the Opposition on this issue. The Government's defence of Couch ranged from the desperate 'we all make mistakes' to the argument that somehow it was all Ian Fraser's fault. Somewhere in the middle came Jim McLay's curious justification that nearly all of Couch's mail was running in Couch's favour. He seemed to be saying that anyone perceived by the public to be that right couldn't be all wrong. But you could tell his heart wasn't in it.

Listener, July 4, 1981

T he Springbok tour dominated the political landscape for much of 1981. I found it impossible to ignore, and even more difficult to rein in my own feelings. I was passionately opposed to the tour and yet had to sit down at the typewriter and force myself into an artificial state to write about it calmly and fairly. Often I didn't make it. It was easier if I stuck to pure farce, like this piece. It provoked a lot of angry letters from pro-tour people complaining about how I had insulted Errol Tobias. I was even the subject of a complaint to the Race Relations conciliator and in due course got a silly little letter from Hiwi Tauroa advising me to be more careful.

Traveller's Tales

Atropa Belladonna Hotel
Anaheim, Los Angeles
July 17

Dear Danie,

Greetings, little brother. Did you get my postcard from New York? So much has happened since we left home three — or was it four? — days ago. There were demonstrators at New York but I wonder if they realise just how little effect they have on us and how they only harden our resolve to make this sacred and historic trip the great success it deserves to be. As our manager was telling the air hostess only yesterday, the strongest steel is forged on the hottest anvil. So far most people have been very kind to us, partly because we are posing as a Namibian team en route to an international underwater bagpiping championship in Tierra del Fuego.

It was very kind of yourself, mother, father, little Frik and Greta to see me off at the airport. Tell father I was deeply moved by his parting gesture of pressing a battered old address book into my hand. 1956 was a long time ago, and a lot of the girls will have shifted, but I was grateful nonetheless. Both on and off the field I hope to emulate father's proud record as a Springbok.

We went to Disneyland today and everyone thoroughly enjoyed themselves, except for the 'Great Moments with Lincoln' display. There a large animated model of President Lincoln delivered a tasteless and quite uncalled-for attack on slavery. While most of us could deal with it maturely and recognise it for the crude propaganda it really was, poor Errol Tobias and Abe Williams shifted uncomfortably from one foot to the other.

Keep this to yourself, Danie, but some of the chaps took advantage of the opportunity to see some dirty movies banned back home and they sneaked out last night to see *The Sound of Music* and *To Sir with Love*.

If you think black girls are sexy back home, you should see the talent here. Some of the chaps have been propositioned by black girls called 'hookers' . . . yes, that's what they call them here, but the lads are reluctant to 'scrum down' just in case the Immorality Act is extra-territorial.

I have been a good boy and go to bed reading the Old Testament aloud. I can't wait to get to New Zealand.

Your brother, Okkie

Sandown Park Hotel
Gisborne, New Zealand
July 20

Dear Danie,

I can't believe it! This is the most exciting thing that has ever happened to me. I am on New Zealand soil. It has rained continually since we arrived but nothing can dampen our spirits. It is so green and beautiful here. This morning when I woke up I thought I could see through the driving sleet a lovely blue perimeter of hills, but when the cloud lifted momentarily I saw that they were only policemen. There are policemen everywhere. Police with walkie-talkies. Police with dogs. Police with helmets and riot shields and already it is making a lot of us homesick. Especially Errol Tobias, who yesterday saw a Maori demonstrator get shoved around a bit.

The demonstrations so far have been pretty tame affairs. Nearly everyone from the Prime Minister down seems to want us here and I am sure we are going to have a great tour. The antis said they would make such a racket they would keep us awake at night but already some waitresses are doing that anyway, and I don't think there can be many people opposed to the tour, because last night there was only one person shouting and all he could say in a high-pitched effeminate way (so typical of homosexuals and communists) was 'more pork' over and over again.

Don't tell mother, it would only upset her, but her carefully wrapped parcels of corned wildebeest were confiscated at customs along with the vibrator I purchased for Greta in LA. Poor woman. She will just have to come to terms with her Durban neurosis. I hope mother and little Frik are keeping up with their pistol practice.

We are settling in nicely here and have got over the worst of the jet-lag. I really like the Kiwis I have met so far. Very friendly most of them, though a few (and the press are the worst offenders) just can't seem to separate politics from sport. I went shopping this morning and got cheered later in a pub when I said

that I supported racial equality and that as far as I was concerned all black people were equal.

There has been a lot of talk about South Africans and New Zealanders dying alongside one another on Italian battlefields. This is true. And, as I have told some Kiwis, it wasn't easy for people like our Uncle Heemie. Afrikaners like him, imprisoned for their pro-Nazi sympathies, had first to break out of South African jails, smuggle themselves across the South African border, hitchhike up the African continent, cross the Sahara on foot, swim the Mediterranean, and on joining the Allies fight for the side they didn't agree with. Surely the supreme sacrifice in anyone's book.

I must retire now. Our first practice run was truly gruelling. Claassen had us forwards running repeatedly headfirst into an iron girder. Still, I suppose I can count my lucky stars I wasn't a Springbok back in the grim unimaginative win-at-any-cost days.

Your brother, Okkie

Gisborne, July 21

Dear Danie,

I got another telegram from mother yesterday. Could you please tell her that while I appreciate her offer of having the servants do my laundry if I airmail it home, there are plenty of servants to do that for me here.

Very strange some of them are, too. I met a sweet young Maori maid in the corridor this morning and I asked her if it was true that Gisborne was the first place in the world every day to see the light and she replied that if that was the case we wouldn't be here and someone called Bob Bell wouldn't be the MP.

Very enigmatic, but I must say the other Maoris we've met have been delightful people. Warm and friendly — certainly a cut above our own tinted countrymen. Their welcome on the marae last night was truly memorable. They taught us a lesson about human dignity and the need for all races to meet and mix.

This tour has hardly started but already it has done so much good. Good old Johan spoke for us all on the bus and on the way back to the hotel when he said that before the tour full integration in South Africa was 400 years away and now it was barely 350 years away.

I was moved to tears by the whole thing, but then that big ox Hennie Bekker was standing on my foot. I must finish now. Tomorrow we play our first game. Oh boy!

Yours proudly, Okkie

Listener, August 8, 1981

Rugby, Racism and Fear

When journalists and politicians are being pious here on the Hill — something we try and limit ourselves to doing only when we are awake — we like to imagine Parliament ceasing to be an arena for petty politicking and instead addressing itself solemnly to the great issues of the day. These might include the economy, unemployment, housing and our energy options, but more often than not, debate on these matters finds the chamber half-empty and half-awake and the Press Gallery down to a bleary-eyed handful.

Human nature being what it is, we prefer a good scrap, as was demonstrated recently when Brian Talboys walked from the House rather than withdraw and apologise for accusing the Opposition of sheer cowardice. Within seconds of the start of the confrontation the Press Gallery filled with reporters and, down below, members poured into the chamber and sat bolt upright in their seats — adrenalin no doubt coursing through their arteries.

The spat had its origins in the PM's uncomfortable admission at his last press conference before shooting off to the royal wedding that he 'believed' he had told Ces Blazey to call off the Springbok tour when they met late last year. Unfortunately for the PM the NZRFU chairman had no recollection of such a request being made. (Labour's Russell Marshall later joked that the Government was led by a Prime Minister who remembered things that weren't said and by a deputy who couldn't remember things that were.)

Armed with the discrepancy between what the PM said and what Blazey said, the Opposition set about attempting a snap debate on the matter.

But they were too clever. That same afternoon the Attorney General introduced the Official Information Bill, and although the Opposition agreed with much of it, they wasted a lot of time on it and in the end left themselves only 25 minutes for the snap debate.

(This Bill closely follows the Danks committee's proposals on the release of official information, and while the Opposition thought the legislation had a long way to go, Government members like Mike Minogue thought it was a good first step. Even Chairman Mao once said that the longest journey always starts with the first step.)

Given the Speaker's acceptance of the Opposition's argument that a snap debate was warranted, the Government naturally enough wanted to know what time, if any, would be given to them for rebuttal. Bill Rowling's assurances of ample time only further incensed them and there followed a spate of spurious points of order designed solely to eat into the time before the House rose at 5.30.

In the face of this orchestrated attempt to 'kill the ball' the Speaker warned against the use of fraudulent points of order. Shortly after that Talboys made his 'sheer cowardice' charge on the grounds that the PM was out of the country and unable to defend himself. Speaker Harrison, obviously hating every minute of it, had no choice but to ask his old friend to rise and apologise, but Talboys stubbornly remained seated while various senior Government members came up and whispered to him.

While some (like Jim McLay) went alternately white and puce with indignation at the Speaker's request, others (like the canny Jim Bolger) seemed to appreciate the event for what it was — a contrived piece of political theatre.

The Minister of Foreign Affairs, who just the day before had been so masterful and dignified in yet another tour-related debate, was deliberately putting his own distinguished reputation on the line to protect the reputation of his boss. By accusing Labour of cowardice he helped to deflect attention from the PM's credibility. By making the smear — knowing that Labour were required by standing orders to raise the matter when they did, whether or not the PM was in the country — he came to the aid of the party. Government members clapped him as he bundled up his notes and walked defiantly out of the house.

Parliament is the highest court in the land and Talboys in fact broke Parliamentary Law by defying the chair. Apparently this is perfectly in order if you feel strongly about what you perceive to be an issue of principle. Indeed, others may applaud as you break the law.

It was obvious at Gisborne and Hamilton that many anti-tour protesters felt much the same way. If you feel strongly about what you perceive to be an issue of principle, you are prepared to break the law.

People will go to extraordinary lengths if they feel moral right is on their side. They will tear down fences (something Bruce Beetham quite correctly condemns, mostly on the grounds that if all the fences in this country are torn down he will have nowhere to sit). They will also invade pitches — and in some cases spread broken glass and carpet tacks, even though the whole apartheid debate is based on a revulsion against institutionalised violence.

On the other side, some rugby spectators at Hamilton behaved as if the interruption of their sporting pleasure conferred extra rights on them. The right to assault people in the streets. The right to chase people onto private property and assault them again. And the right to threaten to blow up HART supporters' homes if the tour is called off.

Separating these two factions were the police, whose demeanour at both Gisborne and Hamilton was dignified and restrained. If our image abroad has taken a denting over this tour, the image of our police — refraining from splitting skulls when many in the

Hamilton crowd wanted them to do just that — will perhaps redress the balance a little.

Separating the two factions is not easy. Cartoonist Murray Ball, among the protesters who marched across a golf course towards the Gisborne ground, was aghast to see some people clambering up a bank and tearing at the fence. 'Hell,' said Murray's brother, 'there are 17,000 of them and only 300 of us. Why are we letting them out?'

I was in Wanganui at the time of the Hamilton battle, watching the television news with a group of people who wanted the tour to go ahead at any cost. They just couldn't see why something as simple as a game of rugby should cause so much fuss.

After loudly abusing the demonstrators my companions informed me that the media were to blame for nearly everything. It later transpired that the angry rugby fans bent on vengeance at Hamilton reserved a special viciousness for journalists, especially television journalists.

Maybe television and radio have given the tour issue exhaustive coverage, but it's hard to see what is so wrong about that. The tour has been news. Maybe the same people who don't want to know what is going on in South Africa also don't want to know what is going on in their own country.

The tour, the Government now tells us, is no longer about apartheid and instead has become a question of law and order. The PM himself concedes that the Government may have to go to the polls on a law and order ticket. While this will probably work to their advantage it must be bitterly disappointing to the Government, who were so looking forward to defending their control of inflation, their general economic record and their celebrated growth strategies on the hustings in November. Sigh!

Listener, August 15, 1981

In the Big League Now

Long before you actually sighted the Logan Campbell centre at the Auckland Showgrounds it was obvious where the annual conference of the Social Credit Political League was being held. Portraits of BCB in green and gold decked the gates (they remained undefaced for four days, without a single policeman in view the entire time), and to get to the hall itself you trekked across a carpark speckled with cars and camper-vans painted green and gold. Only Social Crediters would willingly destroy the resale value of their vehicles for the cause. They have at various times been dismissed as the aristocracy of used-car salesmen but if that is so, they are used-car salesmen with heart.

The vast concrete and steel hall, designed to withstand both rock concerts and a direct nuclear hit, stubbornly remained chill despite the bright spring sunshine and the best efforts of two huge industrial heaters brought in to disguise the fact that we were all being deep-frozen for some journey into the past or the future, though I could never quite tell which.

Still, there was no disguising the warmth of the 500-odd delegates and observers. They were genuinely friendly, relaxed and unpretentious people, delighted to see that the news media were taking them seriously enough to turn up in large numbers. And absent were the swirling eddies of resentment and hostility both to initiates and outsiders that are clearly observable at the conferences of the other major parties.

While bizarre green and gold pantsuits were still evident, polyester is still the fabric of choice and cheap hairpieces still abound, Social Credit conferences have lost, probably forever, the image of being a psychiatric ward on a four-day outing.

The league has become slick. There is a new deftness and polish at the top. Some of this has been achieved with remarkable economy. The sparsely furnished stage, with its flag and kowhai logo and pyramidal lectern, would have cost a fraction of what Labour and National spent, yet coupled with a largely unmanipulated conference it made superior television. Credit for this goes to the younger men like league president Stefan Lipa. While hardly a charismatic figure or riveting orator he appears to have virtually no ego problems and was content with being quietly and crisply efficient in the chair. Save for the last morning, when the final policy debate disintegrated in confusion.

Policy was first considered in workshops and came back with various recommendations like the disconcerting 'accept in principle', and the discussion often led to motions like 'I move the motion to accept their rejection not now be put . . .' Having patiently listened to endless speeches on the mechanics of *how* they could win, the final burden of deciding *what* they could win with almost proved too much for the delegates. At one point Lipa cautioned them wearily, 'We are starting to get into debatable material now . . .'

Getting into debatable material was clearly not what this conference was all about. Avoiding unpleasantries like that is part of what the new deftness and polish is all about. Yet in spite of the attractive new logo and catchy campaign song (half classic rock ballad, half singalong anthem), this conference was not so much a sophisticated political gathering as dry wedding, talent contest and school prizegiving all rolled into one.

It remains, for instance, the only major party which still stops for morning and afternoon tea. There was no fridge full of beer for the press but we were more than welcome to join them for refreshments and lunch. Lunch consisted of four sandwiches and a Mallowpuff encased in Gladwrap.

The talent quest overtones were apparent in the opening address by Commander Ian Bradley. The dashing former Navy man, removed from the service in controversial fashion, gave an at-times electrifying speech on the need for honour and accountability in public life, as well as launching a withering attack on the state of the Navy. Just having him was coup enough, and having him speak so well, and dress so horrendously in order to fit in, gave proceedings a tremendous start. Delegates bubbled about his contribution for days.

The talent quest continued the next afternoon with the battle for deputy leader, a position made vacant by Jeremy Dwyer's retirement from public life. Candidate after candidate selfconsciously extolled themselves, one aspirant assuring the conference that his experience as a policeman, a cabinet-maker and a funeral director made him the right man for the job, and another awkwardly and joylessly insisting that contrary to rumour he had a very good sense of humour. But it was really only a two-horse race between handsome Garry Knapp of the new wave and blunt Kaipara farmer Nevern McConachy, darling of the old guard.

Knapp appeared to have it sewn up beforehand, but the wily McConachy kept winning support right up to the last minute. In the end it was the speeches that mattered and when McConachy somewhat aggressively said they couldn't do without him, conference immediately voted to show they could. Knapp's speech was quite masterly. He began by paying tribute to Dwyer, earning rapturous applause for this consideration, and finished by insisting he was all but deputy leader these days anyway. His victory speech was even more impressive and he told a now delirious conference that with their help he was going to change the direction of this country.

What BCB thought of this reception — the sort of reception that used to be exclusively his — is not clear, but he seemed pleased enough. Social Credit finds itself in the rare position of having perhaps the handsomest leader and deputy leader of any party in our history. Two teddyboys at the top. One ageing, the other still living in the fast lane. The irony of course is that neither man really looks as though he belongs in the league. Their poise and appearance set them apart.

The other great talent quest was the debate on the shape of the future. Whatever their reluctance to come to terms with the here and now, Socred are fond of talking about the past and especially fond of discussing the future. This gets them away from specifics and into generalities, which are much safer, and this session was of a very high standard.

George Bryant, the league's liberal conscience, gave a thoughtful address on the need for a vision of a new society. The star of this session, though, was Socred's other ex-Navy catch, Commander Dick Ryan, formerly director of the Commission for the Future and now candidate for North Shore. Ryan spoke on the recent 'Televote' survey and with commendable sleight-of-hand argued that the future option most people wanted was in fact the very option Social Credit offered.

The considerable force and authority of Ryan's speech ensured that complete attention was paid to him but unfortunately every word was weighted with the same power and as he hardly paused at all I thought it was an address better suited for delivery through a pipe to an engine-room.

The fact however that people like him are attracted to the league demonstrates that it must be taken seriously. It doesn't really matter that the league is not bothered by details of policy. Getting elected is more important. Besides, people have had enough of details. There are no votes in details.

You've got to admire people whose basic approach to most social problems is that they are unhappy about them, and, when pressed for specifics, reply they are *very* unhappy about them.

Listener, September 19, 1981

Trails and Tribulations

When elections are complicated by contradictory variables as this one was, trying to calculate a likely result is the stuff of which splitting headaches are made. Totally unable and unwilling to face the complicated mathematics involved, some of us on the campaign trail resorted to older, more primitive and time-honoured methods like voodoo and parapsychology. We kept a tally of omens both good and bad for the main parties.

When Rob Muldoon visited Whaka and Pohutu the geyser was silent, we knew National's lead was steadily being eaten away. When Bill Rowling visited Whaka and Pohutu was shooting up a storm, it was plain to anyone with half a brain that the parties were neck and neck, with Labour, if anything, in front. But then in Wanganui Labour's Russell Marshall was present at the launching of a rubber liferaft and a sliver of glass from the champagne bottle deflated the vessel as it hit the water. After that it just had to be close. But how close? Indeed should it have been close at all?

In theory, Labour should have led from the start. They didn't, of course; they went into the campaign trailing National by 10 percentage points. And, again in theory, Labour should have won going away — and it's now history that National held on. Why?

I would like to take you now to a sophisticated dinner party in the capital a third of the way through the election. I was seated next to property millionaire, author and horticultural attache to the National Government in exile (viz Derek Quigley) Bob Jones, and naturally enough we chatted about a subject dear to both our hearts — authors' royalties. After that we got on to politics.

'Bob, a poser for you,' I said loftily at one point. 'If Labour were, for the sake of argument, the Government at the moment, given the record internal and external deficits, the galloping inflation, the record post-war unemployment, the zero economic growth these last six years, the exodus of some 120,000 people in the same period, the ministerial scandals, the general sense of social unease and division, how long would they last on November 28?'

The confidante of prime ministers grinned at me. 'I'd say about half an hour after the polling booths had opened for business.' The grin widened further. 'That's the beauty of living in this country, Tom. We have excellent double standards in these matters. We will forgive National Governments much more than Labour, and quite rightly so in my opinion.'

Even before this strange campaign began it was clear that there were really only two places for a mature journalist to be on election night: Ecuador or Peru. Unfortunately I had to choose between Rob Muldoon in the Auckland University Rugby Clubrooms in the Tamaki electorate and Bill Rowling in the Richmond Town Hall in the Tasman electorate. I opted for the latter. For Rowling the results would be especially loaded. Muldoon's position in history was secure; Rowling was fighting for much more. This could be his last chance to break the stereotype of the also-ran, the perennial loser. It would be night of triumph and vindication — or more pain and rejection.

Six-thirty on the big night and Richmond looks like a ghost town. All the bars in the pub at one end of the main street are deserted. Down the other end at the Social Credit HQ a Vauxhall Victor and a couple of motorbikes sport green and gold ribbons. Around the corner big outside broadcast vans parked outside the hall indicate that tonight's the night. Old ladies and young men arrive with plates of food. A lone scooter zooms past. 'National!' shouts the pillion passenger bravely. 'You need your head read!' ripostes one of the men.

Journalists congregate to discuss the TVNZ Heylen poll timed for release at 7.30. It is supposed to put Labour well ahead, but no one is sure if it is to be believed. Private radio's Barry Soper begs for details, is given half a clue and shoots off to outscoop the corporation with their own poll. No matter that it subsequently proves to be wrong. Inside the hall when television watchers see Ian Fraser give the details of the poll and Sir John Marshall predict a Labour win by 10 seats, people start to celebrate the victory they are convinced is theirs.

Bill Rowling is swept shoulder high into the hall. But the euphoria is premature; others huddled around radios are getting a truer, grimmer picture. Gradually it dawns on everyone that the big win is not to be and many turn away from the television sets, some to nibble listlessly at the big supper, some to get into some serious drinking, and others to join in a singsong. Two Maori women with guitars lead them in jaunty ballads but eventually the rhythms and harmonies dissolve into an aimless mournful chant.

When it is clear that Labour are not going to make it, the chairman of the local electorate committee, who is also a member of the local trades council, climbs on stage to introduce Rowling. A bitterly disappointed farmer starts to scream 'It's you trade unionists that have destroyed the Labour Party!' until he is bundled away. Rowling gives a gracious speech telling them that all is not lost. It's a brave, calm performance and he steps down to comfort some weeping supporters. Others again lift him shoulder-high and rush him across the room to the bar, knocking an old lady to the floor as they go. Once there, as though he didn't have a care in the world the Labour leader leads them in a rousing rendition of

'We Shall Not Be Moved'. A group of lads who have had too much to drink hoon around in front of the cameras when they're rolling and, having taken the precaution of wearing cricketers' pads beforehand, kick one another on the shins when they're not.

Dejected but still concealing his real feelings, Rowling leaves the hall with his family. It is only later at a press conference and in a *Truth* column that he blames the New Zealand public for the party's defeat. This is the stuff of private conversation and is quite unworthy of public release. In a democracy you can't blame the public; you can only blame your own inability to change enough people's minds.

In understandable contrast, the post-election relief of Prime Minister Muldoon was almost infectious. 'These days,' he chuckled to Karen Sims on *Newsmakers* on the Sunday, 'I even suffer fools gladly.' Adding that this election had been the one Labour had needed to win, and that they had had everything going for them. He had the air of a man who had just been rung by the hospital and told that there had been a mistake with the X-rays; he wasn't dying after all. It was someone else. For the moment the PM luxuriated in the reprieve. There would be time enough later to punish the clowns who had mixed up the X-ray plates.

Mid-campaign, I had got the impression that Rob Muldoon was a man at last at peace with himself. A man ready to accept the nation's verdict in a state of Zen calm. At that point he was, of course, so far in front that the defeat he might have to accept was unlikely. Later, Labour's claim of secret Treasury reports casting doubts on the think-big projects was confirmed in the face of his persistent denials; defeat loomed large and he didn't relish the prospect at all.

Journalists travelling with Muldoon were con-

vinced that over the final days the old master himself thought he was a goner.

His last address in Palmerston North was that of a man seemingly close to disintegration. At times he completely lost the thread of his arguments, and in a voice thick with strain he attacked assorted journalists in the crowd. Attacks on the press from Rob Muldoon are nothing new, indeed they are as much a part of his stage routine as is 'Moon River' to Andy Williams, but on this occasion there was no benign disdain, just raw hurt and accusation. The following morning he taped his final broadcast to the nation and the consummate television performer looked unwell, stumbled over words, and generally gave the impression that it was all over bar the gloating of his opponents. If that is the case, and I may be guilty of reading in between the lines on his temple, then he had every right to look elated with the narrow win.

The Labour leader, on the other hand, at this stage had looked and sounded like a winner. Rowling had no doubts. Indeed the tumultuous reception accorded him in Auckland in the final week, where 2300 people jammed the Town Hall and the adjacent chamber while another 200 or so stood outside and heard his address relayed over loudspeakers, was billed by party president Jim Anderton as a 'victory rally'. We connoisseurs of omens in the press exchanged knowing glances at that remark. There is an old saying in voodoo politics: you never count your chickens until they have come home to roost.

What went wrong for the Labour leader? Is the Bob Jones dictum true? Will it take extraordinary incompetence on any government's part before the people turn to Labour?

The answer to that is probably. With politics in this country now being a three-ring circus, the anti-government votes in the outer rings tend to cancel each other out and any wily ringmaster worth his grain of salt should rule indefinitely, even with 60 per cent of the votes going against him.

Traditionally it has been assumed in this country that people turned to Labour when times were hard. This is largely a myth, both here and in Australia. No New Zealander or Australian willingly votes for a redistribution of income when there are increasing numbers of people earning no income at all. That would be madness. People here, as they did in 1972 and just as the French did recently with the election of Mitterrand, are more likely to vote for the leftist party when there is relative affluence. Only when there is more conspicuous wealth will New Zealanders take the extraordinary step of moving, albeit minimally, to the left and having some of the wealth, albeit minimally, redistributed. So there. And over the last three years extra wealth has been conspicuous by its absence.

The problem then for Labour and Social Credit is two-fold: each must first convince the electorate that a change of government is necessary, and then that they alone are the true alternative. And on top of that, as George Chapman observed on election night, the nation was really fighting two elections. One in the country and provincial centres, and another in the cities.

Provincial cities like Invercargill and New Plymouth, and rural electorates like Marlborough and Gisborne needed only the suggestion of an anti-Government swing to fall but National managed to hold on, and in some cases actually increased their majority. While the think-big policies definitely worked to Tony Friedlander's advantage in New Plymouth and to a lesser extent to Norm Jones's in Invercargill, the lowest common denominator of National's improved showing in the provinces was the Springbok tour and Rob Muldoon's at times coarse appeal to patriots. As one journalist wryly observed, 'Why not, there are a lot of coarse patriots out there.'

Because the tour never featured in any of the public opinion polls as an area of continuing concern, Labour and Social Credit foolishly assumed no news was good news. (The trouble with public opinion polls is that they don't ask the right questions. They should have asked people, 'Are you prepared to change your political allegiance just so you can watch the Springboks but are too ashamed to publicly admit it?')

If George Chapman is correct, and there were two elections being fought side by side, then it follows that there are two New Zealands.

The two New Zealands are not confined to the obvious polar opposites like Gore and Auckland Central. They can occur only kilometres apart within the same electorate, as I discovered on the road with Bruce Beetham.

One lunchtime I accompanied Beetham to the cafeteria at Borthwicks' Feilding works. It was the very same cafeteria where in my youth I had spent some six summer vacations. Many of the same guys were still there and while the Socred Leader cleared his throat I was busy shaking hands. It was a hot afternoon, the heat of the kitchen adding to the sunshine coming in the windows, and men who had just come out of cool rooms and freezers perspired freely. Beetham promised not to take up too much of their lunch-hour, concentrated on Socred's tax policies and told them how National were trying to get rid of him at all costs. He stressed that National were hoping Labour supporters who voted Social Credit last time would drift back to the Labour fold. He reminded them that only by voting Social Credit could they defeat National; Labour had no show of taking the seat.

From the floor he was asked about seats like Palmerston North that Social Credit had no show of winning. Would Social Credit be advising its supporters to vote Labour there? Beetham looked momentarily nonplussed and without actually endorsing the idea didn't rule it out entirely either. 'Good answer chaps?' he grinned at the press later. He got on the whole an attentive hearing. Transistor radios were not turned up for the Woodville races. In my day visiting dignitaries risked arriving in one piece and leaving, suitably vacuum-packed of course, in about seven.

After that it was on to Ohingaiti, a small community in the north of his electorate. There Socred women busied themselves making tea and arranging goodies for their BCB. Young mothers with infants waiting patiently with a few cockies for their MP. Outside the sun beat down. Wild flowers grew along the roadside, birds sang, and late snow flecked the distant Ruahines.

BCB discussed the cost of loan money, rural depopulation and allied matters until the topic of strikes and freezing works came up. Suddenly many in the small gathering got angry. 'How do you keep the works killing in a dry period?' There were dark mutterings about freezing workers' wages. 'The job is supposed to be seasonal,' complained one farmer sipping a cup of tea and nibbling a piece of sponge, 'yet they earn that big money all year, and if they don't they get it back in tax.' 'Yeah,' said another. 'We're told to get our stock ready for a Sunday so we dag them, yard them. The truck-drivers have to cart them. We don't have our weekends off . . .' 'Nor do we get double time,' mumbled someone else. The hostility and frustration towards freezing workers, people working downstream in the same industry, was immediate and obvious. Beetham made sympathetic noises and eventually, though no siren sounded, people got up, handed in their teacups and drifted out to their cars to natter a bit more before moving away.

Although National worked very hard and spent, according to some estimates, $80,000 attempting to win back the seat, it was clear to me that Beetham would hold on. National's confident predictions of taking back the seat didn't go to waste though. While pretending to be unfazed, Beetham to some extent was taken out of play by National's tactics. They managed to tie him down in Rangitikei for much of the campaign, well away from the volatile north where Social Credit had a real chance of doing well.

For Social Credit this election was to have been the big push, the springboard for total victory in 1984. While they did make progress, mainly in urban areas, they did not get the percentage of votes they had predicted. Nor did the extra votes they received translate into extra seats. They may have to accept that their natural constituency will always be small and their growth will depend on growing alienation with the other parties.

The Nats ran a very shrewd campaign. They wanted

to concentrate on the growth strategy rather than their general economic record, and obligingly the other two parties allowed them to do just that. The growth strategy was the National Party's equivalent to Socred's economic reform. It was untried and therefore could only be proved wrong in theory.

By and large Muldoon held his own in this area with his complex and confusing charts. Many of us expect economics to be confusing, and night after night whole halls of people were clearly comforted by the sheer incomprehensibility of his arguments. As he said he would, in the main he ran a low-key and constructive campaign, mentioning Colin Moyle's resignation from Parliament only when he was taunted about the Marginal Lands Board loan affair. He said later that the only strain he was under was resisting the urge to tear Rowling's guts out, which he reckoned he could have done easily. The week I spent with him he was very relaxed, almost affable.

Derek 'Colonel' Quigley was welcomed in from the cold, the PM visiting his highly marginal Rangiora electorate — to open a few projects and christen a vineyard — for the first time since 1975. On stage that night in the Christchurch Town Hall they were Dereking and Robbing, Robbing and Dereking to such an extent I thought they were about to exchange signet rings.

Rowling, as in earlier elections, ran the most relaxed and accessible campaign of all three leaders. He had the odd beer with the lads and those journalists fond of an early morning jog were welcome to join him. His was perhaps the most gruelling election itinerary of all, and sleeping badly, bothered by a nervous rash and perhaps eating only one proper meal a day, the Labour leader sustained himself with a deeper hunger for victory. He really believed he would make it this time and by any objective assessment had the best leader's campaign. But again he started too far behind too late.

Labour had too much policy on offer. No matter that, as they claimed, it was the most carefully worked out and costed package they had ever released. In the end their promises were too ephemeral and they failed to properly address themselves to lingering resentments over the Springbok tour.

For all parties the election result had some unpalatable messages. For the rest of us the news was much better. In spite of predictions of voter apathy, the impressive party machines, and voter appreciation that this election did matter, resulted in a commendably healthy 90 per cent turnout. In the main it was a cleaner, more courtly election than either '75 or '78. And the wild volatility of the '70s has been supplanted by more considered voting patterns.

This time round the abilities of the candidates seemed to count more than usual. More women were elected. Defeated Wellington Central MP Ken Comber set new standards of grace and generosity when congratulating his successor. And we have a Parliament that National barely dominates. The next three years could be rewarding and fascinating for all of us.

Listener, January 2, 1982

I have been 'sacked' from the *Listener* twice in the last 11 years. The first occasion was in June of 1976. The All Blacks were touring South Africa, it was the time of the Soweto riots and I was pretty steamed up about things. I wrote a piece transferring the riots to New Zealand. They were in Otara and were the work of an oppressed Pakeha majority who were subjected to a form of apartheid imposed by a ruthless, self-righteous Maori minority. The transposition worked neatly and that article remains the most reprinted thing I have ever done.

At the time though it contrasted rather bluntly with Ian Cross's editorial line about bridge-building and the like. I knew he wouldn't particularly enjoy it so I didn't linger long when I dropped it off. About an hour later, back in my Karori home, I got a phone call from him in which he expressed his concern. He accused me of continually challenging his authority and writing deliberately provocative material pushing my own point of view rather than mocking the views of others. He said he wouldn't print it. I said sadly it seemed like the parting of the ways then. Just as sadly he agreed, adding that I left him no choice. There was only one editor in magazine and he was it. We said goodbye to each other and I hung up.

I wanted to cry. Working on the *Listener* had always been too good to be true anyway. Things would just have to return to normal. I would go back teaching or something. I looked out the window and it started to snow. Something locals said hadn't happened in years. Slowly the valley whited out. I cheered up enormously. It occurred to me that anyone who got sacked only to have it start to snow immediately afterwards was born to write. That night I was to be the first speaker in the Ngaio Winter Lecture series and I hadn't yet written a speech but it didn't matter now, I could tell them how I'd just been dismissed. I was savouring my martyrdom while down below in the street children wrapped warmly against the cold spun deliriously among the falling flakes.

Then the phone rang. It was Cross. 'Damn you boy,' he harrumphed, 'I'm going to print it after all.'

I told him he would never regret it and he chuckled nervously and said I wasn't to do this sort of thing to him again.

I skipped around the lounge not worrying any longer about the lecture. Later that evening my good friend Burton Silver of Bogor fame came to pick me up in his battered, rusting, draughty Morris van and we drove cautiously along slushy streets to the Ngaio hall wondering how many people would brave the snow and cold to attend. In the event the place was full of loyal column readers, little old ladies in the main, one of whom grabbed my arm tightly in her gloved hands and told me proudly she had come all the way from Upper Hutt. I could do no wrong. There were anguished, angry cries when I told them melodramatically that I had just been fired and ap-

plause when I added that less than an hour later I was put back on the payroll.

My second dismissal was not as short and sweet. It was in September of 1981 at the time of the Commonwealth Heads of Government meeting in Melbourne. Having covered a regional conference of the Commonwealth in Delhi the year before in the midst of considerable controversy I thought it was important that the *Listener* attend the Melbourne meeting as well. At first Peter Stewart agreed enthusiastically but as it drew nearer he seemed less keen and began to equivocate as to whether I should attend. Eventually he left on a trip to the United States, without telling me anything, but leaving instructions I wasn't to attend.

I was angered on a number of counts. Firstly there was the way the trip was torpedoed. If Peter had told me much sooner to my face that the Melbourne trip was off — for whatever reason — I would have been annoyed and disappointed but would have accepted the decision with no more than the usual backstage grumbling.

Secondly, the conference, in the wake of the Springbok tour, promised to see our PM slugging it out with leaders from Black Africa. By deciding the *Listener* would not be there we were opting out of an important debate, and events that were to have implications for the New Zealand general election only a few weeks away were not to be described for our readers.

Finally, on a more personal level, I thought that in not sending me to Melbourne the *Listener* was in effect apologising for sending me to India. Saying to the PM, we made a mistake then, but look, we have learnt our lesson.

Steamed up, complaining bitterly to colleagues in the Press Gallery about the infamy, I admitted that if I had the money and somewhere to place the article I'd take annual leave from the *Listener* and go to Melbourne anyway. Radio New Zealand's Trevor Henry suggested I ring Martinborough publisher Alister Taylor, which I did immediately. Within minutes the deal was finalised. He would bankroll me and I would write an eight-page article for his glossy magazine *The New Zealander*. As I was boarding a plane for Melbourne the editor of *The New Zealander*, Deborah Coddington, released a somewhat gloating press statement to the effect I was now on assignment for them.

It was hardly the ideal homecoming present for Peter Stewart and it came as no great surprise a few days later when Helen rang me in Melbourne to read out a letter I had just received from the *Listener*. My contract had only a few weeks to run and I was told no further work would be required from me; included was a cheque for $1800 paying me off. In the same post was a letter from our bank manager asking could we please do something about our overdraft, which now stood at $1900.

It seemed I was out of work and $100 down. On my return I went to see Stewart and was told that I could rejoin the *Listener* in six months or so when all the fuss had blown over — after all, I had often talked about needing a break. In the meantime I was not to write the article for *The New Zealander*. I said I couldn't do that because I had given my word, and asked if I could stay on just to cover the election but Stewart said that wasn't possible and I left the office in an angry daze.

What happened after that is complicated. It is sufficient to record here that while no job offers poured in and I was getting jumpy about paying the bills, lots of letters of support did arrive from people as various as trade union officials, pensioners, High Court Judges and Government MPs. I don't know what sort of mail Stewart received (except where people sent me copies) but I do know that a letter from my friend A. K. Grant tendering his resignation in protest was a crucial factor in my reinstatement. The *Listener* could survive the loss of one satirist, but not of two. I will also always be indebted to Gordon Campbell, who adopted the Henry Kissinger role of tough-talking intermediary between me and Stewart.

Eventually I was put back on the payroll and Peter and I agreed to describe the affair as a 'family row' which, in a real sense, it was. I was allowed to continue as before *and* fulfil any contractual obligations I had taken on during my time in limbo. I ended up on the campaign trail writing for the *Listener* and doing daily reports for Private Radio. I was a very bad radio journalist and mercifully I have never been asked back. I also finished the article for Alister Taylor, but it came out well after the elections and sank virtually without trace along with the rest of the publication.

Best of all Peter Stewart and I got on suprisingly well afterwards. Somehow in the midst of some quite tense exchanges we developed an improved regard for each other and I enjoyed the rest of my time under his benign stewardship.

That Melbourne Conference

Melbourne Monday September 28:

Melbourne has been described as the largest lawn cemetery in the world and flying in over Port Elizabeth bay at night provides little evidence to the contrary. Unlike Sydney or Los Angeles where a foul incandescence lights up the horizon, Melbourne, at least from our Jumbo, looked like a glow worm cave on strike. I hate landings but there was a new deeper apprehension to this one. I was coming to Melbourne in search of a big story and if nothing happened I was going to look pretty damn foolish.

Down on the concourse a message came over the speakers calling 'Don Scott' to the CHOGM media desk. Was this an omen?

Still they were pleased to see me. They had been there since six that morning and had processed some 400 journalists in the last 24 hours. I was the last that night and they rushed me out to a waiting car. In between giving instructions to our nervous driver who had been imported from another state just for CHOGM, the guy in charge told me solemnly that everything said inside the car could go no further and I braced myself eagerly for dramatic revelations. He had nothing to say of course and it was left to me to liven the conversation.

'What was the purpose of Harry Lee and Lord Carrington's quick visit to Wellington this weekend?'

'Giving him the message to do a hose job on Gleneagles no doubt?'

'Worse than that,' I replied, 'They came out with the express intention of drugging him.'

'Really?' he grinned uncertainly.

'You bet. When he gets on board Tamaki One tomorrow he'll be so laced with horse tranquilliser Merv Norrish and the others from Foreign Affairs will have to hold him by the elbows.'

'You're kidding?'

'What would you do if you were in Carrington's position? I mean ask yourself?'

Tuesday September 29:

The Royal Exhibition buildings (the REB locally), built over a hundred years ago, are to generations of Melbourne school children a dread and terrible place. Within its vast interiors thousands of pupils from all across the city gathered to sit certificate examinations.

Commonwealth summit meetings are a form of exam — everyone goes home with a pass. This year only one leader will fail: but I am getting ahead of myself.

That first morning down at the REB, once through the impressive security cordon, journalists swarmed through the halls with the mindless jubilation of children at a trade fair — pausing at any one spot only long enough to snatch what was free before moving

on. It wasn't hard to see where the 1.7 million Australian dollars had been spent. Facilities included a news agency, bank, duty-free shop, post office, two pie and sandwich counters, two bars, several lounges, three television studios, radio and television editing booths, a 23-hour telex service, a shop selling Aboriginal arts, and an exhibition of Australian photographs.

Elsewhere the leaders would enjoy even more elegant lounges and their own coffee bar. But it was the circular conference room itself that exemplified the care and no expenses spared approach to the whole meeting. Here, so there could be no distractions, the walls and fittings were a soothing dark brown, the only splash of colour being the specially woven carpet in the centre, with its green map of Australia emblazoned with a gold CHOGM symbol. The leaders themselves would sit at a circular table, hollow in the centre, some 22 metres across. The length, Sonny Ramphal said later when calling for good sportsmanship, of a cricket pitch.

Predictably, many, including the Opposition leader Bill Hayden, and some in his own Treasury, were of the opinion that Prime Minister Malcolm Fraser had been excessively lavish, and the costs would not be worth it. Fraser though had invested a lot more than money. Both personally and politically he had a lot at stake. This summit was to be the crowning achievement in his long and thus far unsuccessful campaign to give Australia a place at the top table of global politics. At home his very survival as leader of the Liberal Party might depend on its success.

Domestic criticism he had to expect but Fraser could hardly have anticipated or appreciated the 'bucket job' as the Aussies call it he received from the first of his guests to hold a press conference down at the REB.

Robert David Muldoon was running late, but the press would forgive him provided he was good copy. They were not to be disappointed. He moved swiftly to the microphone and although unusually pale, the face on TV monitors around the room exuded a ruddy authority. He began insisting he would be raising Gleneagles, and indicating that if there was not acceptance of his view that New Zealand had fulfilled its obligations, then his Government would pull out of the agreement altogether.

It was a gritty 'taking care of business' performance, spoilt by what seemed to me to be a taunting journalist from Bangladesh whose English wasn't very good, and by a very sharp response to a journalist from Black Africa talking about sporting contacts with South Africa being an emotional issue in some African countries. Mr Muldoon leaned into the microphone, jutted his jaw, and replied 'There are some people who think only folk with black faces have feelings ...' You could hear breath being sucked in all over the room. For a few seconds it looked as though the press conference was going to take an ugly, poisonous turn, but the PM regained his composure and the moment passed.

(This aside was the cause of considerable debate among the New Zealand press. I was outnumbered by those who thought the remark, while unfortunate, was a biological truth. That being the case his remarks made about as much sense as saying 'There are some people who think only folk with black faces have duodenums . . .')

Asked whether he would be producing his now celebrated dossier on the human rights records of some Commonwealth countries, the PM grinned and said, 'Let's see what happens.' Informed of this response at his press conference Ramphal bravely insisted that other leaders might respond with their own dossiers.

For some weeks prior to Melbourne the Commonwealth Secretariat had been attempting to compile a dossier on human rights violations in Godzone. Doubtless if completed it was a thin book, but it couldn't have been thinner than the PM's own masterly summation of the human rights situation in New Zealand. With commendable sleight of hand he reduced all our deficiencies in this area to the question of whether boys and girls should get separate prizes in painting competitions. Naturally the place broke out in laughter and from then on in things went pretty much his way. Indeed he was enjoying it so much he was reluctant to leave, and up the back Fred Dobbs, from Dobbs-Wiggins McCann-Erikson, looked very pleased with his most important client.

Filing out, one Australian journalist commented gratefully, 'Compared to Malcolm Fraser's Easter Island statue impersonations that was terrific.' 'Yeah,' said another, 'He may be a clown but he's a good one.' After that opening performance Ramphal's silken metaphors were something of a let-down, though the Secretary-General did get in a few licks of his own. The recent Commonwealth Finance Ministers meeting, he said, was well attended and the best yet. Not shifting it from Auckland in the wake of the Springbok tour would have been an 'insult' to the rest of the Commonwealth. The Gleneagles agreement was not a choice between active prohibition of sporting contacts and genteel expressions of displeasure.

Asked to comment on Mr Muldoon's threat to withdraw from Gleneagles, the normally effusive Ramphal could only reply, 'Did Mr Muldoon really say that?' He would not speculate on what action other countries might take against New Zealand if that happened. 'Sorry to disappoint you,' he said at one point, 'but people haven't come to Melbourne punching.' He hoped the press would focus on the profound issues like the world economic crisis. But even as he spoke the Aussie press at least were busy composing headlines in their heads like 'CHOGM SPLIT OVER SPORT' and 'FRASER FACES S. AFRICA ROW'.

Malcom Fraser hosts news media reception:
With its 25-year waiting list and 9-year probationary period before you become a full member, the MCC is one of sport's holiest places. Yellowing bats lined the walls along with notices advising that ties or cravats must be worn at all times. If the room symbolised anything, high above the famous oval, a vivid jade in the dying light, it symbolised the value of 'mateship'. That and the enduring power of old money. It was entirely appropriate that Malcolm Fraser, 'the crazy grazier' to some, the man who once vowed to replace politics with sport on the front page, should decide to entertain the press here. We sipped gin and tonics and nibbled canapes as he moved slowly amongst us, like a whale against a tide of herrings.

Two South African journalists, JJ and Bruce, who I had met earlier that day, approached me and asked if I would like to go with them to hear Robert Mugabe out at Monash University. They made it sound slightly illicit and to them it was. 'To be born a white South African,' JJ would explain later 'is to know original sin. Even though you hate the fucking place man, you are condemned to spending the rest of your life in perpetual atonement.'

Dashing off to catch Mugabe was just another step in the long road of guilt exorcism. With Bruce at the wheel, a huge map unfolded in his lap, we were soon hurtling east down a motorway not sure if we were headed in the right direction. Suddenly with a flashing of lights a motorcade with police outriders zoomed past on our right. 'That must be them!' JJ screamed. 'Don't lose them.' Bruce dropped down a gear, chopped into the outside lane, and planted his foot. Racing up behind the last car aroused suspicions. Security men turned around to see who was chasing them. You get a feel of what it's like to live in a police state when you drive with South Africans. 'Jesus,' JJ muttered, 'those bulls probably think we're BOSS agents. They'll probably shoot our tyres out and we'll end up wrapped around a power pole!'

Instead they shot through a series of intersections against the lights and left us far behind. We arrived at Monash, flashed our press passes and burst through the crowded foyer into the huge auditorium just as Mugabe was about to speak. The place was jampacked and I sat on the floor beside a black woman nursing a beautiful infant boy so tiny I could have accommodated him in my shoulder bag. While his mum listened in awe, as did everyone else, junior wriggled in her lap, the bright lights dancing on the miniature gold crucifixes he had hanging from each ear. Mugabe apologised for being jetlagged before giving his standard speech on the evils of apartheid, his hopes for Zimbabwe, and the need for national reconciliation and acceptance that the blacks were now in charge. Even tired he was very impressive, but not enough for JJ and Bruce, who wanted him to say something new and withering about their homeland so they could gleefully put it on the wire and make a few Afrikaners choke over breakfast.

Heading back into the city I commented on Mugabe's physical delicacy and almost balletic poise. 'Funny thing you should say that,' said JJ. 'When I was last in Salisbury I heard that while he was in prison he got his wang chopped off.'

'Bullshit,' said Bruce. 'That sounds like a real Rhodesian army lie to me.'

'All I'm saying is, that is what I heard.'

'Well it will be bullshit. Those bastards are always spreading crap like that.'

Wednesday October 30 — the opening:
Helicopters circled warily overhead. Army snipers

patrolled rooftops. Plainclothes policemen mingled surreptitiously with shoppers. Mounted horsemen held back a big crowd, most of whom seemed to think the Queen would be present. The Royal Australian Navy band played jauntily. And journalists were everywhere, like avenging locusts, ready to strip the occasion of every edible fact and nuance. Not much was happening of course, so every time a horse disgraced itself the shockwaves from notebooks being snapped open ricocheted up and down Swanston Street.

Prime Minister Muldoon, who got perhaps the biggest cheer from the crowd, was escorted into the Town Hall, somewhat cryptically to the strains of 'Tie a yellow ribbon around the old oak tree'. A nasty diplomatic incident was averted when the band refrained from playing the theme from 'The Empire strikes back' for Margaret Thatcher.

Inside, the special rostrum that Tammy Fraser had helped design was a riot of colour. The central bed of flowers was supposed to symbolise a boomerang but succeeded in looking more like a floral clock that the hands had fallen off. While most leaders paid attention to the various speeches Harry Lee disdainfully scribbled notes and our Rob slumped forward, propping up his jaw with one hand, hardly bothering to clap with the others.

Opening the meeting, Malcolm Fraser said that relations between developed and developing countries were the most critical problems facing the world. 'Those who fail to understand the gravity and drama of the issues disguised by the rather bland term 'North-South' dialogue,' he said 'are guilty of a serious breach of historical imagination.' Margaret Thatcher, whose hair looked like it was held aloft by girders, and who was to shortly insist in her own speech that the world needed to produce more wealth rather than redistribute the wealth it had, looked at him sharply.

'Such people fail to see,' continued Fraser, 'that behind the abstractions and arguments are the reality of starving children, people dying in the prime of life because of the lack of elementary medical services, despoiled environments in which good farmland is reduced to desert, and the endless grind of impoverished hopeless lives.'

It was a very impressive speech, adding to the growing realisation that Fraser's foreign policy is more sincerely held than he has been given credit for. Certainly many in his own party are not happy with his strong line on Southern Africa, and through one of those happy accidents that make this job occasionally fascinating, it seems I ended up seated next to one of them. The Speaker of the House, Sir Billy Sneddon and Lady Sneddon, who should have been downstairs with the rest of the gentry, were somehow shunted in with the press, and maybe this slight contributed to the strangled mutterings and huffing that punctuated Fraser's speech and rose to a muted crescendo every time a darker hued leader talked about inequality and the need for justice.

Lady Sneddon was more concerned with the problems blushing attendants had handing the microphones and rostrum to succeeding speakers, and kept repeating, 'You can tell a woman didn't plan this.'

Later. At Ramphal's reception for leaders and the media:

Colin Legum, longtime African correspondent for the *Observer* (he supplied Robert Mugabe with law books when the Zimbabwe Prime Minister was in one of Ian Smith's jails) guided me across the crowded cocktail party towards the Tanzanian President, Julius Nyerere. 'Mwalimu,' said Legum, respectfully removing a semi-permanent cigar from his mouth. 'I want you to meet a New Zealand journalist who is an enemy of Mr Muldoon's.' Mwalimu's intelligent, surprisingly boyish face broke in half with a wicked grin. He hugged me and held my hand in his. 'New Zealanders,' he said, 'must be the best and nicest people in the world. I want to thank you all. You have done more for the black man than any other country. Look what happened during the tour! What other country in the world would do so much for black men they have never met? Surely no other country would have. And this is a fact. How can we punish Mr Muldoon? How can we punish New Zealand after what you have done for us? What you good people of New Zealand did has made us black men of Africa so proud.'

Across the room the same Mr Muldoon who couldn't be punished was in fine spirits, and holding an audience of his own. It had been another good day for him, 'Star' treatment in the papers, and now some Aussie journalists were asking him respectfully if he wanted the 100,000 New Zealanders living in Australia to return home. 'Why should we want them back?' he quipped. 'We don't want them back.'

'We love the pig,' a top Australian journalist later explained. 'We use him as a stick to bash Malcolm with.'

Malcolm certainly looked the worse for wear. After a gruelling few days the conference chairman on the eve of the formal sessions was literally grey with fatigue, white stubble on his cheek giving him a frailty and humanity that a terrible shyness is said to normally mask. His appearance was to fuel stories that he was secretly being treated for terminal cancer at a Sydney clinic. But right then other rumours were concerning him. Australian officials were complaining in private that Mr Muldoon was reneging on an assurance he'd made to Fraser to leave the whole Gleneagles discussion to the Canberra retreat. Pressed by the New Zealand press, Fraser wearily replied 'It is my understanding that substantive debate on this issue will be left until we get to Canberra.'

Thursday October 1:

The first working day dawned chill and overcast. The world political situation was the lead item on the agenda. Indira Gandhi was one of the first to speak and the Indian Prime Minister urged the Commonwealth not to take sides in the growing and potentially disastrous rivalry between the US and the Soviet Union. Pointedly she insisted the Commonwealth should move towards a position of non-alignment. She said the money spent on a single intercontinental ballistic missile could irrigate a million hectares, build 65,000 rural dispensaries or feed 50 million children.

She asked Margaret Thatcher to tell the conference the timetable the 'Contact Group' of nations had for the independence of Namibia.

When it was Harry Lee's turn the bright, brittle and wily Singapore Prime Minister unabashedly 'dumped', as the Australians would say, on the notion of non-alignment and came out firmly in favour of the Reagan administration.

Margaret Thatcher was muted in her criticism of the Soviet Union and would not be drawn on the timetable for Namibian independence. Zambia's Kenneth Kaunda, a gentle and deeply religious man, said delegates had to understand the depth of passion and emotion of people who had felt the discrimination of colour. He argued that if Namibian independence wasn't resolved soon the French revolution would look like a Sunday school picnic. When it was his turn Rob Muldoon joined the chorus condemning apartheid, and calling for Namibian independence. If necessary New Zealand would participate in UN economic sanctions against South Africa. Coupled to this carefully worded solidarity was considerable anger directed at those who disagreed with New Zealand's interpretation of the Gleneagles agreement. New Zealanders, he said, were asking why freedoms valued in their country were denigrated by other Commonwealth countries. New Zealanders were angry too, that the shifting of the Finance Ministers' meeting was a departure from the consensus politics previously a feature of Commonwealth decision making. (Actually it was impossible among journalists to get a consensus of what 'consensus' meant. Some of the New. Zealanders seemed to agree with their Prime Minister that 'consensus' was a synonym for 'unanimous decision'.)

Mr Muldoon finished to polite applause and then left almost immediately to brief the New Zealand press contingent. Julius Nyerere, who followed, noted his absence, remarking that he had hoped to thank his good friend Rob Muldoon in person. He said he accepted Mr Muldoon had done all he could to stop the tour and he wished him better luck next time.

At the official briefing Nyerere's contribution was described as good humoured. Muldoon himself felt it was 'conciliatory' and the next morning there were headlines like 'African's move to defuse Springbok issue'. Others, however, stressed privately that Nyerere's contribution, while certainly good humoured, was a devastating, sarcastic and scornful dismissal of the New Zealand case.

Friday October 2:

The availability of cheap and generally excellent Australian red wine was beginning to take its toll. Some of us, more prone to homesickness than others, were going into bottle stores and demanding anything with a creosote aftertaste. With Muldoon seemingly let off the hook by Nyrere my story needed a strange new twist. A fashion parade at historic Rippon Lea perhaps? I knew the others would be either too busy attending a New Zealand press briefing or filing to come and I entertained briefly the notion of a scoop. I knew something was wrong when only four of us clambered aboard the press bus bound for historic Rippon Lea, and one of them was the media liaison officer from the first night at the airport. Outside historic Rippon Lea there were two television crews obviously just as desperate for colour and incident as we were.

Historic Rippon Lea turned out to be a Victorian Romanesque monstrosity set in acres of parkland, and while the lady CHOGs were inside tucking into fresh asparagus, chicken with almond and cherry sauce and orange sorbet, with Wantirna Estate Chardonnay 1981 and Yerinberg Port, the press party, police and chauffeurs had a cold buffet meal in a dilapidated shed listening to the hot wind creaking a giant Norton Bay fig tree. When it became clear that we weren't going to see much of consequence I accepted a lift back into the city. Back at the REB press centre when asked about historic Rippon Lea, I tapped my forehead sagely and said 'Worst attack of food-poisoning the Victorian health authorities have ever encountered. God knows what the final death toll will be. You buggers should have come.' And I walked off with all the quiet authority I could muster.

As it turned out it had been a quiet day anyway from New Zealand's point of view. Those who thought Nyerere's speech was the last word on the Springbok tour hadn't counted on Robert Mugabe. When it was his turn to speak the Zimbabwe leader said it was not a happy state of affairs when your neighbour was attacked by an enemy and someone else played rugby with that enemy. Mugabe pointed out the contradiction in Mr Muldoon's reluctance to interfere in the rights of sportsmen over South Africa and his willingness to interfere in the rights of businessmen wanting to trade with South Africa.

Some observers, perhaps wishfully, called Mugabe's rebuke a 'savaging', but it was far from that and the New Zealand PM was content to tell the New Zealand media that Mugabe was 'poorly briefed'.

Certainly the New Zealand Prime Minister could afford to be magnanimous. For days he'd been the centre of attention, and now it seemed Black Africa had shied away from a direct confrontation. Had he left the conference then he could have come home victorious, but the retreat was still to come, and there the 'Rogue Elephant of the Commonwealth' as one Fleet-Streeter put it, would damage himself more than the fittings.

Canberra Saturday October 3:

Not much happens at retreats. Even less at this one as it rained solidly most of that fateful Saturday and this time it was our Prime Minister's apparel which captured popular imagination – even Margaret Thatcher was overheard by one journalist inquiring in disbelief 'Where did you get that shirt?' While the wire-boys, frantic for something, *anything* to print, diligently scribbled copious shorthand notes on who might play golf with whom if the weather cleared, and who was talking to whom, I was just grateful to be alive.

Our flight up from Melbourne, in dense cloud all the way, was the roughest some locals could remember. 'We hardly ever have to stop serving coffee,' confided an ashen-faced Ansett hostie, as we bounced, like a cattle-truck with flat tyres, through the skies.

At times it was so bad I panicked about never seeing the children or 'Radio with Pictures' again and beside me NZPA's resolute Phil Melchior, purely as a precautionary measure, reached for an air sickness bag.

The afternoon was devoted to sleep, and after that to chatting in the bar with fellow outcast Ian Fraser. We were still there when the rest of the New Zealand press team returned from yet another of the PM's little briefings. This occasion was different somehow. There was no mistaking their anger. 'You should have heard him! You wouldn't believe what he said,' said one. 'It was disgusting,' confirmed another and they argued among themselves as to how 'well oiled' he might have been.

When I heard the tape later I could see what they meant. The voice that came out was so slow and throaty, at first I thought the cassette batteries were flat. He spoke at length and essentially it seemed he'd spent the day trying to buttonhole leaders on Gleneagles, few of whom were interested. 'Most of them say there's no problem, but as far as I'm concerned we've got to have one or two things clear . . . I've told Malcolm it's not tidy yet . . . they're all happy but NZ public opinion is not happy . . .' And he went on in that vein for some time. '. . . I had a chat to Mugabe (chuckle) and he just can't understand why we don't say no visas . . . I suppose when you've been in the jungle a few years shooting people it's difficult to understand.'

In places the flow stopped while he took time out to yawn, and when asked what he wanted he couldn't say exactly, but it was up to Ramphal to sort

something out. '. . . that's why we employ a Secretary-General and pay him a very large salary.' (Ramphal would have been pleased at this elevation, only days earlier the PM was telling the NZ media that in his book secretaries 'take the minutes'.)

Canberra Sunday October 4:

While the leaders of a quarter of the world's population were out at a farm watching a sheep dog display, a group of NZ newsmen sat around the pool at the Park Royal motel and discussed what questions should be asked later that evening. My advice was generally unsound. Having not asked a question of the PM in three years the prospect was suddenly daunting. My fingers began to tingle and I felt unwell.

Lunched with Colin Legum. He had seen Kaunda in the morning and would be interviewing Nyerere in the afternoon. Spent early part of my afternoon lying on bed staring at the ceiling. Rang Ian Fraser. Some comfort in discovering that he was anxious about quizzing the PM as well.

At 3 o'clock Ramphal called a press conference to make an important announcement. It was the much predicted Melbourne Declaration delivered with the now familiar Ramphal over-kill. It would in a very real sense and a very real way reinvigorate the dialogue between the rich and poor countries, declared the beaming Secretary-General. It contained, apparently, 'new intellectual realism' and provided 'the preconditions for the blueprint of a new world' order. But sadly, even as he spoke, some journalists began to yawn and chat among themselves. Still, most of the journalists present were on the Northern end of the North-South dialogue. Third world journalists, many now bunking down two or three to a room in Melbourne hotels, could just not afford the extra expense of coming to Canberra.

If Ramphal was unhappy with the tepid press response, worse was to come an hour later across the city.

The Muldoon Press Club address:

Contrary to expectation and the impression gained on NZ television the PM's address was not sold out. And apart from three tables of journalists in the middle of the room the bulk of the audience were businessmen and High Commission staff and their families. Brian Lockstone, the PM's press officer, warned Ian Fraser that his questions, if he asked any, would be ignored. As this stipulation violated the ethos of the Canberra Press, and as the PM's speech would laud press freedoms, we all encouraged Ian to hold his ground. The speech itself, written almost solely for home consumption, was aggressive, deliberately reactionary in its appeal, and in parts downright cheap. The bit that especially got to me was the insistence that real disgrace about poverty was not the gap between the rich and poor countires,

THE N.Z. NEWS MEDIA LETTING OFF STEAM IN AN ITALIAN RESTAURANT IN LYGON ST...

What time is his first press briefing tomorrow?

SCOTT.

but the gap between the rich and the poor in poor countries. In other words malnutrition is fine provided everyone's blood sugar is lowered to the same level.

If the content was terrible the delivery was snappy, and his handling of questions skilful. When it was Fraser's turn the PM remained seated and a heated exchange between people down the back (one of whom was a NZ Cabinet Minister's daughter) allowed the PM to wriggle free by declaring 'I'll let you fight it out among yourselves. . .' (He answered my question, and as this indicated a return to the fold I subsequently inquired of Lockstone the possibility of a lift home on Tamaki One. As he is inclined to do whenever I ask him anything Lockstone just laughed nervously, and I got the impression that would be OK, but they could only take me part of the way.)

The bombshell of the evening however came with a question on the Melbourne Declaration. The PM was genuinely surprised that it had been released. He then wasted no time in announcing that it had been done without his approval and was a load of platitudes that read beautifully and meant very little. While he could have fudged the issue, as he had with other answers, the PM made a meal out of this splendid opportunity to embarrass Fraser and Ramphal. These remarks, coupled to sections of his speech that attacked conferences such as this one, seemed incredibly belligerent from a man who hoped to enter into closer economic relations with Australia. Indeed one leader told me later that Malcolm Fraser was so incensed he was adamant that CER was off. Publicly Fraser would only say that Mr Muldoon was a guest in his country, and he defended the timing of the release of the Melbourne Declaration, saying Ramphal had checked with all the leaders and an announcement that it would be released soon was made on the Saturday night.

Certainly Indira Gandhi, who followed the PM at the Press Club, and got a capacity crowd, confirmed Fraser's version of events. Asked about Mr Muldoon's criticisms, and the language in the declaration, she crisply replied, 'Frankly most declarations do have platitudes whether we like it or not. But the world is moving ahead even though it may resort to rhetoric and platitudes . . .'

While being a party to the Melbourne Declaration was hardly an act of 'very considerable statesmanship' as Ramphal claimed, it became obvious that Muldoon's views were in the minority. Though leaders of the smaller, and therefore less important Pacific Island states felt that Ramphal didn't so much consult them on what should happen, as tell them.

The Australian press love a larrikin and initially they enjoyed the very good performances put on by Muldoon. But, like a nightclub comic who doesn't know when to leave the stage, he remained too long in the spotlight and blew it. Our Prime Minister has always confused attention with significance but eventually everyone else could see the difference. The Aussie cartoonists were the first to turn on him and the Pryor cartoon from the Canberra Times was one of the best. Barry Soper of Private Radio tried to purchase the original, only to be told it had been purchased five minutes earlier — by Sonny Ramphal.

Melbourne Monday October 5:

Always something of a loner at functions like this one, the New Zealand PM became an even more isolated figure. His constant denigration of Sonny Ramphal, his undermining of the Melbourne Declaration, and finally his unfortunate remarks about Mugabe, resulted in the skies over the REB going dark with chickens coming home to roost. Black journalists I spoke to were incensed. 'Who does he fucking well think he is man,' said a journalist from Trinidad. 'He deliberately makes Mugabe sound like a monkey with a submachine gun.'

Inside the conference the leaders, while more restrained, were just as angry and there were many pointed references to 'bushmen'. Eventually Mr Muldoon made an apology of sorts when he announced that he hadn't meant to be derogatory, only

factual. It was from all accounts a graceless and perfunctory explanation that did little to make amends. Mugabe himself, while saying very little, was extremely hurt and confided the following morning to Nyerere and others that he hadn't slept all night thinking about it.

Personally I don't believe our Prime Minister is a racist, but he is capable of saying things that appeal to racists. One Pacific Island leader who regards New Zealand as his second home, and Rob Muldoon a close friend, was shattered by the turn of events. This leader believes that it could take 14 years for New Zealand's good name to be repaired in the wake of the Melbourne Summit.

But Rob Muldoon wasn't finished yet. On the last day, anxious to get home in time for the 6 o'clock news, he left the conference before it finished, leaving behind a letter for Fraser to read out. This doomsday contribution called on the assembled leaders to accept that New Zealand had done its job under Gleneagles and there should be no more talk of boycotts, and if there was New Zealand would pull out of Gleneagles. Reaction around the table was immediate and hostile. No one spoke in New Zealand's favour and finally it was virtually consigned to the waste-paper basket on Pierre Trudeau's suggestion.

A humiliating testimony to Mr Muldoon's contribution to Commonwealth harmony. Ultimately the only real value of these expensive exercises is whether or not the leaders enjoy each other's company. By and large they do and sometimes out of personal rapport real positive change is made.

Yet our man, for all his endless references to 'Malcolm' and 'Sonny' that imply intimacy and accord, is a remote and isolated figure at these gatherings. While others used Christian names around the table, our PM, along with Margaret Thatcher, was nearly always referred to formally.

At his many press briefings Mr Muldoon at various times mimicked Ramphal, Fraser, Forbes Burnham and Nyerere. The one impersonation he couldn't pull off, no matter how hard he tried, was acting like a New Zealand Prime Minister.

THE NEW ZEALANDER

Cutting Sorry Figures

The PM surveys the rows of journalists below him and smiles slyly out of the corner of his mouth, his tongue diving among his bottom teeth as if attempting to dislodge a sliver of meat. The young television technician making final adjustments to the microphones on the desk blushes furiously. The theatrette is unusually full, and all eyes rest on the two men the PM has with him.

Prime Minister: Okay!... Aaaah yes, I must say I've been following what some of you blokes have been writing about cuts in Government spending and quite frankly most of it is rubbish! It's just nonsense, most of it. I don't know how you do it . . . (He looks up at the ceiling and begins to chuckle, shaking his head from side to side.)
. . . If you've been interviewing your typewriters again, all I can say is most of you need new ones! Ha! ha! ha!!
(As quickly as it came the smile freezes. He puffs out his cheeks and breathes in so deeply through his nose that the small flag on the table flaps wildly and some papers flutter to the floor. He stares coldly around the room and the voice, when he finally speaks again, is much deeper and faintly menacing.)
. . . Accordingly, I have with me David Thomson, chairman of the Expenditure Committee . . .
(Thomson beams, unplugs the pipe from his mouth and gives a small wave, as if being driven in the back of an open-top staff car past cheering troops.)
. . . And of course my Associate Minister of Finance, young Fel . . . young Fil . . . Fo . . .
Falloon (shifting uncomfortably in his chair): Falloon — Falloon, sir.
Prime Minister: Yes — young Falloon Falloon. Anyway, they're here to help clear up the many misconceptions you blokes are helping to spread.
Press: Could we ask Mr Thomson, sir, what the broad thrust of the expenditure cuts will be?
Prime Minister: David?
(Thomson beams, clears his throat, prepares to speak, pauses, pulls out a mirror and comb, adjusts his silver tresses, and taps his pipe against the edge of the table.)
Thomson: Well, broadly speaking, that is to say in general as opposed to specific terms, the overview, as it were, is to grasp the tiger, not to put too fine a point on it, by the nettles and ride it.
Press: Could you give us an exact figure for the cut in percentage terms then, sir?
Thomson: Well, speaking generally, we were sort of ... uh... somewhere in the vicinity of ... so to speak ... ah ... perhaps you could come in on this one, John?
Falloon: Thank you, Mr Thomson. As I understand it, we were aiming at a figure of around 9 per cent.

Thomson: Thank you, John. That sounds about right.
Prime Minister (angrily): That figure is far too high!
Falloon: This is true. These are only approximate targets. We would of course settle for a saving in Government expenditure of 8.5 per cent.
Thomson: We're biting the bullet, and we won't shirk from that, but the trouble with biting the bullet is you never know when you've bitten off more than you can chew, as it were. A figure of 8.5 per cent sounds about right.
Prime Minister (tersely): The figure is three!
Falloon: 8.3 per cent it is then.
Thomson: That sounds about right.
Prime Minister: The exact figure is 3 per cent and that's final!
Thomson: Fine. I can live with that.
Press: Isn't there some disparity between the various figures quoted?
Prime Minister: No.
Thomson: Not to my knowledge.
Press: But surely, with Mr Falloon citing a target of 9 per cent and you yourself, Prime Minister, saying it will only be 3 per cent —
Prime Minister: There you go again! Drawing inferences and leaping to conclusions. Quite frankly I'm getting sick and tired of the sensation-seeking and headline-hunting you fellows indulge in. Mr Falloon was right in the context he was speaking in and I am right in the context I speak in.
Press: In what context was Mr Falloon speaking?
Prime Minister: I shall be having a word with him afterwards to clarify that very thing. Mr Falloon was speaking as a very young and junior Minister. I prefer to leave it at that.
Press: We still don't see how the two sets of figures could be at such variance.
Prime Minister: I don't know why you fellows persist in harping on these matters. I have already explained it pretty fully. It's clear to me that Mr Falloon added the 3 per cent savings in Social Welfare to the 3 per cent savings in Health and the 3 per cent savings in Education and came up with a figure of 9 per cent altogether — surely that's obvious to the meanest intelligence.
Thomson (excitedly): And if we reach 3 per cent in four other departments we'll save 21 per cent!
Press: A figure of $1000 million is being bandied about in respect of the total savings the Government wishes to make. Is this correct?
Thomson: Up to a point.
Prime Minister: No.
Thomson: No.
Prime Minister: You've got to understand that that figure is given in relation to a wage-tax trade-off. We

are talking about an across-the-board tax cut of 20 per cent.

Press: How is this to be achieved?

Prime Minister: The ordinary bloke doesn't care how it's done as long as he gets the cash in his hand. We've looked at a number of areas and to make good the billion dollars or so the tax will cost us we're going to have to introduce some form of indirect taxation — most probably wholesale tax or perhaps cardboard carton and wrapper tax.

Press: Wrapper tax?

Prime Minister: It's very simple. Your groceries will still cost the same but the bags and boxes you carry them home in will cost about $50 each. That will just about account for most of the billion dollars

we have to raise. The rest should easily be met by increasing Government charges in various areas.

Press: How inflationary will this be?

Prime Minister: Who can say?

Falloon: I think I know the answer to that —

Prime Minister: Shut up. You've done enough damage already!

Press: Surely wages will rise to match inflation and people will enter higher tax brackets again and find themselves worse off having to pay for things which are currently free. You're robbing Peter to pay Paul.

Prime Minister: Not at all. If anything, it's the other way round.

Listener, March 27, 1982

They Should Be So Lucky

It was his daughter's birthday party and no one paid the old man much attention. Shrivelled by time and hardship he hovered at the edge of the gaiety looking for an opening. I smiled at him and he attached himself to me like a limpet. His English was poor but there was no mistaking his meaning or the terrible conviction in his eyes. He was Latvian and had spent most of World War II in forced labour camps working for the Nazis. A harsh experience, which for some curious reason left him with a deep affection for the Third Reich and an antipathy to Jews. The Jews, he explained to me, were not to be trusted, because they told enormous lies. With their money and influence they controlled the world's press and spread vicious propaganda.

'Take the holocaust. They claim six million Jews were killed. Bah!' He snorted in disgust. Saliva rattled in his mouth. He held up some bony fingers and leant towards me. 'Such exaggeration . . .Three million! Three million if they were lucky!'

All I could do was excuse myself and move away. You can't dent prejudice of that kind. It may be blind but it's also seamless and durable. It seems there is no atrocity the human mind can't either justify or pretend never happened. You don't have to be a silly old man either. You can be young, well meaning and well educated. I had a very similar conversation about Kampuchea with a Maoist feminist. She was most unhappy about the reports of genocide in Pol Pot's Democratic Kampuchea.

'The West, of course, has vested interests in discrediting the Khmer Rouge,' she said crisply. 'I just don't believe talk about three million people being killed. I'd be very surprised if more than a millon have died.'

To her credit I suppose, she refrained from saying, 'One million — if they were lucky!'

No one knows how many people died under Pol Pot, but if the intention of the Khmer Rouge hierarchy was to rewrite Cambodian history by reducing the population from an unruly, untidy seven million to an ordered ideal of one million, then from all accounts they had made tremendous progress when the spoilsport Vietnamese finally invaded.

The insanity began within hours of the victorious Khmer Rouge (who had just defeated the Western-backed Lon Nol Government) entering the capital, Phnom Penh. According to *Time,* the weary civilian populace was jubilant at first, expecting peace and order after nearly five years of civil war. Instead black uniformed troops began firing into the air and ordering everyone at gunpoint on to the highways leading to the countryside. There were to be no exceptions, not even hospitals, where doctors were ordered to abandon patients in mid-operation. It took two days to completely empty the city, and throughout the country the flushing-out was repeated in every town and city till some four million people had been put on a grotesque pilgrimage to the villages and countryside. Many didn't make it, and once there exhaustion, disease, malnutrition and executions took their toll on those who did.

All this was brought back to me by the recent visit of an old friend, whom I'll call Kevin. We were at Massey together. As editor of *Chaff* he published my very first political cartoons, and a couple of years later he stage-managed my first revue. Shortly after graduation he left for London and eventually settled in New York. I hadn't seen him for more than 10 years when, without warning, he arrived on my doorstep having spent two years working without pay on various aid and relief projects in Thailand, Kampuchea and Vietnam. At Massey he had been a flabby, amusing, somewhat abject young man. The 1982 version, trimmed by resolution, an Asian diet and a daily regimen of taekwondo, exudes charm and confidence, is even more amusing, and has a gritty level-headed compassion.

He was one of the first Westerners allowed into Phnom Penh after the Vietnamese victory and the installation of the Heng Samrin Government. He recalls drily that aside from the conspicuous malnutrition the most arresting sight was the money blowing through the streets like leaves. Under Pol Pot a rare synthesis was achieved. Human life and money had the same value: nothing. Some people made lightshades out of it, others papered their walls with it, and shopkeepers with a fine sense of irony strung it over their doorways like bunting.

He worked at first with an overweight American couple who refused to learn the language and insisted on attending every official banquet — and they weren't lavish affairs — with their own jar of peanut butter and loaves of white, sliced bread.

Of the Vietnamese Kevin says they were obviously in charge but were very discreet and polite about it. For an army of occupation they seemed in the main honourable, and did not commandeer Khmer rice when their own harvest failed. Instead they survived on a lower daily ration of rice than their conquered neighbours. In part this rice shortage stems from the fact that anti-personnel bombs dropped years ago by the Americans still render much arable land unusable. Farmers get mutilated even when driving armour-plated tractors, and some bombs are primed to go off on the second shock, such as when the wife and kids start planting rice days later in the vain belief that the coast is clear.

Still Kevin has no illusions about the Vietnamese and believes them fully capable, as the Americans claim, of dropping the toxic 'yellow rain' on the

nomadic tribes who roam the hills along the Laotian and Vietnamese borders.

Having read some of the meticulously kept 'confessions' Pol Pot's men were able to extract from the prisoners in Tuol Sleng jail — where people would in the end agree to being CIA agents just to hasten their execution — Kevin has difficulty cultivating illusions of any sort.

On the second and final day of his fleeting visit I had to attend an Amnesty International rally designed to draw attention to the plight of people who simply 'disappear' in many countries. Having just come from a part of the world where a whole nation nearly disappeared, Kevin wryly declined to accompany me.

He missed out on a sterling occasion. My contribution was to point out that New Zealand was one of the few countries left in the world where a knock on the door in the middle of the night merely meant someone had run out of petrol or your stereo was too loud. In our comparatively privileged and open society prominent people, apart from Dougal Stevenson and David Lange, do not vanish overnight. Journalists who may get the odd line censored

don't have men in raincoats coming around to censor their breathing.

Afterwards I chatted to Maori activists who felt that New Zealand's own prisoners of conscience and disappeared people — Maoris and Pacific Islanders — were ignored.

At first glance it's an absurd claim. New Zealand militia do not kill babies and small children by slashing at them with machetes and feeding the remains to dogs, as has happened in El Salvador. On second glance, it is obvious that Maoris (12 per cent of the population) are under-represented in the professions and over-represented in prisons and borstals. Ideally they would make up no more than 12 per cent of bulldozer drivers and brain surgeons. Even in Parliament, if the Maori vote carried the same weight as a Pakeha one the number of Maori seats would be seven.

Comparative health statistics make the most depressing reading. Maori children are said to occupy 25 per cent of the beds in Auckland hospitals.

Not everyone agrees, of course. For many it would be 24 per cent. If they were lucky.

Listener, April 10, 1982

Plane Speaking

'Have you heard about the latest Jap camera?' asked the captain. 'This is a beauty,' giggled the co-pilot. 'For God's sake don't attribute it to us!' I never argue with Air New Zealand pilots, especially while we are still high in the air and they have to feel good within themselves for the landing, so I nodded vigorously and grinned encouragingly.

'Well,' continued the captain, 'it's got this absolutely amazing new electronic shutter. The shutter speed is a thousand times faster than any other camera on the market!'

I gave what I thought was a suitably impressed whistle. 'Yeah,' he beamed, 'they reckon it's now possible to take a picture of Bob Owens with his mouth shut! . . .'

Certainly Owens's demeanour since he became Air New Zealand chairman has not been characterised by reticence and excessive discretion. The transport magnate and former king of Tauranga and Mount Maunganui is a man of forthright and well publicised views. Before having Labour Party president Jim Anderton removed from the premises earlier this year, he conceded that his strong views about the Mahon report on the Erebus disaster did not result from having actually read it. More recently, being hundreds of kilometres out at sea pacing the decks of the cruise ship *Oriana* didn't prevent him from reacting angrily to the S. S. Colker and Associates findings on Air New Zealand's financial situation. Contacted by radio telephone, Owens said the report, commissioned by the Treasury, was nonsense and a waste of public money. 'For a Yank to come to New Zealand and tell us to make 2500 people redundant is ludicrous. He's out of his mind.'

The 17-page summary, released without comment by the PM, was a blunt and damning document. The Washington consultancy said the airline was overstaffed, needed streamlined management procedures, and had a history of making ill-conceived and expensive decisions. Apart from going into liquidation and starting again, the airline could merge with an Australian carrier, drastically slash staff numbers to US levels, sell off certain divisions, and immediately try to defer the purchase of the extra two Boeing 747s on order. Certainly the Boeings would be too expensive to fly at the moment and if deferral was not possible the planes should be leased out to someone else. (Some have already suggested the Housing Corporation, while others propose wedging them into the Cromwell Gorge to speed up dam construction, though Derek Quigley would agree to that only if they were sold to private enterprise first.)

If Owens was incensed at the report, his new chief executive Norman Geary, who emerged unscathed from the scrutiny, was more temperate and said that while the airline accepted the thrust of the report it did not accept all of the conclusions.

Having released the report first thing on a Monday morning, the PM naturally enough had nearly a full house of journalists keen to question him on it at his midday press conference. Lately there have been mutinous suggestions that these forums are not all they might be. After the recent CER talks the PM shared the podium with Australia's Doug Anthony only to interrupt his guest whenever he seemed likely to give anything halfway approaching a useful reply to requests for information. At one point a clearly embarrassed Anthony apologised for the bluntness of the answers and the PM intervened again to assure him it was 'quite normal in this theatre I assure you'. Anthony was later heard to remark as they ascended the stairs together, 'It's a wonder you give press conferences at all with the amount of information you give them.'

Anthony wasn't to know, but the aside was quite unfair. When he is not in the business of showing visitors how brisk and firm he is the PM is the Mt St Helens of information. Following ominous rumblings comes an eruption engulfing and numbing all those unfortunate enough to be caught in its path. Not all of it is important and it can be quite dazzlingly irrelevant, but rarely does it serve no purpose.

The morning of the Colker report was a case in point. The PM began apologising for being late, explaining that he had been delayed by a last-minute discussion of the prospect of a change of leadership in the Labour Party. Bets were taken and Ann Hercus was the clear front-runner. That diversion dealt with, he addressed himself to the question of the British retaking of South Georgia and declared himself gratified with this decisive and effective move. Only then could the press get in a few licks about the Colker report and the PM adopted the standard smothering mode of declaring the report both useful and in need of further study. As far as he was concerned there was nothing new in the fact that the airline was in financial difficulty. After that he contented himself with showing off for the benefit of the young photographers on a training course who had clustered down the back.

Since the result of the Taupo electoral case confirmed National's Roger McClay as the member, both the PM and his party have looked a lot more relaxed. With an early election much less of a possibility the Labour Party will find that the brave face it has put on its recent problems will be that much harder to maintain. The familiar mutterings about the need for a new leader are almost inevitable and the PM's remarks about Ann Hercus were designed to boot that debate along.

Since the house began, the eyeball-to-eyeball

numerical equality in the Chamber has produced a dynamic quite unlike any other sessions I have attended in the last eight years. There is a new arrogance and sense of possibility to the Opposition ranks, and with political reversal literally only a heartbeat away, there is among the Government benches a reciprocal humility and acceptance of their diminished status.

No more of that fine careless indifference to the Opposition that both the third Labour Government and this Government had when they enjoyed 20-seat majorities.

Suddenly everything matters and the smallest of measures needs careful shepherding through the procedures of the House. Both sides are still feeling their way. The Government nearly lost one recent division and the Speaker had to exercise a casting vote, while the Opposition are still learning to harness the extra powers at their command. Apart from the new members on both sides of the House, the standard of speeches in the Address-in-Reply debate has not been high. Indeed if Bill Rowling and Fred Gerbic had not questioned the wisdom of continued links between the Labour Party and the trade union movement, most Government speakers would have had precious little to talk about.

The Opposition should be dominant, but a lack of co-ordination and long-term tactics frustrates them.

With David Lange still quiet after his operation, only Richard Prebble consistently worries the Government. Too much time has been wasted on silly business like Mike Moore's National Development Amendment Bill. More correctly it should have been called the Embarrass Mike Minogue and Marilyn Waring Bill No 1. Government members said it was a transparent device and Moore confirmed that by spending most of his speaking time, not arguing in favour of the clauses he wanted repealing, but in taunting the two Waikato members, inviting them to cross the floor of the House and bring down the Government.

You don't persuade a trapped animal to your point of view by poking it with a sharp stick. There will come a time later this session when Minogue and Waring might well cross the floor to help defeat Government legislation. Indeed they might well have crossed the floor on a vote of censure against Ben Couch. Such a vote never eventuated, and instead the Government's most respected younger liberals, Jim McLay and Geoff Thompson, defended Couch on the curious grounds that at least the League of Rights was anti-communist. There will be other opportunities and the Opposition should have the wit to post Minogue and Waring cakes with files as fillings.

Listener, May 15, 1982

Get Up and Glow

Taylor: Now for this morning's bird call. The very last recording of the now extinct Chatham Islands blue tit.
Sound: Chirp! Chirp! Chirrup! Chirp! CLUNK! Aaaaaaggghhhh!!
Taylor: Very sad. Crushed to death when a BCNZ soundman dropped his tape-recorder. Still, as they say, it's a long road that has no street lighting. This is your friend and mine Robert Taylor leaving you with this thought from fox-hunting. Look after the ponies and the hounds will look after themselves. Chuckle. Think about it. Bye now.
Sound: Pip pip pip pip pip pip. DAH dah dah dah, boom diddy boom boom etc.
Perigo: Good morning. Lindsay Perigo and Peter Sledmere here . . .
Sledmere: With . . .
Perigo: Another edition . . .
Sledmere: Of . . .
Perigo: *Morning Report!*
Sledmere: Thank you, Lindsay.
Perigo: Thank you, Peter.
Sledmere: Don't mention it!
Perigo: Welcome to the all-new 'essentially positive' *Morning Report.* Yes, we've revamped the programme following criticism from the PM that we were too negative and were portraying a bad image of New Zealand to the Pacific island states via the soon-to-be-scrapped shortwave service.
Sledmere: I don't think the PM was 'critical' so much, Lindsay, as 'constructive'.
Perigo: Quite. I think I speak for us all in broadcasting when I say we do appreciate the continuing advice and guidance we get from the Prime Minister on how to run things here. After all, he's a very busy man and can't really afford the time. Thank you, sir.
Sledmere: And now the headlines. In the last 24 hours no earthquakes were recorded in New Zealand.

No tidal waves have struck, and there are no reported outbreaks of foot and mouth, rabies, typhoid, malaria or Rocky Mountain spotted fever.

Perigo: Eat your heart out, John Denver!

Sledmere: What was that for?

Perigo: I always come in with a quip after the headlines. You know that.

Sledmere: Not a very nice thing to say about John Denver, though, was it? I mean we all know he's not Mario bloody Lanza, don't we, but the fact remains that a lot of people like him and you were very quick with a facile and catty remark. I don't call that being positive.

Perigo: I'M SORRY, I haven't got the hang of it yet.

Sledmere: I hadn't even finished the headlines anyway.

Perigo: I said I was sorry.

Sledmere: I continue. Police in Auckland, Wellington and Christchurch report that a spate of heads are turning up in car boots.

Perigo: What's positive about that?

Sledmere: Most of them were smiling, so there! It's 7.15 and we cross now to the weather office.

Weather Office: Go-od . . . morn-ing. A . . . de-ep . . . de-press-ion . . . is . . . sit-u-ated . . . south-west . . . of . . . the . . . Kermad-ecs . . . and — CLICK.

Sledmere: Sorry. That's not what our listeners want to hear this early in the morning. Lindsay?

Perigo: Today is Shirley Temple's birthday and on this day 400 years ago Arthur Cruddock invented the toffee apple. Peter?

Sledmere: How many angels can dance on the head of a pin? Or for that matter, how many families can you crowd into one room?
This report from Christine Negus in Christchurch.

Negus: Civic leaders reacted sharply yesterday —

Sledmere: Constructively.

Negus: Civic leaders reacted constructively to welfare agencies' claims that Christchurch needed a transit camp and soup kitchens to deal with the homeless and the growing number of unemployed. They pointed out that while a minority might need food and shelter the overwhelming majority were well-fed and had roofs over their heads. This is Christine Negus in Christchurch.

Perigo: Thank you, Christine. Well, we have the Minister of Housing, Derek Quigley, on the line right now and he has very generously agreed to talk to us. Good morning, sir.

Quigley: Good morning.

Perigo: Not too early for you, sir?

Quigley: Not at all, I was going to get out of bed sometime today anyway. What can I do for you?

Perigo: How is the weather out there?

Sledmere (hissing): Ask him!

Quigley: Lovely. I can see sunlight on the harbour. It's really rather splendid. Is that all you wanted to know?

Perigo: Well, it's this housing thing in Christchurch . . . you know, the alleged shortage and whatnot. Hysterical exaggeration, I'd say — wouldn't you? Sorry. That's quite unfair. Sorry I spoke. Let's forget the whole thing, shall we?

Quigley: Well, Lindsay, I take your point. There is some hysteria involved but to be perfectly fair some of these people do have a low blood sugar level and that can make you unstable. But as for this so-called housing shortage — in New Zealand right now we are only one house short.

Perigo: One?

Quigley: One!

Perigo: That's what we thought.

Quigley: The trouble is, and our political opponents try to make much of this, is that about 9500 families want to live in it. But essentially there is no housing problem to speak of. Certainly we never speak of it in Cabinet. Many of my colleagues, myself included, own at least two homes and for the life of me I find it hard to believe that some people can't even own one. Still, we believe in freedom of the individual and we're not going to make it illegal to not own your own home. If people want to sleep six to a room or sleep in garages, then that is their affair.

Perigo: Quite. About this garages thing, Minister . . .

Quigley: I think the PM put it in perspective when he said most people in the Islands don't *have* garages, let alone sleep in them. The whole point about sleeping in garages, Lindsay, is that people are actually sleeping. Insomnia is a serious social and medical problem all over the world. I was proud to learn that New Zealand men and women actually sleep in garages — after all, there's not much room in your average garage after you've parked an Aston Martin or two.

Perigo: Thank you, Minister. Now we cross to Jack Forsyth at the fruit and vege market. All essentially positive news down there, Jack?

Forsyth: Mostly, Lindsay. Tomatoes are . . . bloody hell! a dollar each, and they're a good buy. Cabbages are coming on too, and at — crikey dick! — $10 a kilo they're a good buy too. Cauliflower at . . . bugger me days . . . CLICK.

Sledmere: With Parliament about to commence soon we cross now to our political editor, Trevor Henry, for an update on politics. Trevor, essentially and positively, what's of interest?

Henry: Well . . . put like that . . . I guess the walls are being painted, though not everyone likes the colours.

Perigo: Sounds like a tricky area to me. We'd better call it quits. That's all we have time for. So it's goodbye from him . . .

Sledmere: . . . And goodbye from me.

Listener, April 17, 1982

Song and Dance

In the gathering dusk and chill wind the Martinborough Town Hall was a warm oasis of lights. Cars nuzzled up to it like piglets about a sow and ladies in wraps and stoles alighted with armfuls of steaming pots and platefuls of goodies. Inside, a television crew set up lights and radio journalists positioned microphones and tape-recorders. The good women adding the finishing touches to trestle tables hadn't known such excitement since . . . well no one could remember quite when.

The South Wairarapa Women's Section of the National Party fund-raising dinner is an annual affair and this year's guest Derek Quigley had been invited months back — when their president had met him at the opening of Parliament and had been 'quite taken' with him. Now of course, with the sacking and everything, interest was running high. The phones had been running hot all week with people wanting to come, there was a waiting list of 15, and they weren't sure they could feed everyone. With Quigley about to make his first public speech since his forced resignation, suddenly it seemed their small township was the centre of the universe. They could hardly believe their luck.

To the press waiting outside in the cold in readiness to buttonhole Quigley the thought occurred that Plains, Georgia must have been a bit like this when Jimmy Carter became President of the United States. The guest of honour was late so the hall tucked into the Blenheimer and accordingly gave him a rousing reception when he entered behind the obligatory piper. Food was rushed out and the locals tucked in heartily while Quigley toyed with his and scribbled on his speech notes.

All the while the music-hall team who'd been such a success during the recent centenary entertained from the stage. Introduced by an MC dressed for some reason as a Mexican bandit, various local stars were greeted with rapturous applause and descended the steps to bump and grind their way nicely among the tables. One song, 'Hold Your Hand Out You Naughty Boy', seemed to apply to Quigley, and 'You Made Me Love You — I Didn't Want to Do It' could have been written for the PM.

When finally it was Quigley's turn he was introduced breathlessly as both a farmer and a lawyer, though in his dark suit and pink unlined face in a hall full of cavalry twill trousers, knitted ties, tweed and wind-burnt cheeks he looked more clerk than cocky. Proof of Quigley's ability, said the chairman, was that when he was forced to leave Cabinet they had to replace him with two men. 'Nah,' whispered one farmer, 'the old bugger was looking for mates.'

Quigley, who can be very engaging and has a nice line in self-deprecating wit in private, has very little stage presence and the speech that followed was at times drab and sterile. That and the effects of the Blenheimer had some fidgeting and others trekking to the toilets.

Still it was a skilfully judged speech, if not riveting in delivery, and most were delighted when they spilt out into the dark, though one got the impression they would have been just as thrilled if Quigley had shown slides all evening. As you'd expect from a keeper of the faith, Quigley spoke mostly in parables, which the hard-news journalists found frustrating.

One parable was about cousin Margaret who voted Labour. He and she both held strong views, but were able to discuss them rationally and still have high regard for each other. Another parable was about a Polish lawyer friend who as a schoolboy had fought the Nazis in the streets of Warsaw and as a consequence had a deep love of freedom and democracy and was a continuing inspiration to Quigley. The implication seemed to be that our respect for one another and our dedication to democratic freedoms needed improving. He talked also of stubbornness being a family trait although when asked nicely the Quigleys were very co-operative people. Dictate to them, though, and they walked briskly in the opposite direction. Countries, too, needed to know where they were going and why. The hall nodded in solemn agreement.

At the close it was vaudeville again when Ben Couch rolled up to the microphones and stole the show. Like his good friend he too had got into trouble from time to time. Indeed it was hard for Cabinet Ministers to get the DCM yet Derek had got one. It meant don't come Monday. The hall rocked with laughter. Returning an earlier compliment, he called Quigley the most honest man in politics (they can't both be right). 'We love you Derek,' he declared finally and led everyone in a rousing 'For He's a Jolly Good Fellow.'

Quigley had every right to be pleased. Couch, who apparently had cried in Cabinet when Quigley was forced to resign, retains his position in that august enclave because he supposedly represents the common man. If that is the case the PM must be worried. It must be disturbing that a gaunt, ascetic ideologue like Quigley enjoys both the respect *and* the affection of so many of his colleagues.

When the sacking was first announced, headlines were quick to describe the reversal as Quigley's third defeat at the hands of the PM. The first two being the attempted 'colonels' coup' and the bid for deputy leadership of the party. In fact it is his fourth hiding, though there is plenty of evidence that he has learnt enough in the earlier bouts to be a formidable opponent in the future.

Shortly after the botched coup, Quigley, having announced his intention to fight Duncan MacIntyre

for the deputy leadership, ended up one night having a drink with some senior colleagues and his boss who was far from pleased at this fresh effrontery. Some quite heated discussion followed, during which the PM several times told him to pull out of the race, and called him a liar. Quigley advised the PM that if he called him a liar once more he would come around the table and thump him. Muldoon looked him straight in the eye and said again, 'You're a liar!' Quigley half rose out of his chair then gave it away. The PM had called his bluff, but Quigley nevertheless remained in the race and the crucial vote had to be delayed so as to deny the Quigley forces victory.

Cleary the two men have considerable, if wary, respect for each other, but respect doesn't necessarily count for much. Tony Friedlander, for example, was part of the colonels' coup but on the PM's return from abroad he saw the error of his ways, spent a week in Queenstown recovering from 'nervous exhaustion' and was eventually rewarded with a Cabinet placing. Had Quigley, after his miscalculation in addressing the Young Nats as he did, pleaded nervous exhaustion and disappeared for a week he would still be in Cabinet today.

Interestingly, after the dumping the PM moved swiftly to see to it that Quigley could retain the title 'the Honourable Derek Quigley'. The former Minister agreed that Muldoon allowed considerably more freedom of discussion than other National Party leaders and said he admired the PM's political skills while admitting he wouldn't want to go on a fishing trip with him.

This mutual magnanimity began to dissolve as the party at large made its feelings known. Some divisions were outraged; Quigley himself was greeted like a hero on his first trip home; Mike Minogue muttered darkly and ludicrously about fascism; Aussie Malcolm rallied to his boss's aid with a speech condemning the right-wingers in his own party, which John Falloon took as a personal attack.

Eventually of course the PM decided it was the media's fault, before attacking some within the party and having another go at Quigley. He wondered if Quigley's newly-expressed social concerns were a road-to-Damascus revelation. A curious choice of words when you consider recent events in the Middle East. Parallels exist. A tough and unpopular ruler surrounded on all sides by enemies makes a bold and ruthless sweep into the National Party heartlands and cripples his chief opponent. An uneasy truce prevails but no one knows for how long.

Listener, July 10, 1982

W hen domestic politics are quiet and I have a column to fill I will often turn in desperation to writing about my family or childhood, or very occasionally if I am particularly aroused I will write on world affairs. 'The Diary of Anna Farouk' was such a piece. I was deeply angered by the Israeli invasion of the Lebanon and found their justifications even more offensive. I have long supported the state of Israeli and still do, but I wanted to write something about the Palestinians that while humorous in a black sort of way depicted them as real people.

The book I chose to parody guaranteed the article would be offensive but just how offensive I had no way of knowing. The piece probably caused more hurt than anything else I have ever written. I got short rude letters accusing me of fascism and long anguished tracts from people who felt profoundly let down and betrayed by me. There were angry letters to the editor and complaints to the race relations conciliator. I was charged with being anti-semitic and fomenting anti-semitism.

It was all very heavy for a while, but then came the massacre of hundreds of Palestinian civilians in the Sabra and Shatila camps in Beruit. A massacre carried out over two days by Lebanese Christian militia men while Israeli troops watched from surrounding high buildings and kindly assisted by the dropping of flares at night.

I stand by everything I wrote except for perhaps the last paragraph. As others have commented it is all too neat and easy to compare the Israelis to Nazis, but just because the inversion is effortless it doesn't make the equation correct. Indeed the equation is obscene, which is why the Israelis do themselves damage when they behave in a manner that invites the comparison.

No matter, if the piece was a cruel lie to many it was, at least to one man anyway, the dinkum oil. At David Lange's fortieth birthday celebrations in the Opposition Caucus rooms, to which the Press Gallery were invited, dear old Mick Connelly came up to me and said, 'How were things in Lebanon, Tom? I read your thing in the mag, pretty rugged over there now I reckon . . .'

The Diary of Anna Farouk

Dear Diary,

It is very hot here tonight. Very hot and very still. My palm is sticking to the paper as I write this. Of course the air conditioning no longer works. Still we are lucky to have power at all, even if the voltage surges so that one minute the room is dim and the next it is as if a flare has exploded silently.

Beirut is very quiet tonight. Nothing moves. Well almost nothing. I heard some machine-gun fire a while back and sometimes an ambulance wails in the distance but we don't mind that. It is when they wail close by that you have to worry. Essentially the streets are empty. There is only the drifting rubbish and the Syrian roadblocks, though Grandad, who doesn't like the Syrians much after they made a botch of amputating his leg when he was wounded in the Yom Kippur war, reckons that drifting rubbish and Syrian roadblocks amount to the same thing, or that at the very least only the trained eye can tell the difference. My brother Achmed doesn't like him saying things like that and usually asks him where his sense of Arab solidarity is and Grandad says it's back with bits of his leg, scattered somewhere on the West Bank.

They often argue like that but tonight they are silent. In the radio news, they said the Israeli ambassador in London was the victim of an attempted assassination. Achmed and Anwar my younger brother, who is only 12, cheered. Grandad swore under his breath. He said it wouldn't surprise him if the Israelis shot their own man — anything to create

an excuse to invade Lebanon and shoot Palestinians. Achmed disagreed. He feels the Israelis have long since stopped feeling any need to contrive excuses to shoot Palestinians.

Anwar felt that even sending the madman Begin a whoopee cushion through the mail would be considered a provocative act and he doubted that our PLO would stoop to assassination attempts in foreign capitals. Achmed blamed the Syrians but Grandad disputed that on the grounds that a Syrian marksman would have missed completely. I don't get to contribute to these top-level discussions. I just clear the table, which isn't easy when the boys are stripping and cleaning their beloved Kalashnikovs and tossing coins to see whose turn it is to have the bullet. Grandad retired early but I saw him staring at the ceiling. The thought of another war saddens him. He is determined to die on Palestinian soil and to that end always carries with him a small bag of pebbles he gathered in Jerusalem. That way he is ready even if the Israelis get us with a direct hit.

Dear Diary,

Last night I had a vivid dream. I was walking in the hills behind Beirut with Grandad and the air was sweet with the smell of thyme and cedar. Then a terrible wind came up and black clouds and thunder and I woke up crying. The room was full of dust and smoke. Part of the wall was gone and the apartment block across the street was gone too. There was just concrete and debris and a lot of people screaming.

The Israelis came five days ago. We heard they had crossed the border and were advancing up the coast, then one fine morning the F-15s and F-16s came in waves to drop their bombs. The bombardment went on through the night and all the next day. We had to abandon our rooms and go to a cellar. While the earth over our heads thudded we listened to the radio.

Reception wasn't very good but we learnt that the madman Begin wasn't after a square millimetre of Lebanese territory. He just wanted the citizens of Galilee to no longer have to suffocate in bomb shelters day and night. Achmed swore and said bitterly that all the Israelis wanted was 'breathing space'. Anwar was convinced that all the Israeli soldiers must hate Arabs. Grandad said this wasn't the case at all. They just took orders from Defence Minister Ariel Sharon and *he* hated all Arabs.

Dear Diary,

We have had to leave our cellar. The Israelis' tanks are now on the edge of the city but shell us only intermittently because of the ceasefire which is now in force. Food and water supplies are running low but Achmed turned up with a newspaper from somewhere today and we learnt that Princess Di and Prince Charles have had their baby. Naturally I was pleased though my brothers did not share in my excitement. The maternity hospital across from the dugout we currently occupy was shelled by the Israelis yesterday. Most of the children died instantly.

Dear Diary,

Food shortage now critical. Last night I had to casserole the newspaper and share it among 10 men. The Israelis as well as bombing us are trying to starve us into submission, Grandad is getting restless.

This morning he eyed our dwindling supply of brackish water, rose to his full height, stared into the distance and hobbled to the door, saying he was going to see a man about a camel and might be some time. He disappeared around the drums filled with concrete and the sandbags and there was an angry burst of mortar fire and within seconds he had flung himself back through the entrance saying it hadn't taken as long as he thought.

I wish Anwar and Achmed were here. They are trying to get into East Beirut via the sewers and bring back some food and water. They missed our beloved PLO Chairman Yassir Arafat this afternoon. He came into our rubble-strewn avenue surrounded by bodyguards. He wore a white khefya, a khaki shirt and a silver pistol in a holster of plaited brown plastic. Thick bulbous lips protruded out over a receding chin. How my heart went out to him. I tried to offer him some of my newspaper casserole but within seconds he was gone. Grandad understands Arafat's deep sorrow. He points out that the Jews spent 40 years wandering in the Sinai wilderness on their way home to the promised land. Think what the Palestinians could achieve with a good road map and a reliable convoy of four-wheel-drive vehicles.

Dear Diary,

Today Israeli Skyhawks flew overhead, glinting in the sun and dropping pamphlets instead of bombs and anti-personnel devices like the cluster bombs. We were warned the pamphlets were contaminated but we read one of them anyway. The Israelis were offering us Palestinians safe passage if we gave ourselves up. Achmed tore it up angrily and said it was a ploy.

He scattered the fragments in the wind which rather put the kybosh on the soup I had planned. Who wants grapes, white figs, arak, kebab, grilled liver, tomatoes, yoghurt, onions and fried eggs for breakfast, I asked. They all said they would love some, and somewhat coolly I replied wouldn't we all, and turned on my heel having made my point.

Dear Diary,

I am very scared now. The shelling continues and whole neighbourhoods are ablaze day and night. Achmed and Anwar did not return from their last trip to East Beirut. Well some of Achmed did, and Grandad gave up his beloved pebbles to bury his grandson in the correct earth. Grandad is now convinced the Israelis are hell-bent on killing us all. Perhaps he's right. I pray for the safe release the Israelis have promised.

Dear Diary,

Can this be true? We are saved. What's left of us, that is, will be allowed onto the boats. They are sending trucks for us in the morning. They are very apologetic. At such short notice they will have to be cattle trucks. We don't mind. Then for public health considerations there will be delousing. Everyone will strip off and hop into the showers. I can't wait.

Listener, July 24, 1982

Dam Blusters

Dr Erich Geiringer is convinced that if the topsy-turvy course of events here in the capital proves anything it proves there is a patient God. Every Monday the good Lord delivers unto the Labour Party a host of things with which to bludgeon the Government and by week's end they have cocked them all up. (I used the term 'cocked up' advisedly. I know that TVNZ has introduced a new list outlawing certain expletives but I'm assuming this column will be read after 8.30 at night, and/or every reader will be accompanied by an adult.)

With inflation in the second quarter of this year leaping to an annual rate of 20 per cent; with the director of the Institute of Economic Research, Brian Easton, suggesting that up to 20 per cent of the populace lived below the 'poverty line'; with the imminent closure of the Patea freezing works and the loss of 800 jobs there; with the virtual collapse of the proposed Aramoana smelter; with the threatened mothballing of the Clutha river hydro schemes; with all this, the Government should be groggy and on the ropes. But, wily old pugilist that he is, the PM knows that the key to avoiding a knock-down is to keep moving, irrespective of the direction, and consequently we have an administration that is still standing and a Labour Party that looks badly concussed.

The masterstroke was the wage and price freeze. A wage freeze alone was what he really wanted but that would have been too obviously unfair so the PM headed for the fridge with the entire economy to put wages in the freezer and prices in the butter warmer.

The move is easily the most Draconian measure of its kind since wartime regulations, and one former Treasury head describes it as more socialist than anything contemplated by previous Labour governments. Many officials were critical of the move on the grounds that it solved nothing in the medium and long term, but the PM, who regards the day after tomorrow as belonging to the dim and distant future, knows full well that in the medium term he is unlikely to be in power and long term he'll be somewhere else introducing 3 per cent cuts in harp allowances and the like.

The PM, who specialises in striking while the irony is hot, introduced the freeze despite his own previous utterance that such measures rarely work, and at the same time made a mockery of all the calls within his own party for a more-market, free-enterprise economy. A friend of mine argues now that wholesale nationalisation of industry can no longer be discounted.

As part of the old one-two the PM then neatly blamed the Clutha impasse as it is known in polite circles, or balls-up if you are reading this after 8.30, on the Opposition parties in general and Brian Mac-Donell and Mike Minogue in particular. The mess is entirely of the Government's making and Energy Minister Bill Birch (whose name offends many conservationists yet didn't make the TVNZ list) responded in a most extraordinary fashion by claiming the High Court's ruling, that the water rights application should go back to the Planning Tribunal, showed 'Our faith in the democratic process was misplaced.' Former High Court Justice Peter Mahon was moved to describe the remark as savouring of fascism.

To be fair to Birch, when the High Court decided that the end use of the power should be a factor in consideration of a water right application for the high dam the Government had the unenviable choice of (a) inventing new uses for the power in the wake of the smelter's demise or (b) taking the relatively simple step of empowering legislation. Obviously the Government would rather build the dam first and worry about using the power later. If the worst came to the worst we could give it away or offer so much Southland lignite for every thousand gigawatts consumed. According to the Coalition for Open Government's Keith Johnstone the Government could easily have returned to the Planning Tribunal with a proposal to electrify the main trunk line and install spotlights all the way down the line so passengers could look at the Southern Alps at night.

Empowering legislation however was not to be the simple solution it first seemed. Both Opposition parties were indeed in opposition and Mike Minogue, who has opposed this sort of legislation in the past only to capitulate at the last minute, made it plain he would not be moved this time. In a situation where he should have taken to sobbing at his desk, the PM naturally went on the offensive. He ignored the constitutional wrangles and concentrated on the number of jobs that would be lost if the work on the dam had to stop. He stopped millimetres short of advising workers' wives and families, if and when the money ran out and the kids needed bread and shoes, to go along to the shops and charge everything up to Minogue and MacDonell, the Labour MP who wanted to support the high dam.

About then Labour and Social Credit, who had been trumpeting about the rule of law being paramount, began to look queasy.

What followed was the great exodus of politicians to the dam site, where, surrounded by burly construction workers and afforded little protection by their canary yellow plastic helmets, constitutional niceties doubtless seemed less compelling. Quite wisely the PM declined all invitations to visit Cromwell. He would have been the target of a lot of anger, unnecessary duplication as Bill Rowling was already receiving much of that anyway.

One can understand the workers' concern. Up to 600 could have lost their jobs and nightly they returned home to distressed families. It was the uncertainty. At least the 800 workers at Patea and the extra 4000 unemployed this month had the quiet satisfaction of *knowing* they had no jobs. Also there is a romance about hydro construction. It's part of our 'young nation on the move' mythology. How many television commercials about the DFC, cars, and chewing gum can you recall being filmed in a slaughterhouse where the workforce is mostly Maori? It's just not the same.

Labour's solution to the conundrum was first to suggest that the work could proceed if the Government passed an Order in Council declaring the Clutha to be of national importance. This of course would amount to much the same interference in the judicial process as afforded by the loathsome empowering legislation. A Labour delegation later visited three Government Ministers with a package which among other things proposed fast-tracking the Planning Tribunal and construction of a low dam. After cursory scrutiny the Government emerged to dismiss the compromise.

An angry Rowling insisted afterwards they wouldn't have had time to 'hitch up their trousers' before running to the news media. Actually Jim McLay had time to hitch up his trousers, adjust his tie and powder his nose before meeting the press.

The debate, however, as it evolved was not so much about a high dam versus a low dam as about high cunning versus low cunning. While Labour proved deficient on both counts the Social Credit compromise is a masterly amalgam of the two. First they delayed until the Government had summarily tossed out the Labour deal. Having contemptuously rejected one deal, the Government was obliged to go through the motions of considering the second package more carefully. Second, Bruce Beetham came up with the idea of allowing the Planning Tribunal to run its course and if the decision was unfavourable getting Parliament to convene itself as the highest court in the land and quash the ruling. Rather than change the rules in the middle of the game to ensure victory, the Government would merely alter the score at the end.

There were attendant conditions as well about irrigation schemes and a nod to the workers at Patea, along with the Government having to promise in writing that it would never again rain on Mother's Day.

At the time of writing Controller and Auditor-General Fred Shailes, who has the power to stop work on the dam, seemed well disposed to the Socred scheme. My own solution is the Controller and Auditor-General De-empowering Bill but as we say here after 8.30 that would be like using a sledge hammer to cure scrotal mange.

Listener, July 31, 1982

Signal Success

Friday

Here I am in Wellington the same day the National Party are holding their 46th annual conference in Hamilton. I can hardly believe my good luck. Political conferences are hard enough but four days at the Te Rapa racecourse is more than I could bear. The very thought sends shudders down my spine. Not that I have anything against Hamilton. They say a lot of nice people come from Hamilton and it's just the ones that stay that give the place a bad name.

Right about the time Sir George Chapman is delivering his final and most serious warning to the party and calling for unity I am here in the capital buying a plastic bucket and Napisan. That's partly why I couldn't go. Many months ago in a weak moment I promised my wife I would take two weeks' annual leave when our child was born. I still have obligations to the *Listener* and the nation though, and have resolved to faithfully monitor the said conference by reading all the newspapers and watching television at the appropriate time. In some ways this would be a bold and innovative approach; I would be telling the public what they already knew.

Unfortunately I am serving up pudding during the 6.30 news so from the outset I am condemned to tell the public less than they already know which is even more bold and innovative than I had intended. Ian Fraser's conference highlights programme is on at the ungodly hour of 11.40 p.m. and thanks to our latest addition I am not getting the requisite amounts of sleep a grown man needs, but I am not allowed to complain as my nipples are neither (a) cracked nor (b) being sucked at four-hourly intervals.

I cope very well with *Yes Minister,* doze off a bit during *The Body in Question* and defy anyone to stay awake during *Cleo Laine and James Galway.* I am instantly alert though for *National Party Conference 1982.* Interior shots of the Te Rapa racecourse bring memories of the 1977 Royal Tour flooding back. It was here that two Fleet Street photographers nearly came to blows over the fact that it could be Saturday in New Zealand and only Friday in England. I had to intervene with the explanation that thanks to the arbitrary placement of the international dateline New Zealand was the first place in the world to get the sun. Then as now one couldn't escape the feeling that this was a dreadful waste.

Next up is Ian Fraser looking cool and professional and with him is Professor Keith Jackson from Canterbury University. Jackson has a moustacheless beard, modern wire-frame spectacles that somehow look horn-rimmed, and a high-domed forehead. The total effect is one of vague but prodigious intelligence. His enthusiasm for politics never seems to flag, though I suspect that if you chained him to a bus shelter for three days without food or water and only lolly wrappers to read he would still describe the experience as absolutely fascinating. Ian Fraser points out that Sir George Chapman's speech wasn't exactly what the delegates wanted to hear, that the PM's handling of the economy has come in for much criticism, and that Derek Quigley got a warm reception. Jackson says that there are strong undercurrents afoot and clear signals are being expressed by the delegates.

Saturday

Terrible night. New baby obviously believes itself to be a possum or some other nocturnal creature. My view expressed at 3.30 a.m, 4.00 a.m. and 4.30 a.m. that you spare the rod and spoil the child falls on deaf ears. Suffering badly from lack of sleep I am still required to referee the second half of Jacob's soccer match. Jacob and others object loudly and at length when I award a penalty to the other side. I eventually have to approach parents of the boys in other team with a view to forming a flying V at full-time to protect me from my own lads. Unused to this much physical activity, I develop painful cramps in calf muscles of both legs and should have no trouble staying awake for conference report.

Had hoped to read the *Evening Post* but Jacob is our paperboy and whenever he is short we are the first house to miss out. In spite of cramps I fall asleep in front of the telly and wake up in the middle of a film about the last days of Hitler in the bunker. Crazed and shaking he stalks the bunker ranting and foaming about betrayal. I drift off and wake up to find the screen filled with the PM delivering his leader's address to the party faithful. I'm confused at first but then the reassuring images of Ian Fraser and Keith Jackson hove into view. Fraser doesn't think the PM has told the party what they want to hear and Jackson says there are strong undercurrents and clear signals reverberating about the hall. Observers at the conference rate the PM's address highly. It was, according to some, a skilful lesson in political pragmatism. Essentially the PM says you can't do anything in politics unless you take the people with you.

What you can't do in one year you do in two. What you can't do in one term you do in two. Party faithful are now worried that what you can't do in one century you do in two. Newspaper stories tell of growing resentment after the PM's address which probably accounts for the fact that at the social function which follows the entire dance floor does the hokey tokey. Desperate people do desperate things.

Sunday

Young Nationals hold their AGM and the Attorney General, Jim McLay, tells them: 'You have a white Anglo-Saxon privileged look about you and

for that matter you have a distinct white Anglo-Saxon privileged sound about you.' In other words they look just like Jim used to a few years ago. Pressure definitely building up. Looking white, Anglo-Saxon and privileged used to be, like Anzus and the nuclear family, the cornerstone of our way of life.

Sir George Chapman, the man who once said he'd rather have a company directorship than a knighthood, is farewelled and given his own home computer. What has happened to monogrammed cufflinks and crystal decanters?

Choosing a successor, Jackson tells Fraser, has added greatly to the strong undercurrents and clear signals being reverberated around the hall. The lobbying has been intense and Jackson wouldn't like to have to pick a winner at this stage.

Monday
A very bad night. The dog, clearly displeased by the new arrival, retaliates in the only way she knows in the early hours of the dawn. I am finishing the last of the mopping up and sterilising the squeegee when I learn from the radio that Sue Wood is the new president of the National Party. I shrug off fatigue and give a weak cheer. Apparently she won by a country kilometre in the second ballot.

Delegates frustrated in their efforts to debate party philosophy as a late remit are jubilant at the result.

On television Wood exudes a relentless niceness and speaks in PR shorthand, but it would be wrong to see her victory as only a symbolic gesture. Behind the amorphous charm there beats a steely intelligence and disciplined ambition. Ian Fraser wondered if she could stand up to the PM. Keith Jackson wasn't sure. Elsewhere, however, there were strong undercurrents and clear signals that many in the party expected her not only to stand up to him but to tower over him as well.

Listener, August 21, 1982

Whipping Yarns

Donald Charles McKinnon is the Senior Government Whip. Jonathan Lucas Hunt is the Senior Opposition Whip. They sit opposite each other in the Chamber in benches directly behind their leaders. Most days you can see them gesticulating at each other across the floor, one or the other performing a peculiar semaphore to attract attention until they both bob down and exchange information via telephone.

The new phones, with their glamorous pushbutton dialling to reduce noise, were McKinnon's idea. They do more than save him the five-metre stroll to Hunt's bench. From the sanctuary of his bench McKinnon can ring anyone in the building and keep in touch with Cabinet Ministers anywhere in the country. Traditionally Whips like to know where their members are — and with a working majority of one McKinnon *has* to know. The New Zealand Parliament requires a relatively large quorum, 20, and it is the Government's job — or more specifically McKinnon's job — to keep enough National members in the House to maintain both a quorum and a majority. It's not easy but the honourable tradition of 'pairing' helps. The system is widely misunderstood but essentially it means that if some Government MPs have good reason for being absent the same number of Opposition MPs will agree to abstain on any division.

It is probably best likened to a primary school swimming lesson where every child is given a 'buddy' and at a peep of the teacher's whistle all the buddies stop frolicking and hold their hands together aloft. If you had an even number of children to begin with, a solitary child with one arm aloft is proof that someone is dead on the bottom. If every child has a buddy the teacher has nothing to worry about unless through some cruel twist of fate a pair of children are dead on the bottom.

Having been granted pairs or buddies, of course, it is the Whip's job to see that no one wanders off early to the dressing sheds. When the present Minister of Works, Tony Friedlander, was the Senior Government Whip, vigilance took the form of tartly expressed notes to offenders. One night a few years back Norm Jones left the Chamber briefly, to return to a signed curt warning that if the bench was empty again all future leave could be cancelled. Jones was about to foam at the mouth when he noticed that Ken Comber a bench or two away had just been called to a phone in the lobby. Comber quite rightly prided himself on his record as a sitter in the House; his service was above and beyond the call of duty as well as common sense. To Jones it seemed the perfect time to slip the note onto his desk. The member for Wellington Central returned jauntily to his seat, radiating his usual goodwill until he glanced down and saw the message. Burning with indignation Comber bounded to Friedlander's desk demanding an explanation from the pale and hapless member for New Plymouth.

Being a Whip is a rigorous and at times unpleasant and thankless job, but both McKinnon and Hunt take issue with the legend that a good Whip has to be hated and feared. Both take pride in the fact that they were elected unopposed by their respective caucuses.

If anyone served the right apprenticeship for the role I suppose it was McKinnon. His father was a Major General, his brother is headmaster of Wanganui Collegiate, and McKinnon himself was the founder organiser and tutor of a very successful Paremoremo Prison debating club. He had a relaxed easy manner with the prisoners then and the same nonchalance pervades his dealings with his charges in a very different sort of prison today. He strolls about the House with the big-boned gait of a farmer, a sleepy grin on his face, but he says he can never drop his guard for a moment. The Government drew a division earlier this year and although the damage was minimal the psychological blow was painful. His colleagues were shaken in a way outsiders wouldn't understand. Still they appreciate the sense of proportion McKinnon brings to the job. Everything matters but ultimately not that much. 'If we miss a division,' he grins, 'obviously we can resubmit the measure when we have the numbers. It is not that serious but if anyone does happen to miss a vote I will almost tear them to pieces!'

The role of a Whip has been described as falling somewhere between head prefect and matron in a boys' school, but McKinnon likes the analogy of a halfback between the executive and caucus. Hunt prefers to see himself as Labour's equivalent to David Thomson, the Leader of the House. It's a job Hunt wouldn't mind when Labour return to office.

Hunt's credentials for his current job include a spell as a Junior Government Whip and later the job of acting Speaker during the term of the third Labour Government. Like McKinnon, he thrives on the job.

Hunt has a deep affection for Parliament as an institution. In his 16 years in the House, unlike almost everyone else, he has hardly aged at all and is becoming something of an institution himself. He believes in the Norm Kirk dictum that you should read a page of the Standing Orders a day. 'There are only four or five people here who really understand Standing Orders.' He shakes his head in lofty regret. He doesn't so much stroll around the Chamber as strut like a well-fed seal, brushing his lapels with his fingertips and whispering instructions to the troops out of the corner of his mouth, his lips barely moving at all. Yet behind the fussy, sometimes pompous

manner there lies considerable patience and kindness. Colleagues who have personal or domestic problems — which, given the number of new members with young families, is a growing occurrence — are readily granted leave. Hunt bridles at the Social Credit accusations of a cosy relationship between Labour and National on pairs. Hunt insists the system is rigorous but humane and he cites proudly the letter of appreciation he received from Duncan MacIntyre's son when the critically ill Deputy Prime Minister was granted a pair earlier this year.

McKinnon wonders why some pairs are granted and others turned down. Recently Bob Bell and Ben Couch were excused for electorate duties while two Ministers supposed to address conferences were refused. Looking at the legislative programme, McKinnon took a risk and secretly dispatched them anyway, which left his side without an operating majority. Labour lost the opportunity to score a 'psychological blow' when three of their members were given leave to go to the movies. Annoyed at the refusal of pairs in the first instance the Government deliberately publicised Labour's lost opportunity, albeit a slight one, to score a psychological blow of their own.

McKinnon was the publicist for that but he stresses that there is no element of one-upmanship between the Whips. Although they seldom mix socially, apart from the odd morning tea with the Speaker, the relationship is one of mutual trust and respect. A relationship which must survive the unpleasant messages they are often obliged to deliver on behalf of their bosses. Both men work closely with their leaders to shape strategy and tactics in the House and select committees. For Hunt this means arranging who will speak on what and when, and to this end he keeps meticulous records of how long every colleague has spoken. McKinnon doesn't bother with charts. He likes the freedom to manoeuvre at short notice. He has more room to move in that he can control, in consultation with the Leader of the House, the daily legislative load. Recently the Government deliberately introduced five tax measures on the same day. 'If stuff is going to hit the fan you might as well load it up and slow down the blades!' he grins. 'We know every newspaper in the country only has one front page.'

Neither man enjoys admonishing colleagues or dealing with battered egos. Maintaining morale is partly their responsibility and in the process they learn a lot about their colleagues' strengths and weaknesses. They have to lead by example and every day Hunt is at his desk before 8 a.m. and rarely home before midnight. McKinnon has had three hours' leave this year.

Listener, September 18, 1982

Loss Leader

Who will lead the Labour Party into the next election? If Bill Rowling was just half as good at winning elections as he is at beating back challenges to his leadership the question would never arise. Even his critics in the Opposition caucus ruefully concede the member for Tasman will be difficult to dislodge. The party at large regard him with an affection bordering on ferocious and at their last annual conference they demanded some say in any future leadership contest, though the mechanism for computing this input was never defined.

This affection, which Rowling assiduously courts while pretending not to, is made up of equal parts of respect and sympathy. There is something strangely unifying in a party that feels sorry for its leader and sorry for itself. It may not be in the party's interest and sometimes it certainly isn't in Rowling's.

It grew out of the humiliations and reversals he has endured on their behalf and it invites him to endure even more. On occasions it threatens his physical well-being. On election night in '78 dejected supporters valiantly lifted their defeated hero aloft without checking the height of the ceiling and he was thumped into the rafters. Last year in Richmond when the early election results looked good for Labour he was borne into the town hall shoulder-high and only quick thinking on his part prevented serious concussion when they came through the door. Later the same evening, with victory ebbing away, tipsy supporters lifted him unsteadily on high and a frail old lady was knocked to the floor.

It is Rowling's tragedy that he is not wired for the hurly-burly of opposition. The skills which would make an excellent Prime Minister are of little use in the bull-ring. He is altogether too gracious and reserved. These qualities serve him well in defeat. For three elections now reporters have admired his dignity and composure in the face of extreme disappointment. Last year in Richmond, talking to the press in his own home the day after the election, his eyes red-rimmed with fatigue and sorrow, he saw to it personally that everyone had a chair or was comfortable before the questioning began.

Some in the Labour caucus are prepared to forgo dignity in defeat in favour of unabashed glee in victory and the press can slug it out among themselves for the chairs. Not that David Lange, were he to succeed Rowling, would behave like that if he led Labour to victory in the next election. Glee would be strictly abashed and the victory toast would be limited to half a glass of diet cola per man.

It now seems certain that the Lange camp will challenge Rowling next February when the leadership vote comes up in caucus. First there was Rowling's announcement after his long trip abroad that no one else in the party was quite ready to be leader. Shortly after that, he claimed — 'not immodestly', as he put it — that being leader required a significant amount of political experience, which only he had. This hurt some of his colleagues and delighted Government members, who weren't slow to say it added insult to injury and at the next Labour caucus everyone agreed that any MP comparing their own ability with that of others would in future be censured.

While designed to take the leadership battle and its attendant divisions and bitterness off the front pages, this resolution could pose problems in other areas. Members are prone to shouting 'Good speech!' when one of their number has resumed his seat — now this reflex bravura will have to be accompanied by the qualifier 'Not that all our side's speeches aren't good, mind you ...', which will dampen the effect somewhat.

Second, the latest public opinion poll on preferred leaders puts Lange well in front of his boss. The Lange camp were hoping Rowling would walk the plank quietly but now it seems open mutiny is necessary and the polls will lend daring to their ambition. (Such a move will not please the party at large but the Lange camp can point with some justification to Jack Marshall's replacement as leader of the National Party. The elevation of Rob Muldoon was not wanted by the party hierarchy or the rank and file but the parliamentary team saw the change as necessary to achieve electoral success.)

The poll in question was taken while Rowling was overseas and confirmed what everyone on the Hill already knew — that Lange had acquitted himself very well in his leader's absence. Even to the extent of threatening to expel people who leaked information to the media about the party's finances. It was a stern warning to some of his more rash supporters. The leak was designed to discredit party president Jim Anderton, a Rowling supporter, and it came from some zealot in the Lange camp hoping to dent the grand designs Anderton is presumed to have.

It's all a little unsavoury and perhaps unnecessary when you consider that Labour and National are virtually level-pegging in the polls. Rowling the reluctant Leader of the Opposition is a different proposition on the campaign trail. He performs very well there, making up a lot of ground, but Labour's problem is that it seems to go into every election a good 10 points behind. With the parties now so close, Rowling must be itching to have another go and Lange must be wondering how big a part he played in the narrowing of the gap.

With Lange better suited to the rough and tumble of the chamber and Rowling the ideal campaign trailer, obviously the best interests of the Labour Party would be served by sending Rowling overseas

I'm the only one battle-hardened enough to lead the Labour Party

Runner Up c.78 · ALSO RAN c.75 · No 2 in 81

indefinitely and leaving Lange in charge of affairs in the House. Then when the next election is announced Rowling could return and take over from the pacemaker for the last lap. It is such a simple solution that you can guarantee the Labour Party won't think of it and the clawing and scratching for position will continue until February.

Should Rowling be defeated he wouldn't want to hang on as deputy so there is another, quieter struggle for that potential vacancy. As a healing gesture the new deputy would probably come from the Rowling camp. Accordingly Russell Marshall and Ann Hercus are out and running. Hercus is hitting the Rotary circuit with her charts and graphs about borrowing and public spending and Marshall is going up-market talking to United Nations Associations and the like.

Marshall, who is praised for his contribution to the Imprest and Supply debate by no less a person than the PM, has decided to repay this embarrassment by outflanking the member for Tamaki and calling for changes to the world economy even more radical than those advocated by the PM.

The PM reiterated his case for a new Bretton Woods conference at the regional Commonwealth summit in Suva and won a qualified victory of sorts when the final communique 'noted with appreciation' the proposal. Originally it was 'welcomed' but in the face of Australian opposition the wording was diluted.

Clearly the Australians hadn't forgotten or forgiven the PM's sabotage of the 'Melbourne Declaration' at the last Commonwealth summit. The PM called that 'words, words, words', but it seems that words like 'appreciation' do matter if you are on the winning end.

The PM and Fraser have clashed at the last three Commonwealth Heads of Government meetings, sometimes quite bitterly. The PM's latest suggestion — that Fraser's reservations about his proposals were based on his inability to understand them — won't help, and it came as no surprise when Fraser announced on his return to Canberra that a signing for CER was still a long way off.

Some people never learn. Some people can't see the Bretton Woods for the trees.

Listener, November 6, 1982

National Government speeds up 'fast track' planning procedures. (Open Government Report, December 1982)

All over Bar the Doubting

The scenes on the third floor were almost without precedent. Not since the early 70s, when these rooms were part of the Prime Minister's Department, had there been such drama and excitement there. Big changes were in the wind and more than 40 journalists and technicians had congregated in the long corridor. The red and black power cables feeding the gear of the four television crews ran like the entrails of a terrible beast down the yellow carpet to the old cabinet room where the crucial caucus meeting would take place.

Inside, one Labour MP who had arrived early, sat contemplating the seven pictures of former Labour leaders. 'I have been given riding instructions from my LEC,' he confided with a sly smile, 'but they'll be staying in my pocket.'

Outside under the heat and glare of the television lights his colleagues gathered nervously for their last cuppa before the big moment. Russell Marshall glided past, calm and serene. Bill Rowling attempted light conversation with David Lange, who managed to look suitably solemn. Party president Jim Anderton looked like he hadn't slept. Ann Hercus's smile was creased with tension. Grinning broadly Mike Moore announced that he knew he was the ugliest contender for deputy leader. The man who was eventually to beat him by one vote, Geoffrey Palmer, arrived unruffled, jacket draped casually over his shoulder. He'd just done 20 lengths of the Beehive pool and looked like a man who either knew he had it won or genuinely didn't care either way.

Eventually Opposition Chief Whip Jonathan Hunt shepherded his flock away from the tea urn and we were ushered down the corridor and the caucus doors closed. It took less than an hour but it was a nervous time for us as well. There was more than the future of the Labour Party at stake. More than the future of the country. Some of us had made predictions and now had vested interests in the outcome. So we listened to the distant bursts of applause much like doctors listening to a heart murmur. What did it mean?

Forty-five minutes after they had gone in, the doors opened and a jovial Rowling, flanked by a less pleased Anderton, led out Lange and Palmer. Amid the sounds of scribbling and the clicking on of cassettes could be heard tiny sighs of relief mixed with quiet groans. Lange expressed his relief that it was all over. Palmer, genuinely dazed, could only give a silly grin and say he felt humble.

Their colleagues pressed past us in the corridor and the general response seemed to be one of relief tinged with euphoria. For a few, the result came as a shock. Hercus could not conceal her hurt. She went straight to her room, where close friends guarded the door. If the party at large were divided over who should be leader they were at least resigned to the fact that the country as a whole was for Lange. Given that imperative they wanted a deputy of their choice and 35 LECs are said to have instructed their MPs to vote for the Lyttelton wonder woman.

As with Marshall, this support did not translate into votes. She received only nine of the 43 votes cast and was eliminated on the first ballot. Some of her colleagues doubtless felt that the push for her election was orchestrated by the Anderton machine. Others considered how well she would work with Lange, all too aware of the problems that arise when the people in charge are incompatible. Hercus, before leaving for overseas, released a press statement pointedly congratulating Palmer and omitting any reference to Lange.

Mike Moore, who wanted the No 2 spot just as desperately, was just as disappointed. But he delivered personally around the Press Gallery a gracious press statement congratulating both Palmer and Lange. The dark circles under his fierce blue eyes looked freshly nuggeted and he seemed even more like an old boxer than ever. While free of self-pity he made no effort to disguise his sorrow. 'You spill your guts for the party and this happens . . .' Then the grin returned. 'Judging from who was on my list and who was on the others we have about 60 people in our caucus!'

Had Moore been elected, Lange would have been delighted. But it would have outraged some Labour MPs, one of whom threatened to resign and force an immediate by-election.

The also-ran for leader, Russell Marshall, seemed quite unperturbed by defeat, exuding the Methodist equivalent of Zen calm. He'd seen to it that Lange wasn't elected unopposed and was pleased about the deputy leadership too. Although a close friend and admirer of Hercus he eventually opted for Palmer as the best complement to Lange.

Others who voted for Palmer instead of Hercus did so on the grounds that as the leadership had been decided like a popularity contest there was no need to treat the race for deputy in the same way, so the will of the party was tacitly ignored.

Whatever Lange thought privately, he appeared delighted with the leadership mix when he and Palmer held their first press conference. Asked about the combination he used an old trick of the PM's to describe it himself and define for the public their response to it. The pairing, he said, could have come straight from a manual and the chemistry was immensely attractive.

The conference was a lively affair, frequently interrupted by laughter as Lange fielded questions with an awesome battery of quips and bon mots. In the main he sought to establish that it didn't matter that

he wasn't an economist, and that the charges against him that he was lazy were untrue, the work of his political enemies, and didn't worry him at all. (In truth the charges come from friend and foe, and he is sensitive to the criticism.)

All in all it was a good start, even if a little like a child's birthday party — lots of colour, glitter and dazzle, but precious little food value.

The *Newsmakers* special, however, taped a few hours later with Ian Fraser, was considerably less assured and at times chillingly inept. He sounded all right. It was what he said that was disturbing. Lange has said of himself that his greatest political strength is his ability to articulate a vision and Fraser invited him to unveil it, and shrewdly let him go without interruption.

Lange began by saying he had a conviction that New Zealand was a richly endowed country with an unmatched population mix, adding that this vision wasn't really a vision because he could see it already in a school in his electorate. Still, he wanted to 'communicate the incredible richness in the living experience of the people who are put together'.

'If I talk about these things in terms of a vision it is because they are rooted in me,' he said, and went on to explain that this vision came partly from the fact the state intervened to give him free school milk. A little worried he asked out loud: 'Can you communicate a vision rationally?'

He wanted to be a person who really wanted to say something for himself and for the people he felt for. These things would at times be emotional and not necessarily utterly coherent. 'But I tell you it is what the Labour Party's about!'

He carried on some more about supporting creative people. He had a conviction about that too, then he conceded he could 'articulate these things or write them'. Then, tossing in the towel altogether, he added: 'I'm simply saying, accept me as a person with a soul and not just a mechanic.'

Small wonder that Palmer, who had earlier been describing himself as the backroom boy and Lange as the great communicator, was within hours intervening politely with, 'What I think David was trying to say . . .'

Listener, February 26, 1983

Dilutions of Grandeur

I have had occasion in the past to describe the PM, somewhat coarsely perhaps, as being a tough, pragmatic man with both his feet and his knuckles planted firmly on the ground. Early in his Ministry he was like those ute commercials you see on television. He could, it seemed, go anywhere and when he did it was the jeep that shook. He was so fierce it was said that when he shouted half the Cabinet disgraced themselves and his echo came back and apologised for interrupting.

Ah yes, they were happy days, but things change. Journalists are always writing off sportsmen and politicians on the reasonable premise that eventually they must be proved right, but still it can be fairly said now of the PM that there is a borrowed quality to his authority. And even more disturbing from his point of view are the mutterings from within the National Party that a mortgage sale might not be a bad idea.

Talk of a decline in the PM's powers is misleading, however, unless you measure the depletion against the original stockpile. The power he appropriated by sheer force of will was staggering, so even as the erosion accelerates he remains a formidable figure. Certainly there is only minimal diminution in his ability to inspire psychic dread in those who encounter him at close quarters. One senior gallery journalist confesses that he has no problems dealing with the PM if he prepares himself emotionally beforehand, but a meeting without warning in a corridor will weaken him at the knee and set his heart thumping. Others are just as susceptible. Crossing from Parliament to the Reserve Bank on foot one day last year, the PM virtually brought traffic to a halt and had pedestrians scattering out of his path. It was as if there had been a secret police warning about a pear-shaped man on the run with gelignite strapped to his chest who wasn't to be approached under any circumstances.

For all that, his few press conferences this year have been curiously understated affairs. He hasn't actually come out in a sweater yet and sung 'Moon River' but he's come close. While the tickings-off of the news media have not been entirely abandoned, the reprimands have had a half-hearted, reflex air about them. He hasn't bothered with the new Labour leadership, apart from some bored asides. Indeed his best effort on the issue to date has been to suggest that while David Lange might wake people up, Geoffrey Palmer would put them back to sleep again. While neat enough in its own way the remark is patently untrue, as anyone who has heard Palmer speak in the House will attest. Whenever Palmer is on his feet the Health Department insist that the BCNZ broadcast proceedings at half power. Members in benches near the Christchurch Central MP, it is true, have some-

times been found slumped and inert in their seats, but tests later have shown that concussion from the shock waves was responsible. The PM's denigration of Palmer is rooted not so much in reality as in the fact that Palmer was one of the original Citizens for Rowling and rather than changing his name by deed poll, undergoing plastic surgery or emigrating to Brazil, the former professor of law had the temerity to join the Labour Party and then run for Parliament.

Various explanations have been put forward for the PM's new mellowness. Some insist it isn't mellowness at all but indifference. Others put it down to his age. Not even Prime Ministers, they insist, can escape hardening of the cerebral arteries. Neurones pop their clogs at truly alarming rates shortly after the first child comes home with the bill for his or her high school uniform, and with the PM now a proud grandfather time alone will have taken a terrible toll. Thus, according to these observers, he may be suffering from senile decay of the anger and hostility centres of his frontal lobes. The corollary to this argument is the suggestion that elsewhere in the same lobes there exists a nice personality in mint condition because it has hardly ever been used.

This is supposition and my guess is that the PM is relatively benign because he has his mind on other things. He has the distracted, preoccupied air of a man dealing with intractable problems. Indeed his own staff have indicated that on his recent trip abroad the PM, instead of burying himself in official papers or sleeping as is his usual practice, spent many an hour just staring out at the clouds.

This gazing into the middle distance, focusing on nothing in particular, has also been a feature of his recent press conferences. Coupled to this is an unusual reluctance to discuss anything in any detail. In regard to the strike at the Marsden Point refinery expansion site, apart from one brief outburst when he suggested the 16 hapless British riggers caught up in the row might be sent home if they didn't work, the PM was not very responsive.

Asked by gallery journalists what would happen if various proposed solutions didn't work, the PM's stock response was: 'That question hasn't arisen!'

If questions weren't rejected because they were questions that hadn't arisen, they were dismissed firmly but politely as questions that couldn't be answered in the context in which they were asked. No one actually got to ask him, 'When that question arises, Prime Minister, what will you do then?' Not that he would have said much more. The 'that question hasn't arisen' response is a better blocking device than 'no comment'. It is just as worthless but sounds more forthcoming.

This is not to say he is absolutely silent on everything. There are two issues which he addresses with

They said it couldn't be done! Yet he came out of nowhere to save the world economy...

glee. One is the imminent physical collapse of the Australian fast bowler Dennis Lillee, and the other the imminent financial collapse of the world's banking system. These both deserve our immediate attention. As for everything else, the humdrum considerations that fill the gap — the state of our economy, the rising unemployment rate, the factory closures, the dilemma of what to do when the wage freeze ends, the problem of phasing out SMPs — all of these remain questions that haven't arisen.

This is understandable, and if I'm not wrong I heard him on Sharon Crosbie's radio programme defending poor Cuba against the infamous Common Agricultural Policy of the EEC. This makes considerably more sense than talking about the teacher surplus or the debate over whether the police should carry guns.

On the same programme he told La Crosbie that the Meat Board deficits just looked bad. Asked how long farmers could continue to be propped up he replied without hesitation, 'A year or two . . .' (What happens after that is another question that hasn't arisen.) He pointed out that should the world economy collapse in the meantime then of course things would be different. Not that he was that pessimistic really. 'I am postulating the beginning of an upturn,' he said boldly near the end.

In many respects his fascination and fixation with the world economy has given his speech a modular structure. The same analogies and homilies recur repeatedly, but in different order and with different emphasis. He mentions the need for a new Bretton Woods almost as often as Lange talks of Mangere and 'my people'. The only difference in their verbal Lego sets is that Lange's is New Zealand made and has lost less of its sheen.

Listener, March 5, 1983

SOCIAL CREDIT 1951..
SOCIAL CREDIT 1981
SOCIAL CREDIT 1983

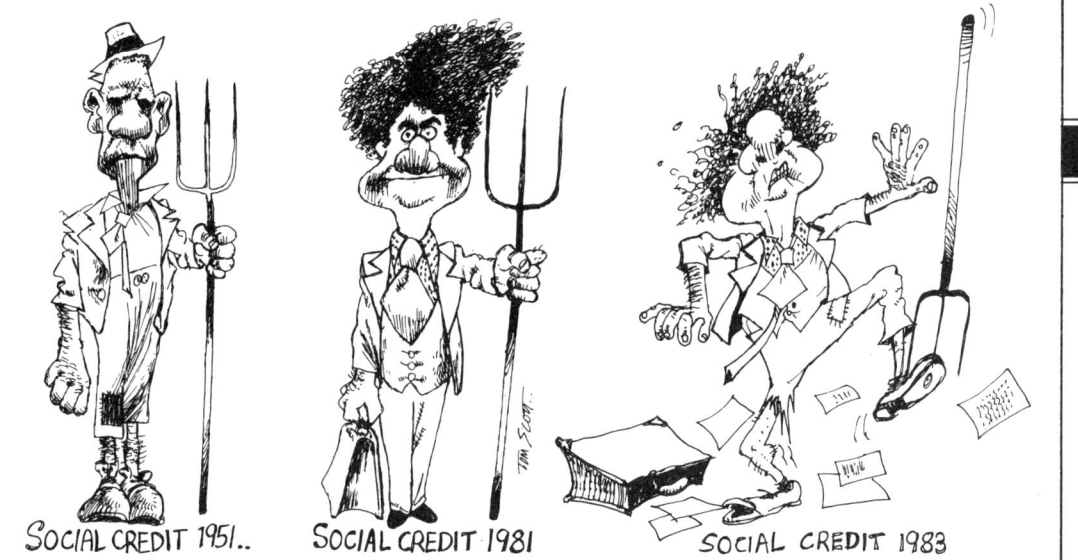

April 1983: after scaling dizzy heights in the early months of 1981, Social Credit start into a long, remorseless decline. (Straight Furrow)

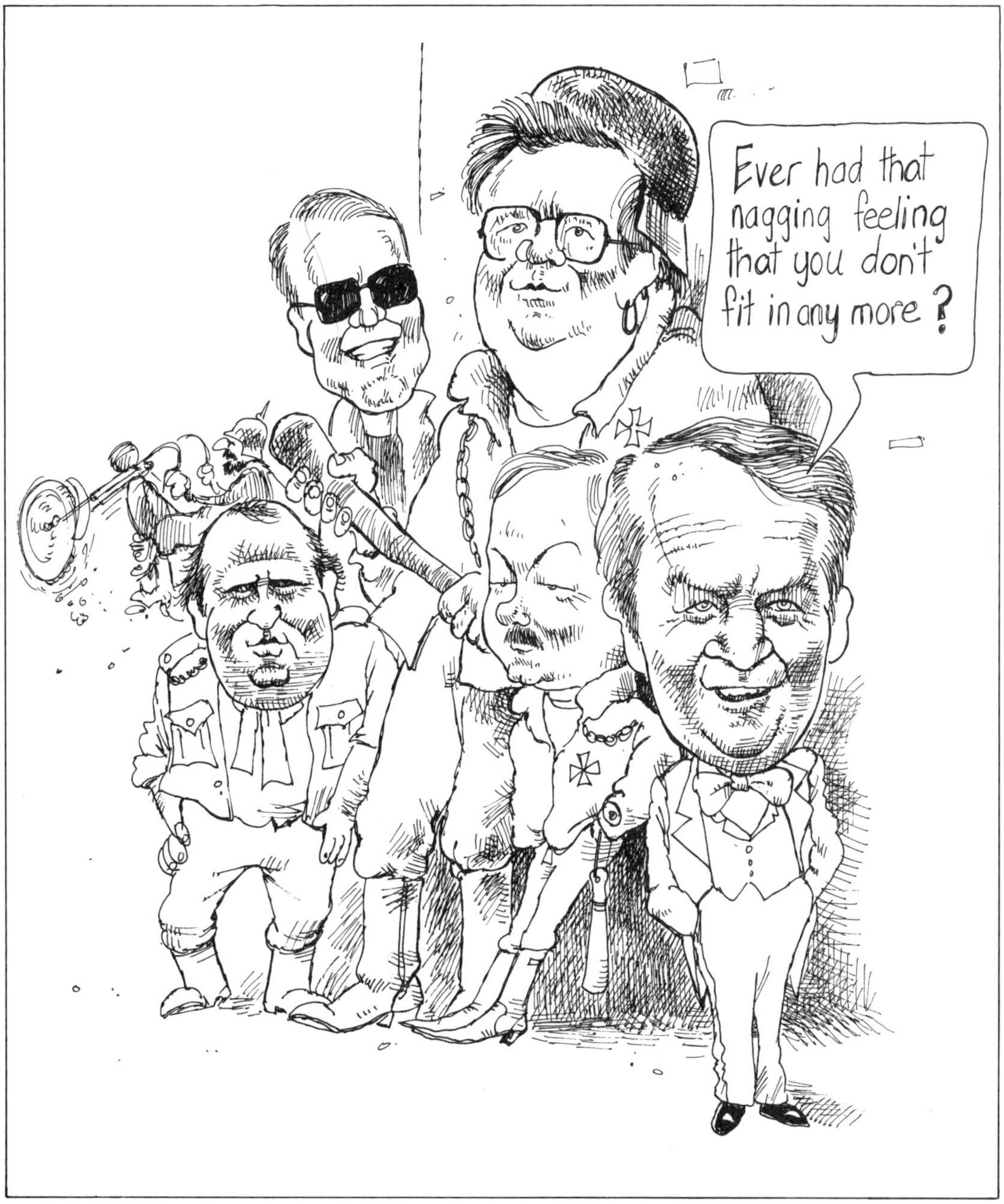
Ever had that nagging feeling that you don't fit in any more?

Bill Rowling announces his intention to stand down next election. (May 1983)

Labour Intensive

High on the walls next to the fake medieval swords and armour, small heaters blazed away to no avail. 'What is this place?' someone whispered. 'I'm not sure but when I was a law student we used to hire it out for stirs. The floor used to be awash with beer — that was before they got carpet . . .'

There was a crackle of feedback as Fran Wilde stepped up to the microphone. 'Thank you for coming to this Victory for Labour rally tonight,' beamed the Wellington Central MP to the hall two-thirds full of party faithful huddled together in little clusters to keep warm. 'Aaah excuse me Fran . . .' A confident young man who just had to be a teacher rose to his feet. 'Could you do something about the microphone levels, we can't hear you very well back here.' Adjustments were made. 'Is that better?' she asked. There were cries of affirmation from others and the young man nodded.

'Not a bad turnout considering we are competing against the weather and *McPhail and Gadsby,*' continued Wilde with a grin, 'but who needs *McPhail and Gadsby* when you can have the real thing!'

She gestured in the direction of the two men sharing the small stage with her. The star attractions, Sir Wallace Rowling and Jim Anderton, smiled modestly.

Insisting neither of them would speak for long, she paid Rowling lavish compliments in her introduction. 'I can't bring myself to call him Sir Wallace yet!' she laughed. 'It'll take some getting used to, so Bill will speak to you now . . .'

'People have been so nice to me lately,' began Rowling with a sly smile. 'After this business I read so many nice things about me in editorials I concluded I had died and no one had bothered to inform me!' The hall laughed affectionately and he went on to say he had no regrets. He'd made a lot of friends in politics. 'Friends . . .' he said extending his arms forward, 'they're the ones that stab you in the front!' He didn't mean that. He was relaxed about things. He was in good shape and so was the Labour Party. It would be the next Government and while it would need to exercise restraint in office it mustn't, he thundered solemnly, 'sell out to orthodoxy!'

The fourth Labour Government would inherit terrible problems and would need an investment strategy to create more jobs. There would have to be stabilisation policies and tax equity. Labour would have to get its priorities right. It would need discipline and just as Bob Hawke had done across the Tasman it would have to practise the politics of national reconciliation. Just like the third Labour Government before it, the next Labour Government would have to give a lead to the Third World countries. 'We cannot — we dare not — let them down,' said Rowling sternly. Adding, to further applause,

that there was no room in the Labour Party for squabbles on nuclear issues.

He said then he could feel Fran kicking him in the shins so he concluded on the question of leadership. There were special parameters to it. Sometimes a leader had to stand above and be seen to stand above the political process. It was a leader's responsibility to remind us that in the final analysis we were all New Zealanders.

Later that night he would be glued to the radio following the fortunes of the New Zealand cricket team in England. 'If we can unify over a cricket match or football match,' he implored, 'why in the name of God can't we strive for some excellence and unity of purpose in the economic area!'

'I must admit,' said a grinning Jim Anderton when it was his turn, 'I had some difficulty getting my mouth around Sir Wallace when I met him tonight for the first time since his great honour.' The party president praised Rowling for his balance, control, maturity and dignity under pressure, comparing Rowling's courage in defeat with Malcolm Fraser who in the same predicament broke down and cried. That done, Anderton got on with the job of entertaining the troops. To delighted laughter he read aloud from a letter sent to him anonymously from a disgruntled Nat. The letter addressed to 'Dear party member' was from the Tauranga branch of the National Party and warned that 'manpower was thin'. It complained that the National Party was getting a lot of stick from the news media, from the Labour Party, and from its own members. Notwithstanding that, it pleaded: 'We beg you to renew your membership!'

There were more jibes and taunts before he got serious and told them that the Government had lost its moral authority. Sacrifices weren't being shared and inflation and unemployment had to be solved together. If the National Government followed the course of the Thatcher Government in Britain we would have over 250,000 people out of work. 'I can remember a time,' he drawled, 'when Muldoon went up and down the country saying there were 800 people out of work and wasn't this a terrible indictment of a Labour Government.'

Its collective memory stirred, the hall bristled with indignation. 'Where are those charts on borrowing and inflation now?' asked Anderton sarcastically. 'You'd need a *Towering Inferno* ladder to get to the top of them!'

More soberly, he cautioned against jubilation at Labour's lead in the polls. National's popularity had gone up three per cent since the last election. Labour's gain was solely at Social Credit's expense. Labour's harvest was of negative anti-Government votes. These had to be cemented in place as positive pro-Labour votes. This hadn't happened in the past

and there had been only two Labour Governments in the last 34 years. This was because they survived only one term. The challenge for Labour now was not to win office but to stay there. For this they needed what they had lacked in the past — a strong electorate base. And for this they needed money.

Ah money! The mere prospect of a chicken raffle sent ripples through the hall. But no, the Labour Party has progressed beyond that. Anderton started talking about automatic banking transfers and some people gasped. So far he'd been to 40 such meetings and had 55 to go. The response had been great. Money was coming in at the rate of $10,000 a week. By the end of the year they expected to raise over $400,000, a sum well ahead of their initial target.

It wasn't all that new really cajoled Anderton. Miners in the Coromandel saved sixpence a week for the Labour Party in the '20s. Walter Nash used to go to the Railway workshops in Lower Hutt every payday and collect a bob per man. This generation, said Anderton, had an obligation to generate the same kind of loyalty. The money that went with the commitment would keep Labour in power.

People with red folders containing bank transfer forms moved among the audience handing them out at the end of each row like collection plates. 'I don't have a pen on me,' said one relieved voice, to be followed seconds later by: 'My God they come with pens on them.' 'No you can't take them home with you,' said Anderton, reading a hundred minds. 'We know what would happen to them. Fill them in now with your name and address and we'll phone you in about two weeks' time to get the rest of the details.'

Using an engaging mix of banter and aggression he soon had nearly everyone scribbling away merrily. Commencement date was June 20 and the bit about 'until further notice' meant people would be told when to increase their monthly donation. There was nervous laughter. Only joking, beamed their president.

Supper of tea, sammies, sausage rolls and sponge cake followed with Wilde insisting it all be eaten as it had all been paid for. Rowling and Anderton posed with pensioners for some snapshots and the rest filed out, some laden with surplus food, into the cold night. David Lange's name had not been mentioned once.

Listener, July 9, 1983

The Philosophy of Confusionism

The studio lights dim, throwing the small but excited audience into darkness. The floor manager raises one arm and conversation stills. All eyes are on the black leather swivel chair that seems to float in the centre on a single shaft of light. To one side, illuminated by another spot, sits the ageless blond question-master Peter Sinclair, nervously licking his thin lips and shuffling his papers. The floor manager gives him his cue.

Sinclair (smiling nonchalantly): Good evening and welcome to *Mastermind.* Our first contestant is Reon Mudgeway, a Dargaville beekeeper and amateur gynaecologist . . . (A small man in a check shirt and thin, stained suede tie and crimplene suit shuffles awkwardly to the chair trailing clouds of dandruff.)

Mr Mudgeway has chosen as his specialist subject the policies of the Opposition leader David Lange on the nuclear threat and visits of US warships. (There is an audible gasp from the audience while Mudgeway nods anxiously.) You have two minutes starting now. What in Mr Lange's own words has characterised the recent debate in New Zealand on the nuclear threat?

Mudgeway (without hesitation): Confusion!

Sinclair: Correct. And what sort of confusion in Lange's view is it?

Mudgeway: Unfortunate!

Sinclair: Correct. And where does Mr Lange think this unfortunate confusion has come from?

Mudgeway: It arose in the heat of debate.

Sinclair: Correct. And who helped provoke that debate and ensure it was heated by advocating changes at variance with existing Labour Party policy?

Mudgeway (screwing up his face and closing his eyes): Oh dear . . . I know this . . . I'll have to guess. The people of Mangere?

Sinclair: So close, but I can't accept that. The answer I wanted was David Lange. You knew that all the time didn't you? (Mudgeway close to tears can only wring his hands despairingly.) Now. In March Lange called for a review of Labour's official policy on the visit of US warships and he warned his party not to get sidetracked by what?

Mudgeway (still rattled): Loose women?

Sinclair: No. He warned against getting sidetracked over whether the vessels were nuclear powered as well as nuclear armed.

Mudgeway: Of course! (He strikes himself a blow with some force on the side of the head.)

Sinclair: What sort of abhorrence does Lange have to nuclear weaponry?

Mudgeway (cheering up): Total and unqualified.

Sinclair: Correct. In March of this year what was the essence of his proposed policy changes?

Mudgeway: As Prime Minister he would *trust* the Americans not to send a warship to New Zealand if it was nuclear armed.

Sinclair: Correct. What does the authoritative *Janes Fighting Ships* say about nuclear powered warships?

Mudgeway: It says that nuclear propelled warships are invariably nuclear armed.

Sinclair: Correct. Why is it then that successive commanders of the US Pacific fleet have a policy of non-disclosure on whether or not nuclear weapons are carried?

Mudgeway: They are hoping the Russians will think *Janes Fighting Ships* is the title of a book for girls put out by a feminist collective to break down sexual stereotypes.

Sinclair: Correct. In March what was Lange's attitude to the visit of nuclear propelled warships?

Mudgeway: He would assume the commander was fully cognisant of his total and unqualified abhorrence of nuclear weaponry and he would turn a blind eye to the nuclear propulsion bit.

Sinclair: I'll accept that. What would happen though if the nuclear reactor went into melt-down while the warship was in port?

Mudgeway: Lots of other people would be turning a blind eye as well.

Sinclair: The answer I have written down here says drop the American embassy a terse note asking them not to let it happen again. But I'll accept that. What is the essence of Lange's latest stand on the visit of US warships?

Mudgeway: Disclosure. Commanders must disclose whether or not they are nuclear armed and/or nuclear propelled. If they are nuclear armed they can't come here. And if they are just nuclear powered they can't come here either — at least not until safety procedures can be devised and enforced.

Sinclair: Fair enough. This represents an about face on Lange's part — true or false?

Mudgeway: True.

Sinclair: Wrong.

Mudgeway (desperately): FALSE THEN!

Sinclair: Wrong. Sorry but this was a trick question. The answer we wanted was neither as it is too early to tell yet.

Mudgeway: Bloody hell!

Sinclair: Does Mr Lange's latest statement accord with current Labour Party policy?

Mudgeway (pausing thoughtfully before replying cautiously): Aah . . . sort of?

Sinclair: Yes, well done. What does Lange say to those who argue that he has in fact had a significant change of heart?

Mudgeway: He says in that case the English language has taken a terrible thrashing.

Sinclair: Correct. And what does the Prime Minister say?

Mudgeway: He says Lange's statement is an abject capitulation to the something something in the something . . . (He holds his head in his hands and thrashes about in his chair.)

Sinclair: You'll kick yourself when I tell you . . .

Mudgeway: I know it! I know it! . . . Sorry.

Sinclair: An abject capitulation to the left wing of the Labour caucus . . .

Mudgeway: Of course! (He throws his head back in anger and fresh dandruff wafts upward like drifting gun-smoke.)

Sinclair: When do US warships visit New Zealand?

Mudgeway: Just before Labour Party annual conferences.

Sinclair: Correct. What don't our politicians want in their own backyard?

Mudgeway: French underground testing.

Sinclair: Wrong. Mongrel Mob headquarters. Since embarrassing his party with his comments back in March what has been Lange's response to repeated invitations to appear on *Sharon Crosbie* and *Newsmakers*?

Mudgeway (now visibly exhausted): Pass . . .

Sinclair: Correct. You have answered 14 correctly which is a very good score. Now we welcome retired schoolteacher and Gore housewife Dawn Saunders to the chair. Her specialist subject is the industrial relations policies of Jim Bolger . . . (A squat, cheerful woman in sensible tweed clothing eases herself into the hot seat.) Dawn you have two minutes starting now. What is the thrust of Mr Bolger's moves about intention to introduce legislation to get rid of the unqualified preference clause?

Saunders (brightly): I dunno. Make voluntary unionism compulsory I suppose.

Sinclair: Correct. And what did Mr Bolger tell his caucus colleagues when they asked him what would happen when the bill came into effect?

Saunders: Oh dear, I haven't the faintest idea . . .

Sinclair: Correct. Your next question is . . .

Listener, July 30, 1983

Lend Me Your Ears

Midway through his recent overseas trip the PM turned 62. He didn't think the occasion merited much fuss, but after the draining and disaster-ridden Caribbean leg of his odyssey his staff thought otherwise and purchased a cake and an 'Oscar the Grouch' birthday card for him. On the eve of the IMF/World Bank meeting, on a warm Sunday evening, the PM obligingly invited everyone across to his suite in the old wing of the Washington Sheraton for drinks. He was in a good mood and didn't mind that the cake was decorated in Social Credit colours. The ever-present, ever-vigilant secret service agents, however, speculated that it might be poisoned and insisted others taste it first. When no one dropped dead the PM was allowed a piece.

There were no presents as such, but then the yellow-paged summaries of the news from home were present enough. Apart from Trade and Industry Minister Keith Allen's attack of 'diabetes' in the House one night the feedback for most of the journey couldn't have been better from the PM's point of view. The Labour Party were brawling amongst themselves and his own lads were preoccupied with industrial problems at Marsden Point. This allowed him to concentrate solely on the task in hand – saving the world economy – and one present he would dearly have loved was tangible proof that he had made ground and persuaded more people to his cause.

He certainly tried hard enough. He pushed the case for a 'new Bretton Woods' with a single-minded ferocity that exhausted his aides and perplexed other politicians. In Trinidad, after the PM had been championing the rights of Third World nations at a press conference, Mark Lalonde, the Canadian Minister of Finance, was moved to comment in exasperation, 'I didn't know Mr Muldoon was black!', a sentiment shared, but more delicately expressed by Nigel Lawson, Britain's Chancellor of the Exchequer.

In Washington, Paul Keating, the Australian Treasurer, was no less cynical. Interviewed by the Australian *Financial Review* about our PM's campaign, Keating responded: 'Mr Muldoon has had a very big international problem with his rugby union policy a few years ago – I would therefore understand his interest in repairing his image with developing countries. That's his problem not Australia's.'

Every New Zealand official I spoke to ruled out the theory that Muldoon was on a journey of personal atonement. They argued that his sincerity was beyond question. 'He really does care,' sighed one senior aide. 'He is a complex man. He is well known and respected, but he is not an insider's insider. He is a lonely isolated figure to some extent and this feeling of not belonging – of never belonging no matter what – helps him relate well to smaller poorer nations.'

I was told the key to understanding the PM's crusade could be found in an interview he gave last May to Briar Whitehead in the Christchurch *Press*. The PM talked freely about his religious beliefs. The Bible, which he read often, was the 'divinely inspired word of God' and faith 'a great heart-warming sustaining mystery'. His initiative for the reform of the international monetary system was 'in accordance with the will of God'. New Zealand didn't need to get involved, he said, but, being a white affluent community, 'When I say something as Prime Minister it makes more impact than if a Black African leader says it'.

By the same token something said by President Mitterrand of France has more impact than the same thing said by the leader of a tiny nation in the south-west Pacific.

But then one of the express purposes of his crusade is to persuade those whose utterances have real impact. To influence the influential. To get the big boys on to his wavelength. This, it seemed, wasn't all that hard. Often one conversation was enough. 'A lot of people haven't done their homework on this,' he explained in Washington, shaking his large head sadly and adding, 'I had to educate the new British Chancellor . . .'

Okay, okay, assuming the PM's objectives were noble and his heart pure, how successful a trip was it? From New Zealand the assessment was easy. Journalists and political opponents had no trouble concluding it was a failure. From America it was much harder to tell.

When you travel with a politician in a foreign country you vapour-trail them like a heat-seeking missile. You are obsessed by the red glow up ahead, to the exclusion of the rest of the sky. It was particularly hard for Radio New Zealand's Dick Griffin and the *Herald's* Greig Shand. They had to file almost daily and, as many of the PM's activities took place behind closed doors and at private functions, they were at the mercy of the PM's version of events. Inevitably these were patently self-serving (as the PM told one audience, the job of the politician was to take the facts 'and put them in the best possible light') and interspersed with the tales of triumph were heart-stopping moments where he screwed up his eyes and asked them if they were reporting his speeches fully.

His final set-piece address to the Kennedy School of Government at Harvard University, Boston, was most informative in that it gave us a chance to view the PM and his audience close-up and test their reactions afterwards.

The speech was dense, and heavy going in places, and some of the earnest young men and women in the small lecture theatre went quite glassy-eyed, but the PM put on a show for them during question time. He was chatty, relaxed, anecdotal and for the first time advanced beyond description of possible solutions, admitting nothing would happen until America came to the party, and that there was no likelihood until after the elections were over.

Elections were the bane of international conferences. As soon as you got agreement on anything someone always said, 'Yes, but I've got an election coming up at home and what we have just agreed to would be politically unacceptable'. He had a theory that every country in the world should hold its elections on the same day every five years. That would give the world four years in which to govern.

When he wasn't making them laugh he was grim with foreboding. He talked at one point about how people had become jaded with the subject of world poverty. 'There is aid fatigue,' he explained, while almost everyone in his official party had slumped forward onto the desk, showing there was such a thing as Bretton Woods fatigue as well.

For this audience, though, the subject was fresh and at the end one young man thanked the PM for his 'fascinating address'. 'I am going away,' he exclaimed, 'more despondent than I have ever been in my life.'

Other students were just as enthralled. 'Very direct, very impressive,' said one. 'Very personable,' said another. 'We are honoured to have him here,' gushed a lecturer. 'Yes we are,' chimed in a colleague. 'And he was speaking to postgraduate students from all around the world — a room full of the Robert David Muldoons of tomorrow.'

The PM, who is not averse to a little idolatry, was still pretty chuffed when I spoke to him later. While insisting there wasn't a vote for him in it back home, he was pleased with the whole exercise. He had set himself modest goals and had actually spoken to the audiences he wanted to reach. He was getting his message across. The US Treasury were undertaking studies on the issues he raised, and events since the IMF meeting — like the arrest of the President of Argentina's Central Bank on his return from Washington — confirmed the worsening crisis. Success couldn't be measured in column inches of newsprint. It was more important to reach the decision-makers. Take his two live interviews on cable television. While the number of viewers was small, research showed the average viewer as a businessman earning an income of $70,000. Then there was his article on the op-ed page of the *New York Times*. Malcolm Forbes of *Forbes* magazine, who had taken the PM cruising on the Hudson, read the PM's article when he got home.

'Had he seen it before,' beamed the PM, 'he said he would have put it up on the noticeboard of the boat.'

Listener, November 12, 1983

December 1982: John Clarke of Fred Dagg fame says that the New Zealand economy has entered a 'Whoop! Whoop! Pull up! Pull up!' phase.

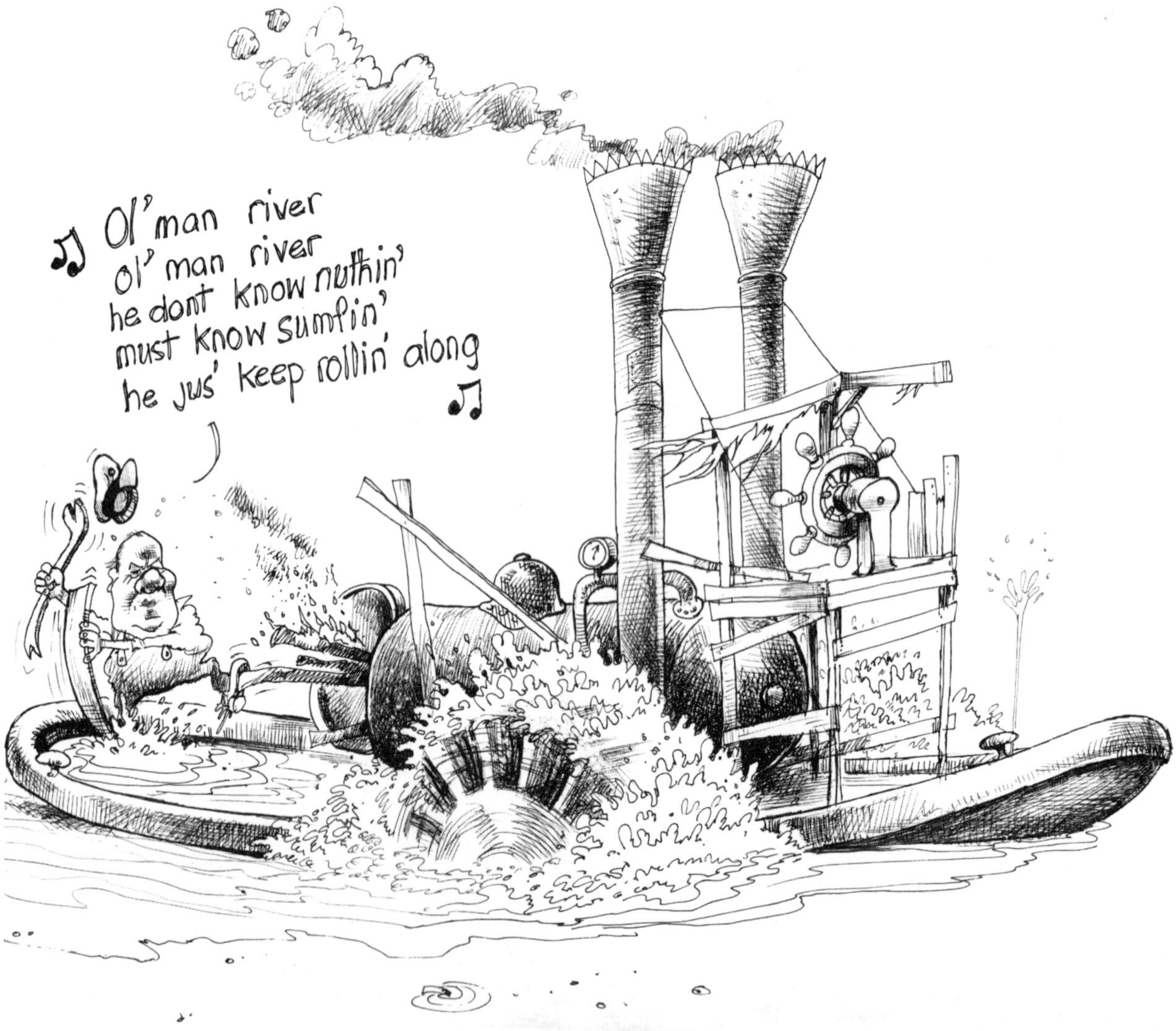

♪ Ol' man river
Ol' man river
he dont know nuthin'
must know sumpin'
he jus' keep rollin' along ♪

September 1983: the New Zealand economy continues to worsen, not that you could tell by the demeanour of Prime Minister Muldoon.

September 1983: Paddy MacGuinness, editor-in-chief of the Australian Financial Review, *came to New Zealand on a Government-sponsored trip and went home to say that the New Zealand economy was run on bullying and fear. I did this cartoon and felt pretty pleased with myself until I read that the PM had done much as I had depicted, with much the same results — proving yet again, if proof were needed, that life in this country is so bizarre satire is almost redundant.*

November 1983: publication of Reserve Bank figures on New Zealand's total overseas debt.

The Perishable Dirigible

There is every indication that the best is yet to come.

With the growing prosperity in Asia, New Zealand should be looking very closely at using modern airships to haul our fresh horticulture to market.

Such modern airships could easily carry 500 tonnes at an average of 150 km per hour.

New Zealand has some of the world's best airship design experts. — Press statement by Mr Neil Morrison, Social Credit spokesman on transport.

There was no denying it.

Long before you got to the airport it was an impressive sight.

A green and gold dirigible stretching the length of a football paddock hovered over Rongotai straining at its hawsers.

Made from stretch-and-grow jumpsuits donated by League women up and down the country and sewn together by the good ladies of the Wellington division in a disused Miramar factory, it was more than an end product of thousands of man hours of painstaking labour — it was the embodiment of Neil Morrison's dream.

Bruce Beetham said as much at the opening ceremony.

'This,' said Beetham waving an outstetched arm at the vast zeppelin overhead, 'is the embodiment of Neil Morrison's dream.'

At his side, Morrison cried openly.

It was partly pride and partly pique.

Morrison wasn't happy with the name. He thought BCB 101 was too prosaic. He favoured something more nautical, more noble, yet with a Socred ring to it.

But the planning committee flatly rejected his suggestion of 'The Spirit of Reduced Velocity of Circulation'.

Still, he kept these thoughts to himself when Beverly Beetham stepped forward to cut the ribbon.

Loaded to the gunwales with fresh produce — strawberries, kiwifruit, asparagus and cabbages — the BCB 101 was ready to fly.

So were Captain Garry Knapp and his hardy crew.

'America here we come,' he beamed at the television crew.

'What about the asparagus bound for Germany?' hissed Terry Heffernan, formerly of the Socred Research Unit and now his trusty No 2.

'And Germany,' added Knapp without pause.

'What about the kiwifruit to Japan?' asked John Kirk, who'd volunteered to come and had been accepted as ballast first class.

'And Japan,' Knapp winked straight down the lens.

'Actually,' hissed Heffernan, 'I think the asparagus goes to Japan and the kiwifruit to Germany . . .'

'Oh, shut up!' said Knapp turning swiftly, accidentally rabbit-chopping Heffernan in the windpipe.

'I had hoped to be going with you but my duties as leader make it impossible,' said Beetham with a sly smile.

Knapp led his crew up the gangplank.

The door was shut and at a signal from Beetham, the hawsers were cut.

With an ear-splitting crack, the dirigible, which looked like a giant speckled marrow, leapt skyward, pulling a lot of air up with it and sending hundreds of Socred hairpieces wheeling over the tarmac like mohair seagulls.

Picking himself up from the runway and dusting himself down, Beetham suddenly noted that the airship was headed due south.

'My God,' he stammered, 'they're going the wrong way . . .'

'Perhaps they know a short cut,' ventured Morrison brightly.

From 8000 feet up, through breaks in the cloud you could see the white caps on the waves, but that was all.

Heffernan put down the binoculars, turned away from the salt-sprayed windows of the pilot's deck and shrugged. 'According to my calculations, we should be over New Hampshire by now.'

'Is there any chance at all, Terry,' said Knapp gently, 'that you might have made a mistake?'

'Vermont possibly. Massachusetts or Connecticut possibly. Maine as an outside chance.'

'Geeze,' said Kirk from near the glass.

'Any fool can see we are over an ocean!'

'Any fool, yes,' said Heffernan evenly, 'but not necessarily an expert who has studied the tides and trade winds carefully.'

'Exactly, Terry, so why are we still over water?'

You could tell Knapp was worried, the hair on the back of his hands hadn't been combed for days and his tie clashed with his socks.

'Well, if you want my opinion, these books,' said Heffernan darkly, pointing to a huge pile of textbooks and charts, 'are designed with the two-party system in mind. They make no allowances for a third-party dirigible. Indeed, it is my suspicion that they actively conspire against us. We are anathema to them you see!'

'I say, that sounds a bit far-fetched,' said Kirk, who in the normal course of events loved a conspiracy theory.

'Aha!' said Heffernan. 'What was far-fetched to our grandmothers when they went shopping has, with the invention of the supermarket trolley, become a hop, skip and a jump.'

'I reckon you've got me on that one,' said Kirk limply.

'This is all very well, Terry,' said Knapp quickly, 'but I think we have to accept the fact that we are lost. If only we had petrol for the bloody engines we could use the propellers . . ."

'We don't need petrol, Garry,' Heffernan smiled broadly.

'We don't?'

'Nope. This little beauty is the work of the Nelson/West Coast division.'

'God, I suppose it runs on coal . . .' sighed Kirk.

'It runs on water.'

'Terry,' said Knapp, quietly leading him to a chair and sitting beside him, 'there is no such thing as a machine which runs on water. The technology just simply does not exist.'

'Oh, I dunno,' piped up Kirk. 'My uncle had a thing which ran on water.'

'See!' said Heffernan.

'Really,' said Knapp cautiously. 'What sort of thing was it?'

'A speedboat . . .'

'A speedboat!' exclaimed Knapp, rising suddenly and accidentally kneeing Kirk in the groin.

Three months later, morale was getting low.

The crew went around unshaven and spitting on the floor.

Knapp stopped wearing cufflinks and sometimes appeared on the flight deck with his fly unbuttoned.

Only Heffernan remained unaffected.

He often came into the stateroom at breakfast, whistling the tune of 'The Sloop John B'.

Not that there was much left for breakfast these days. It was either asparagus rolls or strawberries.

'Can't we have kiwifruit just once?' whimpered Kirk.

'Certainly not!' snapped Knapp. 'You know the drill. We have kiwifruit at lunchtime and boiled cabbage for tea.'

As soon as he said it, everyone looked guilty.

Men half rose in their chairs and adjusted their clothing and the terrible stench intensified.

For quite some time, no one could make eye contact and the lacquer on the walls peeled off silently in long yellowing strips.

'I say old man 'whispered Heffernan, 'I wonder if boiled cabbage at teatime is the wisest move?'

'Damn it,' hissed Knapp through clenched teeth. 'Have you forgotten already what the urinals were like in the morning when we had asparagus rolls for tea?'

'I take your point, Garry,' said Heffernan calmly. 'I just make the point that there is now as much hot air in this part of the airship as up aloft.'

'What's making things worse,' said Kirk, 'is some of the produce is going rotten in the holds. That's where a lot of the smell is coming from. We'll need to lower the temperature.'

'We'll have to climb to a higher altitude,' said Knapp.

'To do that, we'll have to dipose of some of our ballast,' said Heffernan.

'You don't mean?' gulped Kirk.

'I have another proposal,' said Knapp. 'We only need to lose about 30 pounds. I suggest we shave Terry's head and trim his moustache!'

Heffernan was about to reply when there was a cry from forward.

'Land ho!'

They all tore forward.

'New Hampshire, is it?' grinned Heffernan.

'No, Island Bay,' sneered Kirk.

'Aha, just as I thought,' beamed Heffernan as they drifted down through the clouds toward the beach.

'Oh, the shame,' muttered Knapp. 'We've been away six months and haven't actually gone anywhere. How do we explain this to the voting public?'

'We don't have to,' said Heffernan. 'We organise a petition for proportional representation when it comes to fair allocation of trade winds. We concentrate on the basic inequality of the weather. This calls for a celebration.'

He whipped a cigar from his breast pocket and pulled out a cigarette lighter.

'No!' screamed Knapp but it was too late.

There was a sheet of flame and a deafening explosion.

Knapp came to on the sand, surrounded by smouldering fragments of yellow and gold cloth.

A dense plume of black smoke spiralled skyward. The acrid smell of scorched strawberries filled the air.

His crew!

He sat up suddenly.

What had happened to his crew?

A charred figure staggered up the beach.

'If the Labour Party and the National Party think they can get away with this sort of thing, they've got another think coming!'

Knapp's heart sank.

It was Heffernan.

Straight Furrow, November 23, 1983

Changed Tunes

The old Legislative Chamber these days is a place of shadows and silence. Chairs and the odd trestle table are stacked in the gloom. Cosy timber panelling rises up from a battered red carpet to the gallery where regal columns of grey marble support the high plaster ceiling. Wan daylight filters through skylights of simple but attractive lead-light glass, dappling the floor with blotches of colour.

Since the abolition of the upper house in 1950 the room has been used intermittently for many things. Speeches from the Throne are delivered here. Visiting sportsmen were sometimes feted here. Conferences, select committee hearings and seminars are occasionally held here. Parties of schoolchildren still traipse through giggling and whispering while its history is explained to them.

The power and the glory, though, are gone. The pandemonium and histrionics of its heyday are over. The only thing now which comes even close are the concerts of the Parliamentary Players. This year, with the irrepressible, indefatigable Roy Amor of the Bills Office in charge, a music hall was organised. Parliamentary staffers as well as politicians took part and when you consider how busy most of them are and how little rehearsal time they had it was a surprisingly accomplished show. For nearly two hours the old Legislative Chamber reverberated to the sound of song and laughter. The staffers took advantage of the occasion to make fun of the politicians and the politicians happily joined in making fun of one another and themselves. A lot of it was corny but just enough of it was sufficiently telling and barbed to rescue the evening from self-congratulation.

While largely a boisterous romp, the concert had some quieter moments. Invercargill's Norm Jones hobbled out to sing a poignant rendition of 'Lilli Marlene' and David Thomson's version of the Christmas hymn 'Mary's Boy Child' was strangely affecting. The Minister of State Services can be unbearably pompous and usually exudes a silken calm, but on this occasion he approached the microphone grey with fear, the lyric sheet fluttering in his trembling hands. The baritone voice wobbled softly and uncertainly at first but gradually gained in confidence with the swell of voices joining in on the chorus.

Others to confound expectation were the Minister of Health, Aussie Malcolm, and Government backbencher Dail Jones. In the past, sometimes unfairly, they have enjoyed social leper status on the Hill and the evening gave them the opportunity to play off against their popular images. Jones, perceived as a killjoy, wimp and wowser, pranced on stage in bloomers to play a pint-sized, spindle-legged, randy Romeo opposite an equally amorous but much larger Juliet. Malcolm, depicted by television satirists as a slobbering sycophant to the PM, delighted in playing his boss in a sketch called 'McFailed and Ghastly'. Malcolm went down on his knees to get the proportions right and with a huge scar painted on his left cheek delivered a wickedly accurate impersonation of the PM. The heavy, aggressive tone was just right and Malcolm can think himself lucky that the PM was in India and that plans to have the show videotaped were scrapped at the last minute. Broadcasting Minister Ian Shearer, who was supposed to play the part of the craven 'Aussie', lost his voice three days before the show and the script had to be reworked into a monologue, which made it even more effective.

There were some nice lines. 'You want to know what KISS stands for do you Aussie?' rasped the pretend PM. 'Well it stands for "Keep it simple, stupid!" ' 'So Aussie you don't want to wind up a lonely pathetic old man by yourself ... That's all right, bring him in and I'll give you a hand! Ha ha ha.'

When it was over many of the participants didn't want to go home. A post-show cast party lasted until well into the morning and degenerated into a freewheeling singalong. At one point, with Associate Minister of Finance John Falloon on guitar and John MacGibbon from Hugh Templeton's office on piano, Labour's Fran Wilde and Kerry Burke led Norm Jones, Falloon and the others in a lusty version of 'The Red Flag' — with Jones by way of balance singing at the end, 'The working class can kiss my arse ...'

No member of the new Socred/Labour-reject alliance participated, but they were the butt of many jokes. Even more noticeable was the Government MPs' obsession with the New Zealand Party. The references were often gratuitous and a little nervous. During the Romeo and Juliet parody the symbolism got confused. Right at the end the alcoholic nurse who was the only survivor wandered past the heap of dead bodies clasping a bottle of gin and a sign saying 'New Zealand Party'. This got a laugh and almost as an afterthought the sign was thrust into the hand of the dead Romeo. This got a laugh too but the significance escaped me and to make things even more confusing all the corpses eventually rose and danced their way off stage.

I can understand, though, why the Government is jittery about the New Zealand Party. The latest Heylen poll shows a dramatic rise in the popularity of the New Zealand Party. For the first time they have moved into third place, one point ahead of Social Credit. Their gains come at the expense of all three traditional parties. National are down from 45 per cent to 41, Labour from 39 to 38. On the preferred Prime Minister rankings Bob Jones has made a similar advance. At 5 per cent approval he heads Bruce Beetham by a point, and again both Rob Muldoon and David Lange drop a couple of notches.

While the Government are still well ahead in popularity the trend is not to their long-term advantage. If the New Zealand Party split the conservative vote in the rural marginal seats, the way is made easier for a Labour victory next year. This could happen despite Labour's worsening position in the polls.

Recently Lange has made a much-publicised tour of the provinces and has enjoyed good audiences, but it is obvious that he is not pulling in the crowds Muldoon did on his roadshow of '74 and '75. Nor are his performances having the same dramatic impact. For parallels to the Muldoon juggernaut you have to turn to the New Zealand Party. Bob Jones is doing to the National Government now what Muldoon did so punishingly to the Labour Government back then.

Jones is making an impact partly because he and his party are political curiosities, partly because he has developed into a canny and engaging operator, partly because he seems utterly fearless and says what he really thinks (a large component of Muldoon's initial appeal) and partly by default. Over recent months the Labour Party's internal wrangles have counted against them, and in the House and in other areas they have gone off the boil somewhat.

Political popularity in this country is rather like being on an escalator; sometimes you are whisked upwards without moving a muscle. For five years Lange enjoyed such a ride. The great danger is that you never really learn why you have been so chosen. Now Lange finds himself on a stair-case moving down, having to run feverishly just to remain in the same place. It must be a bewildering, demoralising experience. Lange's fortunes will change again and if he can hold on over the next few months he will be a better politician for it. In the space of one cruel, demanding year he is being forced to serve the political apprenticeship his earlier popularity seemed to render unnecessary.

Understandably, he is not so sure-footed these days. The hesitation is obvious in his speeches. Speaking to a Fletcher Challenge seminar recently, he offered 'A Labour analysis of where we are as a nation, and where we are going' before adding, 'Quite honestly, it is hard to answer the question about where we are going . . .'

Still he might yet end up in Vogel House and, at next year's music hall, come on stage and sing 'If I Ruled the World'. Bob Jones, the new MP for Ohariu, might wander out after him and bring the house down with a moving rendition of 'If I Were a Rich Man'.

Listener, December 10, 1983